Public Management as a Design-Oriented Professional Discipline

For Catherine, Adele and Alex

Public Management as a Design-Oriented Professional Discipline

Michael Barzelay

Department of Management, London School of Economics and Political Science, UK

Edward Elgar
PUBLISHING

Cheltenham, UK • Northampton, MA, USA

Published by
Edward Elgar Publishing Limited
The Lypiatts
15 Lansdown Road
Cheltenham
Glos GL50 2JA
UK

Edward Elgar Publishing, Inc.
William Pratt House
9 Dewey Court
Northampton
Massachusetts 01060
USA

A catalogue record for this book
is available from the British Library

Library of Congress Control Number: 2019947090

This book is available electronically in the **Elgar**online
Social and Political Science subject collection
DOI 10.4337/9781788119108

ISBN 978 1 78811 909 2 (cased)
ISBN 978 1 78811 911 5 (paperback)
ISBN 978 1 78811 910 8 (eBook)

Typeset by Servis Filmsetting Ltd, Stockport, Cheshire
Printed and bound in Great Britain by TJ International Ltd, Padstow, Cornwall

Contents

Figures

Tables

Preface

I think it's a safe assumption that if you've read further than this book's title, you care about public management, as an enterprise within the academic world and/ or in government-based schools of public administration. And I'm also assuming that you're willing to listen to a case for change, along with considering how you might be part of its realization.

As the title suggests, this book is for bringing about a shift in public management, from whatever it is as a field now, to being a professional discipline; more specifically, the book promotes a twist in public management, towards being a design-oriented professional discipline. This view of public management isn't unprecedented. Some have called for a design-orientation to research and practice; others have called for public management to adopt the mantle of a profession, as opposed to suffering the loose analogies of being an art and/or science. But the sources on which this book draws don't add up to what this book is: an intellectual foundation for public management, as a collective effort to develop and learn professional knowledge, with a clear focus on strengthening professional practice within public organizations – in a phrase, it's an intellectual foundation for public management as a design-oriented professional discipline.

Describing the book as an "intellectual foundation" – and titling it as I have done – sends signals that reading it will be neither a walk in the park, nor an entertaining show. But don't judge a book by its cover, or by the gravitas of its rhetoric. This book is designed specifically to be a page-turner, for one sole reason: it won't work otherwise. One reason is that the book has to appeal to students of the subject, as well as to newcomers being recruited to join this academic enterprise. Otherwise it won't be discussed, and then it won't become a meaningful vehicle for introducing the idea of public management as a design-oriented professional discipline. The book makes use of several rhetorical devices to tackle this challenge. I won't say more, to avoid spoiling the surprise.

This book's main audience is people who teach the subject: long-standing professors in the field like me; disciplinary social scientists who trespass into it; doctoral students in public administration and management; and practitioners who become full- or part-time "pracademics" identified with this subject. Starting in Chapter 1, you'll get to know fictional characters fitting the respective descriptions, namely Marshall, Nora, Olivier, and Petra. However, Chapters 1 and 4 are specifically written to be assigned to masters students and discussed with them.

By the time you finish this book, you should be able to imagine a future where you wouldn't have to define the evolution of public management in successive stereotypes of administrative philosophies, such as traditional public administration, new public management, and digital governance. A future where designing is considered no less important to the professional practice of public management than issue analysis and decision-making. A future where public management is a specialization of choice within the academic field of public administration. And, a future in which public management is looked to as the leading example of a design-oriented professional discipline. If you can do this, then this book will have functioned as intended, in starting an important conversation about the future of public management. I hope it does.

Acknowledgments

Providing a true and fair statement of how people other than me have contributed to this book project, and its outcome, is a standard I simply cannot meet. The main reason is that I worked on this project for nearly a decade.

I will begin by listing the names of people I consider to have fully collaborated on this book project, in simple alphabetical order by surname, because providing brief indications of how much value their collaboration was worth would be silly: John Arvanitis, John Bryson, Terry Colvin, Urska Kovse, Paulo Marques, Humberto Falcão Martins, Sérgio Seabra, Fred Thompson, and Pedro Vilela. My co-authors for Chapter 7 were Masakatsu Okumoto and Hideki Watanabe.

I wish to thank the institutions that one way or another have supported the work on this book: London School of Economics and Political Science (LSE); University of Minnesota's Hubert H. Humphrey School of Public Affairs; Yale School of Management; Japan International Cooperation Agency Research Institute (JICR-RI); and Brazil's National School of Public Administration (Enap). My home institution, LSE, provided the most support: wide latitude to teach public management along the design-oriented lines presented in this book; multiple years of sabbatical leave; a supportive research environment; and Knowledge Exchange and Impact Funding. I was at the University of Minnesota, as a visiting professor, during the autumn of 2015 for a pivotal period in the development of this book, with a room in the library, more than weekly lunches with John Bryson, and opportunities to present and receive comments on my thinking. I was a visiting professor at Yale School of Management, during the spring of 2016, when I was able to teach design-oriented public management to MBA and other students, while refining the purposive theorizing that lies at the core of this book. JICA-RI provided funding for the work reported in Chapter 7, as well as an opportunity to present this work, and the ideas behind it, at seminars at their offices in Tokyo in autumn 2017. Enap provided multiple kinds of support: an opportunity to translate this book's ideas into executive teaching for Brazil's public managers and constant challenges in ensuring all manner of kinds of contact between theory and practice, from September 2016 through now.

Innumerable individuals provided comments on drafts – some of which have long since been relegated to electronic folders that will never be opened, some of which are here. Others have made astute remarks about the project in seminars or informally. I list some of these individuals here: Luciano Andrenacci, Alberto Asquer, Yally Avrahampour, Adele Barzelay, George Bitar, Mark Borkowski, Fernando Coelho, Juan Carlos Cortázar Velarde, Armando Cunha, Francisco Gaetani, Tom Haase, Dan Honig, Hajime Isozaki, Karen King, Bob Kowalik,

Evelyn Levy, Alan Love, Humberto Martins, Natália Mota, Nuno Oliveira, Maria Oset-Serra, Antonio-Martin Porras, Sidney Winter, Henry Yee, and Bob Yetvin.

I am thankful to Alex Pettifer of Edward Elgar Publishing for being the most encouraging publisher that one could ask for.

I would like to underscore the long-standing intellectual friendship and collaboration behind this project, from Fred Thompson and John Bryson, which I expect to go forward from here, as well. As well I wish to thank John Arvanitis, Urska Kovse, and Pedro Vilela for selflessly sharing the burden of getting it done during the autumn of 2018.

To all, thanks for the past – and future – collaboration.

1

Encountering design-oriented public management

You're a master's student, taking a degree related to public policy and government. Along with your fellow classmates, you're shopping for a good elective course. You meet with your academic adviser to discuss what elective to take. You mention four possibilities: three courses in specific policy areas, as well as a higher-level quantitative methods course. The adviser agrees that every one of the electives you're considering would be absolutely fine. You are then asked whether you have considered one of the electives that isn't on your list. The adviser swivels around to tap two words on the keyboard.

One click later the screen shows the course listing the adviser has in mind. It's Public Management: A Strategic Approach. You ask what the adviser knows about it. "Not a lot, but previous students say that it helped them with job interviews, and it then helped them gain a reputation as a great hire." After glancing back at the adviser's screen, you write down the course code that hadn't been on *your* screen.

As you leave the building, you use your smartphone to log into the university's course catalogue and search for the course. The entry on course content says:

> The course provides a management dimension to the study of public
> administration and public program planning. The course focuses on using
> purposive theories of directing, planning, coordinating and controlling – plus
> design-precedents from case studies – to devise jointly-enabling mechanisms to
> tackle challenges in performing the management function in public programs and
> organizations. Through class discussions and case assignments, the course expands
> professional knowledge, improves professional abilities (e.g., sense-making,
> designing, argumentation, and dramatization), and strengthens professional
> competence. It also develops an ability to reverse-engineer public programs
> and organizations so that planning can benefit from experience. The course also
> considers the past and future of public management as a professional discipline.

You click on the link to the university's on-line learning system and search for PA 419. You begin to scroll through the icons and links for Week 1, noticing the course introductory video. You click on the link. As the video is loading, you get a WhatsApp message telling you that your new classmates are waiting for you at the student center café. By then the video has loaded, but you pause it and head for the café.

Moments later, you spot your classmates at a table toward the back. Mercifully, there's no line to order coffee. You tell the barista you want an espresso. As you sit down, Alicia, Bob, Carmen, Dimitrios, and Eva (from China) are comparing their shopping-lists for elective courses. After picking up the conversation, you tell them you've just been looking at a course on public management. Bob says he hadn't seen that listing. You say that you heard about it from your adviser.

Carmen pulls up the course description on her smartphone screen, while you tell her that the adviser remarked that past students felt it was good for their careers. Alicia asks what skills you will get from the course. You say you're not sure, but that the course description says it improves professional abilities and strengthens professional competence. Carmen reads out the list of professional abilities: sense-making, designing, argumentation, and dramatization. Alicia looks skeptical. Those are skills? Bob says you need to be good at these things as a professional in organizations: after all, you can't solve problems without sense-making and designing. Eva says you can't justify decisions without argumentation. Dimitrios says that dramatization may not be a skill, but it's key to the art of leadership. You say that maybe these issues are explained in the course introductory video, which you point to on your screen. Carmen suggests talking about this again after you all have had a chance to check it out.

Unpacking the narrative opener

Let's take a moment to understand and appreciate this short, initial encounter with *Public Management as a Design-Oriented Professional Discipline*. The chapter opens with a narrative. Why? Research about rhetoric and communication has shown that people tend to be more receptive to ideas presented narratively, than to ideas presented argumentatively.[1] This bit of knowledge supports a design principle for writing and public speaking: if the reader isn't ready to be receptive to an argument, then authors and speakers should preface arguments with material presented in story form.

The story you read earlier begins with its characters deciding what courses to take as part of their degree. As a consequence, public management makes its first appearance as a course, which might be unexpected. Is there a reason? A correct guess is that students are among the book's intended readers and, further, that the author imagines students won't immediately care whether public management is a professional discipline. Why introduce the chapter specifically with the scenario of course selection? The communication principle involved is to anchor the meaning of abstract ideas in their experientially-familiar likenesses.[2] Such likenesses are sometimes called "concrete" analogues.[3] They aren't actually concrete: but that's a simple way to highlight that they can be understood without mastering an abstractly-worded code. It won't be hard for readers to imagine what it would be like to consider taking such a course. In combination, these reasons lead to the conclusion that the text is suitably designed to trigger the audience's interest in the character of public management, at least as a matter of momentary interest.

An invitation for studying public management

Your wi-fi connection is good. You click on the arrow icon to re-start the video. A slide comes up with the title: "Encountering Public Management." The professor's voice comes across, but he is not seen. He makes some introductory remarks, and then starts to dig into substance.

This course is on public management. As public management doesn't have a uniformly standard meaning that everyone shares, you need to be told what public management means specifically in this course. Public management is a professional practice. Generally speaking, a professional practice is what professional practitioners are engaged in when they are creating or improving a phenomenon that exists for reasons of intent. Take architecture: it's what architects are engaged in when they are creating or improving buildings for shelter or other purposes. Take engineering: it's what engineers are engaged in when they are creating or improving machines to be used in households and offices, to make products, or to make other machines. So, what is public management? It's what professional practitioners are engaged in, when they are creating or improving public organizations.

That statement is so expansive that it needs to be unpacked. In this course, a public organization is not a list of kinds of attributes, such as a government agency's legal powers, organizational roles, program responsibilities, and budgets.[4] A public organization is viewed more abstractly and functionally, as a mechanism for effectuating intent. Accordingly, "public organizations" is not a classification category, but is rather a kind of mechanism-intent phenomena.

Mechanism-intent phenomena is a new term, coined for the purposes of this course. However, it's not a new idea. Aristotle had some things to say about this idea, which he contrasted with naturally occurring biological phenomena, as some philosophers have recently discussed.[5] The main precedent for the idea of mechanism-intent phenomena goes back to Herbert Simon's *Sciences of the Artificial*.[6] His book was mainly concerned with a broad category of mechanism-intent phenomena: artificial systems, such as machines and buildings.

In this course, the main precedent for thinking about public organizations as a kind of mechanism-intent phenomena is a widely known book by Mark H. Moore, entitled, *Creating Public Value: Strategic Management in Government*.[7] Moore worked out an elaborate argument about public organizations, in which one thesis was that their intent is to create public value. Creating public value is a short-hand phrase for effectuating the realization of collective political aspirations through public programs, while limiting restrictions on individual liberties. Another direction for his theorizing of public organizations is that they create public value by delivering public programs, and by doing other things (including management) that enable program delivery.

The idea that public organizations are a kind of mechanism-intent phenomena is very broad. The reason for breadth is to connect public management with centuries and even millennia-old theorizing about practical questions that lie between institutional design and behavioral choice. A bridge to such theorizing is Herbert Simon's *Sciences of the Artificial*. As mentioned, the kinds of mechanism-intent phenomena on which Simon focused were artificial systems, like machines, buildings, and software programs. A second bridge to such theorizing is Fayol's *Industrial and General Administration*.[8] The kind of mechanism-intent phenomena on which Fayol focused was enterprises. In this course, public organizations are seen as a special case of enterprises.

This course theorizes public organizations as effectuating intent through the performance of enterprise-functions. This idea comes from Fayol, who theorized enterprises much like Aristotle theorized kinds of organisms. Organisms need to perform functions like respiration and circulation: if they do so inadequately, they will become sick, or even die. Enterprises need to perform enterprise-functions: if they do so inadequately, then they will be less able to effectuate enterprise-intent, and even fail entirely.

The list of enterprise-functions in Fayol's theory was a series of nouns: in alphabetical order they were accounting, commercial, finance, management, security, and technical. Fayol went into detail about the enterprise-function of management, by defining its constitutive functions as a series of verbs: in alphabetical order, they were (famously) coordinating, controlling, directing, and planning. Each plays a role in performing the enterprise-function of management.

Fayol's theory of enterprises as a kind of mechanism-intent phenomena is one side of a coin: the other side is that he theorizes enterprises along mechanism-intent lines. That is, enterprises are a kind of mechanism-intent phenomena because Fayol theorized enterprises along mechanism-intent lines. In this course, public organizations are theorized along mechanism-intent lines.

Under the mechanism-intent theorizing of enterprises, functions are said to be performed by mechanism-like phenomena. Mechanism-like phenomena are *for* performing enterprise functions. Given that, the question is what do mechanism-like phenomena *consist in*. In this course, mechanism-like phenomena are *for* performing enterprise functions and they *consist in* context-dependent, non-deterministic scenario-processes.

The idea that scenario-processes perform enterprise functions may not sound familiar, but it couldn't be more conventional: after all, decision-making in organizations has been theorized as a context-dependent, non-deterministic scenario-process since at least the 1950s. And the idea that enterprise-functions – especially management – are performed by decision-making remains entirely current.

Decision-making isn't the only kind of mechanism-like phenomena within enterprises. No less important is a kind of scenario-process that eventuates in decision alternatives: Herbert Simon referred to this form of scenario-processes as designing. Designing is about creating solutions, while decision-making is about choosing a solution to go with. The scenario-process of designing has a sufficiently different profile from that of decision-making that it's important to insist upon the distinction. Accordingly, scenario-processes in mechanism-intent theorizing of enterprises and public organizations are two-fold, at least: decision-making and designing.

Thus, in this course, performing the enterprise functions of public organizations effectuates public value creation (i.e., the intent of public organizations), while their mechanism-like scenario-processes include both decision-making and designing. This sort of mechanism-intent theorizing of public organizations takes the best of Fayol, Moore, and Simon – and consolidates it into one coherent approach.

I will now talk through this course itself as a mechanism-intent phenomenon. The slide you are now viewing presents a high-level representation of this course. I call this high-level representation a "conceptual design": that is a term from the field of engineering design for a diagram that is clear about functions and intent, and that suggests the shape of the technical systems that perform the functions, but doesn't go into their specifics.[9]

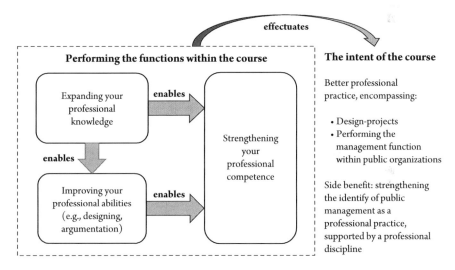

Figure 1.1 The conceptual design of the course

A simple way to read the conceptual design diagram is this: the course will effectuate your being better at professional practice in public organizations in the future as compared with the past. It will do so, above all, by strengthening your professional competence. The course will strengthen your professional competence by both expanding your professional knowledge and improving your professional abilities. I'll now go into details.

Regarding intent, the idea is that the course will effectuate your being better at professional practice in public organizations. Professional practice is *for* performing enterprise-functions, not least the management function, with its constitutive functions of directing, planning, coordinating, and controlling. In relation to Simon's implied mechanism-intent theory of enterprises, professional practice is *for* bringing design-projects – with their constitutive scenario-processes of designing and decision-making – to fruition. Thus, the intent of the course is to effectuate your being better at contributing to design-projects, as well as in otherwise performing the management function within public organizations.

The main *function* of the course is to strengthen your professional competence. Professional competence is a capacity to act in ways that effectuate your professional intent: under this idea, you and your actions are mechanism-like phenomena situated in some locale within a public organization, during some interval of time. Professional competence is partly the capacity to act within a design-project, furthering the scenario-process of designing as well as that of decision-making.[10] Professional competence is also partly the capacity to *instigate* design-projects within a public organization.

In the course's conceptual design, your professional competence is strengthened, in part, by improving your professional abilities. This course seeks to improve four kinds of professional abilities: sense-making, designing, argumentation, and dramatization.

In this course's conceptual design, your professional abilities are improved, in part, by assessing simulated experience in the light of theories of people and practices. Sense-making is theorized in psychology and cognitive science. Designing is theorized in the interdisciplinary field of design studies. Argumentation is theorized in philosophy, linguistics, and rhetoric. Dramatization is theorized in sociology and anthropology. The implication is that learning about theories of sense-making, designing, argumentation, and dramatization is constitutive of "expanding your professional ability."

Let me now explain the direct relation between "expanding professional knowledge" and "strengthening professional competence," according to the conceptual design of this course. The idea is that there's more to professional competence in public management than exercising the capacities of sense-making, designing, argumentation, and dramatization. It takes an ability to make use of theories that consider public organizations to be purposeful phenomena (such as Mark Moore's), as well as the ability to be enlightened by – and utilize – mechanism-intent analysis of specific public organizations and their design-projects, as they have transpired in the past. Otherwise, professional practice might be masterful in form, but lacking in substance.

There's more that can be said about the course's conceptual design, but I'm conscious of the limitation on concentration when receiving information in this aural and video format. Let me make some general points rather than to add detail. First, you'll probably sense that this course has something in common with a normal management course. There's an emphasis on "skills," if you consider sense-making, designing, argumentation, and dramatization to be skills. There's an emphasis on professional practice. There's an emphasis on performing the management function within enterprises. In these respects, the course reflects a tradition of management education, historically associated with Harvard Business School.

Second, you'll probably sense that this course *isn't* your normal management course. There's an emphasis on furthering design-projects within enterprises. There's an emphasis on the professional ability of designing. There's an emphasis on being enlightened by, and using, mechanism-intent analysis of specific public organizations and their design-projects, as they have transpired in the past. In these respects, the course reflects a different approach to management education, one that grew up inside what was historically known as the modern management school, dating back to the 1950s, and that was advocated by Herbert Simon when he was a professor in the Carnegie Institute of Technology's Graduate School of Industrial Administration.[11] The course similarly reflects the design-oriented approach to professional practice that was later advocated by Herbert Simon in his book, *Sciences of the Artificial*. Thus, the conceptual design of this course is infused with an explicit, fully developed synthesis between two traditions of management education, one known, the other not so much. I call this synthesis a design-oriented approach to the professional practice of public management.

When you come to class, I'll explain how this conceptual design is implemented by the course's mechanism-like scenario-processes, to include reading, case discussions, and a very demanding individual project.

You ask Clara what she thinks. She says the course is more theoretical than she would have expected, but on the other hand, what is being discussed theoretically looks like it will be really practical. You say that this is certainly the way it looks.

Clara asks you whether you're going to go to the first class. You say you'll go if she will. She says that she's shopping five courses, but will go along to this one, too.

Preparing to teach design-oriented public management

A week before the first class session, the course professor, Marshall, walks into a small meeting room, joining Nora, Olivier, and Petra, who are already there. Marshall is a full professor who is approaching his twentieth year as a member of the public administration department. He has taught the course in many different ways over this period. Marshall, Nora, and Petra will co-teach, while Olivier will be the teaching assistant. Nora is a recently minted PhD in political science who has just joined the department as an assistant professor; she has no specific academic background in public administration or management. Olivier is a second-year doctoral student in the public administration department; he has not studied or taught public management before. Petra is new to her role as a senior lecturer-in-practice, having decided to take a two-year leave from government service. Their first faculty team meeting is about to begin.

After they all commented on the weather, Marshall stated the main purpose of the meeting is to formalize the faculty team's role and activities, as well as to make sure everyone is on the same page going into the first session of the course. He hands out hard copies of the presentation slide titled "The conceptual design of the course," saying that this is definitely one of those pages they should be on together.

Petra asks Marshall for some clarification about the intent of the course. Specifically, she asks why the intent of the course doesn't include helping

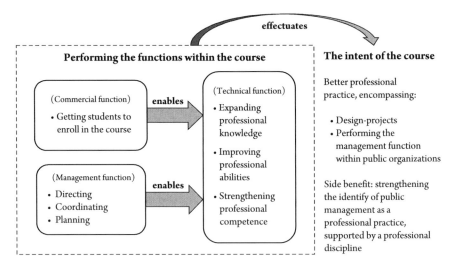

Figure 1.2 The conceptual design of the course: lead teacher's view

students to get a job. Marshall says that he considers getting a job as the intent of a student's degree program as a whole, rather than of this specific course. Petra follows up by asking: Marshall, don't you think more students will take the course if you give them a good reason to believe that it will help them in getting the job they really want to be offered? Marshall says he agrees.

Marshall offers to share his "designer drawings" of the course, as contrasted with the "presentational drawings" that he has presented as "the conceptual design of the course." After shuffling through some loose sheets of paper, he puts the diagram on the meeting table and begins to discuss it.

Marshall says that Petra's asking whether the conceptual design of the course includes a commercial function. The performance of the commercial function will be adequate if students enroll. If students enroll, then the course can perform its technical function, whose constitutive functions are (a) expanding professional knowledge, (b) improving professional abilities, and (c) strengthening professional competence.

Petra looks around the table at Nora and Olivier to see if they seem to appreciate what she considers to be Marshall's pedantic approach to answering her questions. They seem to be keeping neutral faces. She keeps wondering what it's really going to be like to be part of this teaching team.

Petra asks Marshall whether he will tell students that the course will help them with getting offered the job they would like to have. Marshall indicates that he'll now characterize the mechanism-like feature for implementing this part of the conceptual design of the course. He asks every student to form a pair with someone seated to their left or right. He then asks one of them to take on the role of a job interviewer and the other to take on that of a job interviewee. In the exercise, the interviewer says: "I see from your C.V. that you have taken a public management course in your degree program: how do you think it strengthens you as a candidate for this position?" The interviewee has to answer. I give them less than five minutes for this; then I ask them to reverse roles and do the exercise again. After the students have completed their exercise, I ask them what their "partner" in the exercise said that they found to be an especially good line – one that they might use in a true interview. Then I give them a template they can use in scripting their interview responses in the future. It's presented early in the slide deck for the first session of the class. Here's the slide:

A Pitch for the Job Interview

My public management course added a management dimension to my main area of specialization, and as a result, I am now better at gaining and using professional knowledge – about public management and problem-solving – in designing solutions to problems that arise in creating public value through public programs and public administration.

Figure 1.3 Pitching the public management course to an interviewer

---

Marshall asks Petra what she thinks of the interview exercise as a mechanism for performing the course's commercial function. Petra says that she could well imagine that the exercise would win over students who might be put off by the highly theoretical presentation in the course introductory video. An outcome should be for more students to decide to join the course.

Nora shifts slightly in her chair and then prefaces what she wants to ask by saying that she has been taking a compulsory course for new faculty on best practices for designing and evaluating courses. She's planning to write up her experience with this course as part of satisfying the requirements of the new faculty course. Nora says she isn't yet sure how she'd be able to do that. For one reason, the new faculty course instructor says that best practices include formalizing a whole cascade of learning objectives, from the overall course down to its elementary units, such as the individual class session, task, and reading assignment. Nora asks Marshall if the course design has been formalized in this way.

Marshall says that he never had to take a new faculty course, fortunately. Nevertheless, he recently had an experience working with a government-based school of public administration in South America, in order to transfer this course to their curriculum, and the staff there insisted that he comply with their rules that every course needs to have its learning objectives specified. Marshall said it wasn't easy to comply at first, but it felt good when he had finished the task. He saw the value in being able to show others that the course is coherent, even when they didn't know much about the content. He hadn't done the same thing for the course they were going to teach, but he'd be willing to go there if it was important for Nora being able to complete her new faculty course.

Petra says that it would be really helpful for her to know what the learning objectives are, especially as she herself is going to have to learn the material in order to teach it.

Marshall says that the learning objectives should be coherent with two things: one is the course's conceptual design, and the other is the course's embodiment design, which consists in an array of course features: lectures, videos, in-class exercises, case discussions, readings, project assignments, and essays. This discipline of mechanism-intent thinking means that learning objectives represent an understanding of feature-function relationships within the course. He says that a feature worth discussing is the job interview exercise.

Marshall then asks Petra what learning objectives she sees for the job interview exercise. Petra says that the exercise involves more than an interviewee speaking to an interviewer to advance an argument: it also involves non-verbal communication in a situation of face-to-face interaction. The learning objective is then to improve how you perform in front of an audience of sorts. Better stated, the learning objective is to improve how you plan what you'll say and how you'll perform what you've planned to say, or adjust it to surprises as they occur during the interaction. Petra says that she isn't sure what to call this ability, or how to relate the objective to the course's functions.

Marshall thanks Petra for her astute comment. He says that the learning objective she's concerned with relates to the function of improving professional abilities, and that "dramatization" is the term used in the course to refer to the professional ability of planning what you'll say and how you'll perform what you planned to say. The term, and the theorization of social processes associated with it, comes from work by Erving Goffman, a noted sociological theorist. His most famous book was *The Presentation of Self in Everyday Life*.[12] Marshall mentions that last time he checked, that volume had achieved a citation count of 57,000.

Petra comments that she's always taken a certain amount of pride in being able to make use of her personality to influence what happens during meetings – and that was part of her success as a practitioner. But she says she hadn't heard the term "dramatization" before she viewed the video about the course. It's nice to have a word for something that you've always felt was important, she tells Marshall.

Marshall then asks Olivier what learning objectives he sees for the course. Olivier answers by saying that he sees the course as teaching *ideas* about public management. What he specifically has in mind is the idea that professional practice in public organizations involves problem-solving, and problem-solving involves gaining and using professional knowledge. Olivier says he is not sure how to characterize the learning objective, as he is not sure how teaching ideas about public management relates to the conceptual design of the course.

Marshall says that these ideas are presented as professional knowledge. Professional knowledge includes explicit arguments about what public organizations are for, what they consist in, and how they work. Nora asks whether under this definition, professional knowledge consists in normative arguments, much as one finds in political or ethical philosophy. Marshall says that there's no denying that professional knowledge involves normative claims. But such knowledge is not about institution forms or discrete decisions: they are about mechanism-intent phenomena. Marshall says he uses the term "purposive theories" to refer to ideas about what public organizations are for, what they consist in, and how they work.

Olivier asks where he can read about this idea of purposive theorizing. Marshall says that he has just read the page proofs of a book by an academic friend of his, Michael Barzelay, where the idea is developed. Nora asks whether the book presents specific purposive theories of public organizations. Marshall says that Chapter 4 does that, where the specific works examined are Mark Moore's *Creating Public Value: Strategic Management in Government* and John Bryson's *Strategic Planning in Public and Nonprofit Organizations*.[13] For that matter, he adds, Chapter 4 examines works about design-projects and the professional activities of sense-making, designing, argumentation, and dramatization.

Marshall starts to smile broadly at this point. Nora, Olivier, and Petra gaze at him with surprised looks on their faces. Sensing their gaze, Marshall tells them about how the chapter is presented as an audio guide for a tour of a fictional museum called the Public Management Gallery. He intends to assign Chapter 4 to students on courses like the one they are co-teaching.

At this point, Petra looks conspicuously at her watch and then at the clock in the room. She tells Marshall that she will need to get to another meeting soon. Marshall proposes that they go around the room to list issues that the teaching team should take up together in their subsequent meetings, or issues they might want to just talk about informally when the opportunity arises, or to make any other comment. Let's go in alphabetical order.

Nora says that she's aware that the course includes case studies; she wants to know if there's any relation between case studies in this course and case study research that she has done in political science. Marshall says that issue is crucial for the course. He points out that Barzelay's book discusses the relation between case study research in social science and case study research in public management, considered as a Design-Oriented professional discipline, in Chapters 6 and 7.

Olivier says that he's curious about this idea that public management is a professional discipline. Marshall just mentioned it, and the term put in an appearance in the diagram on the conceptual design of the course, in the lower right-hand corner. Marshall says that the idea of a professional discipline is developed throughout Barzelay's book. Indeed, the title is *Public Management as a Design-Oriented Professional Discipline*. He thinks Olivier will be especially interested in the final chapter, entitled, "Designed, not copied: the making of public management as a design-oriented professional discipline," as well as in the extensive glossary at the back.

Petra asks Marshall if she, too, could get a look at Barzelay's book, as it ought to get her started on the right foot. Marshall said he'd send her the proofs as soon as he gets back to his office.

Meeting the author at the book launch

You've made yourself comfortable in your seat at the launch event for *Public Management as a Design-Oriented Professional Discipline*. You're seated next to

Carmen and Eva. You notice that Marshall, Nora, Olivier, and Petra have front row seats. Two figures take their places on stage. One adjusts the microphone and scans the audience. The murmur in the auditorium subsides. The host begins the session:

Host: Welcome to the Academy Theatre, Professor Barzelay. Congratulations on your new book. Thank you for agreeing to speaking at this event.
Barzelay: Happy to be here, thanks for inviting me.
Host: I'd like to begin by asking you some questions about the faculty meeting scene in Chapter 1 of your book.
Barzelay: That's perfectly fine, please go ahead.
Host: As I watched the scene unfold, I wondered whether you might identify with a particular character portrayed in it?
Barzelay: Yes, indeed. The one whose given name begins with the letter M and ends with L. As you get to know Marshall – what he cares about, how he thinks, and how he dialogues with Nora, Olivier and Petra – you'll get to know me, at least as I know myself.
Host: I imagine then that the faculty meeting scene is modeled on actual experience. Are Nora, Olivier, and Petra modeled on actual people?
Barzelay: You know, the ideas in this book have been developing for quite a while, longer than I would like to believe. As these ideas developed, I worked closely with assistant professors, doctoral students, and practitioners. What's important about the characters of Nora, Olivier, and Petra is that they represent the roles that need to become part of the professional discipline of public management. We need to bring in talented young academics from social science disciplines like political science; we need to invest in developing doctoral students in fields like public administration and management; and we need to transform some number of practitioners into outstanding practitioner-academics (or what's called pracademics).
Host: At the end of the meeting, Olivier picks up on your idea that public management is a professional discipline. What prompted you to think about this idea?
Barzelay: Imagine the following scene. You're an associate professor, going through your tenure review. You're asked to meet with the Dean. You sit down, not exactly at ease. In the course of the discussion, the Dean says that he has a hard time understanding what public management is. It's not a substantive area of public policy. It's not a social science discipline. It's taught in the core curriculum, alongside some other courses like statistics. So the way he has resolved his doubt is to view public management as a methodology.
Host: You've made up this scene, no?
Barzelay: No, that "conversation" truly happened. Specifically, in 1994 in Cambridge, Massachusetts, at Harvard University's Kennedy School of Government.
Host: Were there any other influences?
Barzelay: In 1996, during my first year at LSE, Larry Lynn published a much-expected book entitled *Public Management as Art, Science, and Profession.*[14] I read Lynn's concluding chapter as contending that public management is a

professional discipline, with practice being craft-like, and with both scholarship and research being important to the education of professional practitioners. That line made sense to me, and I filed it away in my mind.

Host: What brought it out of the file?

Barzelay: It became relevant again when I started to teach public management to students on an MPA program and in a MSc degree in our Management Department. For a while I presented public management as a form of professional practice. I tied that idea back to Simon's idea that all professional practitioners are problem-solvers and that every professional practitioner brings specialist domain knowledge into the problem-solving process. So, what does that mean for public management? First, it means problem-solving concerns the future of particular public programs and public institutions. Second, it means that public management practice also involves bringing specialist (domain) knowledge about *management* into problem-solving about public programs and public institutions. This framing of public management seemed to go over well with both students and practitioners.

Host: So how did you get from "professional practice" to "professional discipline"?

Barzelay: I got there as I finally settled on the title and chapter composition of my book, *Public Management as a Design-Oriented Professional Discipline*.

Host: That's the book on-sale here, right outside the theater hall, ladies and gentlemen.

Barzelay: I decided that the book had to reach academics – they had to be viewed as the primary audience, in that they would have to endorse the book for students ever to come across it. For academics, it's important to be able to present a "line" about what this field's character is, in my view. The language of professional discipline is meant to fill this need.

Host: A few minutes ago you mentioned that you had filed away in your mind your positive reaction to Larry Lynn's argument that public management is a professional discipline. Does that mean your idea about public management is the same as, or very closely similar to, the one Lynn presented in his 1996 book?

Barzelay: I agree with his book that it is important to take a line on public management. I agree that public management is best labeled as a professional discipline, for many of the same reasons as Lynn's book puts forth. However, I have many reservations about Lynn's overall argument about public management. For one, Lynn's book defines the subject matter of public management too broadly, as performing the executive function in government. I think *that* broad definition hardly distinguishes public management from all of public administration. For another, the idea of professional practice is underdeveloped. Without an acceptably developed idea of professional practice, you don't have all the makings of an idea of a professional discipline.

Host: Do you have a way to summarize your view of public management as a professional discipline?

Barzelay: I do have a diagram that presents an overall conceptual design of public management as a design-oriented professional discipline, if we could project it on the screen.

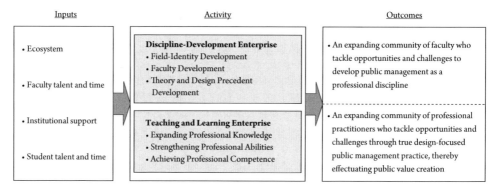

Figure 1.4 Results chain for the public management professional discipline

(The diagram is projected.)

Host: Go ahead, now.

Barzelay: The main precedent for this diagram is the results chain framework used routinely in presenting program plans to funders and other stakeholders. The results chain framework should be familiar to everyone here – in any case, the underlying ideas are part of ordinary systems thinking, you know, inputs, activities, outputs, and outcomes. I've simplified the standard representation by omitting outputs. Let me take you through it.

Host: Please do.

Barzelay: Well, the diagram as a whole represents the professional discipline of public management. It consists in two collections of activities, labeled as enterprises. One is about developing the discipline, the other is about teaching and learning. Both enterprises are designed to accomplish outcomes. The intended outcome of the discipline-development enterprise is an expanding community of faculty – like Nora, Olivier, and Petra – who tackle opportunities and challenges to develop public management as a professional discipline. The intended outcome of the teaching and learning enterprise is an expanding community of professional practitioners who tackle opportunities and challenges through true design-focused public management practice, thereby effectuating public value creation.

Host: I'm conscious that we are bumping up against the end of our allotted time. Perhaps you could just say a few words about your book before we wrap up.

Barzelay: Yes, thank you for the opportunity. I think its intent ought to be broadly clear by now: it's to effectuate the discipline-development enterprise, more than the teaching and learning one, but that's not excluded. I hope the book will enable field-identity development, faculty development, and professional knowledge development. In relation to the teaching and learning enterprise, I think it can be used by faculty in developing curriculum for courses. It can be used by students in expanding their professional knowledge, particularly in giving a broad perspective on that matter. Overall, the book is meant to effectuate public management becoming "great" as a field – finally, perhaps.

Host: I'm sure we would all like to receive a detailed preview of all the chapters of this book, but unfortunately we don't have time today. Thank you very much for the interview. (Turning to speak to the audience.) Colleagues and friends, I think what you have gotten out of today's session is a feel for why the book has been written and how it might relate to your own concerns. You know what it is for. It's clearly designed to effectuate public management's discipline-development enterprise and to enable its teaching and learning enterprise. Whether it has either effect is up to you. Thank you for joining us today.

NOTES

1 Tilly (2006).
2 Lakoff (1987).
3 Heath and Heath (2008).
4 Among many works that view government agencies in terms of such empirical attributes, see Wilson (1989).
5 Ariew and Perlman (2002).
6 Simon (1996).
7 Moore (1995).
8 Fayol (1919/1984). See also, "Henri Fayol: Planning and Administration" https://www.pocketbook. co.uk/blog/2014/07/15/henri-fayol-planning-and-administration/ (accessed April 28, 2019).
9 Cross (2008).
10 Simon (1996) and van Aken and Berends (2018).
11 Augier and March (2011).
12 Goffman (1959).
13 Bryson (2018).
14 Lynn (1996).

2

Rediscovering management: analysis and synthesis

An underlying theme in the previous chapter is that public management's disciplinary identity isn't what it needs to be. As a mechanism to define discipline identity, this chapter starts off by making an historical turn. It investigates paths along which *ideas* have developed: specifically, ideas about professional disciplines, management, design, and public management.

Just a few years ago I came across an historical narrative about North American business schools in the post-World War II period, by Mie Augier and James G. March.[1] This eye-opening book showed that fissures in the management field are deeply evident in its North American history, with the sharpest lines drawn between the pragmatist tradition represented by Harvard Business School (HBS) and the "modern management school." The ideas of the modern management school took concrete form in the 1950s, particularly at Carnegie Institute of Technology's Graduate School of Industrial Administration (GSIA), more than 25 years after the HBS approach had settled into a pattern. Augier and March showed that the institutional forerunner of the modern American management school was the modern American *medical* school, pioneered in the 1910s, at Johns Hopkins University. In commenting on their narrative historical account, Augier and March argue that traces of this episode in the history of management schools – including the intellectual and institutional rivalry between HBS and GSIA – can still be discerned.

This history matters for public management. It matters in a general way because fissures in the management field have shown up as battle-lines in discussions of public management. As this chapter will show, sharp battle-lines came to be drawn, once an approach to public management had taken clear form in U.S. public policy schools, most notably at Harvard's Kennedy School of Government. The person who drew those battle-lines was Lawrence Lynn,[2] by that time a professor at the University of Chicago. Lynn critically opposed ideas identified institutionally with Harvard Kennedy School, where he had previously taught. As made plain by the end of his 1996 book, Lynn's own views, by the time he was at Chicago, carried a strong resemblance to those of the modern management school. Thus, the battle-lines that Lynn drew look similar to what Augier and March found had been very much true of the field of management schools decades earlier.

Going back to the management school history will help put public management in perspective (in part because these management disciplines are not historically independent). Herbert A. Simon plays a part in this story. While serving as a professor at Carnegie, Simon developed his now hugely influential ideas about the character of problem-solving, initially as a critical response to what became the mainstream view of the management discipline at GSIA, patterned on the modern medical school. But Simon eventually left GSIA; and his views about *design*ing, as a distinctive idea about problem-solving, took form later, becoming better-known with successive editions of his *Sciences of the Artificial*.[3] However, Simon didn't come up with a fully formed idea of *management* as a design-oriented professional discipline. The need for one has been discussed in the management field overall and in a couple of its sub-fields.[4] Nevertheless, I would contend that no such idea really yet exists in substance.

This situation is perhaps unsettling. The public management discipline has usually talked about itself as if the key question requiring lucid discussion is public versus private management. The underlying assumption is that ideas about the management discipline are monolithic, that its main debates as a discipline are settled. This assumption might be convenient, but, as Augier and March's book implies, it's not valid.

This chapter analyzes and then synthesizes two approaches to theorizing management, one being Harvard-esque (hereafter, H), with the other being Simon-esque (hereafter, S). The chosen primary bibliographic source for H is one about public management. Specifically, it's *Creating Public Value: Strategic Management in Government*.[5] Its author, Mark H. Moore, did his doctorate at Harvard's Kennedy School of Government in the 1970s and then served as a professor at Harvard, based in that school, for nearly 40 years. Moore engaged fully with Harvard Business School (HBS) theorizations of business enterprises. Like a designer, Moore used the ideas that he came to understand deeply as *precedents* in coming up with a synthesis that would be suitable for public management. While Moore makes reference to his synthesis' precedents, his text didn't provide an extensive account of them.

Let me now turn to explaining the use of Simon's *Sciences of the Artificial* as a basis for identifying S. That volume contains Simon's most well-known theorization of problem-solving; specifically, Chapter 5 is the *locus classicus* of this theorizing. This discussion isn't presented as being specifically about management; the chapter's primary audience was professors of engineering. The reason we can be confident that Chapter 5 is a theorization of management is due to Augier and March's narrative historical account, which explained that Simon's approach to management as problem-solving was developed during his earlier period at Carnegie's business school, when he was working out an alternative to mainstream ideas within the "modern management school."

The Harvard-esque tradition as exemplified by *creating public value*

As I proceed, I will assume passing familiarity with Moore's book, by which I mean some of its ideas stuck with you, but you certainly wouldn't want to be called upon out of the blue to make a well-structured presentation about it.

Taking up first things first, you will recall the initial presentation of Moore's theorization of public management involved narrating a fictional case where the Town Librarian verbalized her thinking about whether and how to take action in the face of a change in the library facility's usage patterns: specifically, in the mid-afternoon period, the library's public rooms filled up with school-age residents of the town. This population of users was known as latchkey children: going to the library was a preferred alternative to spending after-school hours at home, with a factor being the absence of adult relatives during daytime hours. The Town Librarian and Latchkey Children case served Moore's expositional purposes for three reasons. First, the Town Library exemplified a key concept in his theory, which Moore labeled as the "public organization." Second, the Town Librarian exemplified a pivotal concept in Moore's theory, labeled as the "public manager." Third, the Town Librarian's response to the change in pattern in Town Library usage exemplified a further key concept in his theory: "strategic public management." Let's examine these ideas.

In doing this, you need to keep telling yourself that Moore is using this case discussion to *theorize* public management practice. It may seem odd to theorize through a case discussion, but there's a long tradition behind that. If you're going to treat Moore's discussion of this case as theorization, then you will have to look for the structure of ideas. In order to do that it helps to know something about the ideas about management that he draws upon as precedents.

As a point of entry let's take the idea of a public organization. Ask yourself, is this term being presented as a way to *classify* organizations? If Moore were developing a descriptive or, what is the same, a positive theory of organizations, then the idea of public organization would sensibly be conceived as a category. However, Moore didn't develop a positive theory of organizations: he developed a purposive theory of public management. In such a theory, "public organization" isn't a category: it's an idea about a kind of purposeful phenomenon. So, let's go forward on the basis that, in Moore's theory of public management, the term "public organization" plays the role of the kind of purposeful phenomenon with which his theory is concerned.

If we choose to see Moore's theory as a purposive theory and, specifically, interpret the term "public organization" as being the purposeful phenomenon within the theory, then we can follow standard steps to clarify the theory further. If a public organization is the purposeful phenomenon in Moore's theory, then Moore's theory has to say what intent is effectuated by public organizations. So, what is the specific concept within Moore's purposive theory that plays the role of public organizations' intent? This is not meant to be a demanding question. If you glance at the cover of Moore's book, you can't miss it. The role of "intent" in

Moore's purposive theory is played by the three words that form the main title of the book.

If you stare at the overall book title, you might contemplate the relation between the main title (i.e., creating public value) and the sub-title (i.e., strategic management in government). There's not much information in the grammatical symbol – a colon – that sits between the two parts of the title. So we have to guess, while keeping in mind that Moore's theory is a purposive theory of public organizations, for use in the professional practice of public management.

In purposive theories like Moore's, professional practice consists, in part, in using theories of the purposeful phenomena with which their practice is concerned (e.g., public organizations), to channel a practitioner's imagination and deliberative reasoning. The outcome of such cerebral activity is effectively a plan for what such practitioners are going to think and do as they further engage with the situation involving the purposeful phenomenon at hand (e.g., public organizations) in whatever capacity they hold (e.g., managerial roles in public organizations). I'd say that "strategic management in government" is a reference to the professional practice of public management. More precisely, "strategic management in government" is a reference to the sum-total of ideas in Moore's theory that are meant to channel a practitioner's imagination and deliberative reasoning.

For ease of recall and reference, I formalize this discussion of Moore's purposive theory in the following way:

1. Public organizations *effectuate* public value creation.[6]
2. Strategic public management ideas *channel* practitioners' imaginative and deliberative reasoning about public organizations; such activity *eventuates* in practitioners' plans for further professional activity.[7]

If you're familiar with Moore's book, you may understandably react to this involved discussion and its formalization by asking: why not just say public managers create public value? After all, that's one of the most memorable ideas about Moore's book. You can guess my answer: the idea that public managers create public value is like a tag-line, bumper sticker, or sound-bite: it is meant to be a sticky message. The line works because it expresses some of the core ideas of Moore's purposive theory in an exceedingly compact way. That's helpful in establishing Moore's book as a reference, which is a good thing. But, on its own, the idea that public managers create public value isn't that helpful to public management practice, let alone developing public management as a professional discipline.

For professional practice, the most useful role that the line "public mangers create public value" can play is in *indexing* Moore's theory in a practitioner's memory system; in this role, referring to public managers as public-value creators can be used to activate the neural networks that, in turn, channel a practitioner's imaginative thinking and deliberative reasoning about actual public organizations.[8] For that scenario to happen, however, a practitioner's neural networks have to reflect Moore's theory, in its expert rather than sound-bite version. How can such networks come to be formed in the mind? It requires a learning activity,[9] one in which concept acquisition is channeled by reference to a well-structured, purposive theory.

Having made the case for using ideas about purposive theorizing in uncovering the expert version of Moore's theory of public management, let's now return to the task of stating *what it is*, going into more substantive depth. A starting point is to examine the earlier, formalized idea that public organizations effectuate public value creation. Consider the case of the Town Librarian and Latchkey Children. No doubt we learn of aspects of the Town Library, considered as an organization, such as the fact that the town librarian's formal role is located at the apex of the library's organization structure and that the organization's staff identifies themselves professionally as librarians. But much of the discussion of the case is about the library facility's public spaces, usage patterns by clientele group, and accessing library holdings. This information doesn't clash with the idea that the case is about a public organization, provided the idea of technology is a property of the idea of organization. Nevertheless, there's another concept that gives meaning to these otherwise disparate observations: it's the *program results-chain*. The library's public spaces and holdings are *inputs*; usage of the library's public spaces by clients and accessing its holdings are *activities*; information transferred from accessible library resources to the library users' internal and external memory systems are *outputs*. On the basis of this case discussion, then, we can see that Moore's concept of public organization includes two ideas: an *organization* (with its role structure, personnel, culture, contractual partners, and technology) and a *program* (with the inputs, activities, and outputs of a public service operation).

As we think about the structure of Moore's theory, we might want to ask: is there any point making a distinction between the idea of "organization" and the idea of "program"? I think there is. My interpretation is that in Moore's theory of public management, program results chains provide relatively fine-grained information about how any given public organization effectuates public value creation, when that information is compared with the organization's role structures, personnel, contractual partners, and technology. That point – and the conceptual distinction between organization and program underneath it – becomes plainly evident if you manage to work your way through Moore's discussion in Chapter 2 of the illustrative case of the municipal sanitation department and its program of picking up the garbage.

The organization/program distinction has a practical import, within Moore's theory. Recall the statement that, "strategic public management ideas *channel* practitioners' imaginative and deliberative reasoning about public organizations; such activity *eventuates* in practitioners' plans for further professional activity." The implication is that specific ideas about programs and public service operations have a role to play in channeling practitioners' imaginative and deliberative reasoning, a role that is distinct from ideas about organizations. (Thinking about public management as a professional discipline, a different sort of implication is that professional knowledge about public management and program planning should go hand-in-hand.)

We now face a terminological problem. "Public organizations" is a term that means two related things. An organization and a program/public service operation. You could work hard to remember that "public organizations" includes a program/public service operation, in Moore's theory. That's fine, but there may be a better alternative, for which there is a long-standing precedent in management theory. It's the concept of an *enterprise*, which was introduced in the oldest modern theorization of management, by Henri Fayol, written in French and translated years later into English. In Fayol's theory, an enterprise is like an organism that, to survive and thrive, performs functions, which he listed as the technical, commercial, financial, accounting, security, and management functions.[10] The organization – which his text sometimes referred to as "the body social" – is a structure that effectuates the performance of these functions. How does the idea of a program/public service operation in Moore's theory relate to this scheme? It's the public sector analogue to performing an enterprise's technical and commercial functions. How do organizations in Moore's theory relate to this scheme? They effectuate the performance of all of these enterprise functions, and they consist in a "body social." So, my suggestion is that we recruit the concept of enterprise from Fayol's theorization of management to solve a terminological problem. If the term "enterprise" in Fayol's theory is substituted for the term "public organization" in Moore's theory, then Moore's theory could be understood as being about two aspects of enterprises: organizations and programs. (There would also be a symmetry to the contemporary management literature, where the idea of an enterprise covers both an organization governed as a company and a business operated by a company.)

While the inclusion of "enterprise" in Moore's theory would solve a *terminological* problem, it might raise a *labeling* problem. Moore surely was aware of this labeling problem when he chose to use the term "public organizations." As a matter of history, those who translated Fayol's book from French to English were involved in public administration; they translated Fayol's term *"entreprise"* into organization; they had their audience in mind. Moore was being conservative in his labeling. In what follows, I'll use the word "enterprise," because I want to avoid the terminological problem: but if it creates labeling problems for you, please feel free to relabel the idea as public organization, like Moore, or go for something different but slightly less corporate, like "public venture."

Having discussed public organizations, we can turn to the idea of a public manager. Here's a question for you: does Moore introduce this concept as a *category* to *classify* actors, roles, or statuses within government? By now you probably will guess that my answer is no. "Public manager" is a concept within a purposive theory of public management. Concepts within purposive theories aren't classificatory categories. Does that mean that Moore says *nothing* about the "properties" of the concept of public managers? No, it just means that when Moore is presenting his theory of public management, public managers isn't a classificatory category.

To see the difference, let's take a quick look at the meaning of "public managers" as a category. A key property of public managers is that they are biological individuals; another key property is that they work within the institution of government. The question then becomes how the concept of public managers is differentiated from the concept of biological individuals working within the institution of government. One differentiating property is that public managers work within public bureaucracies; they are not legislators or judges. That is about all one can say about public managers, by listing this category's *defining* properties.

One can say more by listing *typical* properties. For Moore, a typical property is that public managers are appointed to their jobs; to be a public manager and elected is atypical, as might be the case with U.S. jurisdictions with "long ballots," where, for example, a state-level secretary of state or attorney general would gain office through elections. How a public manager becomes appointed to their jobs is not a property of the concept of a public manager; for this reason, referring to public managers as bureaucrats would be terminologically incorrect. One could perhaps say more: for example, that a typical property of public managers is that their positions are managerial, where this property is a constellation of more specific properties, such as holding of grant of (conditional) authority in relation to coordinate authorities or hierarchical subordinates. So, now if you were asked to define what a public manager is, you'd know what to say. It's a category with defining and typical properties (as listed), within which can fit some atypical cases (such as elected public managers).

At the risk of pointing out the obvious, the idea of a public manager within Moore's purposive theory of public management *is related to* the idea of a manager in purposive theories of business management. By analyzing this relationship, we will get on the road toward understanding the idea of a public manager. Not only that, we will come to see how Moore's theory is Harvard-esque, which will prepare the ground for later discussions.

In analyzing the relationship, consider that Moore's book was published in 1995, following a gestation period of about a decade. The book's content was developed during a period when Moore was active in developing curriculum for executive programs for public officials, with the collaboration of a few Harvard Business School professors, identified with the area of general management and business policy. In form, the curriculum design was modeled on executive and MBA education, as it was practiced at HBS and at other institutions that had followed its lead. The form included case studies of administrative situations as they had been shaped by earlier events. Classroom discussion focused on issues posed by such a situation, as they would be formulated by specific actors caught up in it, in accord with their organizational role. Participant discussions were facilitated, guided, and summed-up by the case teacher. While the form of the curriculum design was a replica of teaching at Harvard Business School, the content was meant to be specific to public management. Moore's book is the product of this history.

Case method teaching of business management was established at HBS in the 1920s; its precedent was case method teaching of legal practice, which had come to be established at Harvard Law School during the previous 25 years or so.[11] It stands to reason that basic ideas about professional practice exhibited in case teaching in the Law School were absorbed into the teaching of business management. And what ideas were those? One of those ideas was *casuistry*.

Casuistry is a form of practice employed to reach and explain decisions in life. The basic idea is that, even when there's consensus on principles of what's right to do, there's still lots of room for disagreement about what's right to do, in particular circumstances. Room for disagreement is particularly wide when circumstances throw up a dilemma, as circumstances often do. When that happens, there's no alternative to leaving it to individuals to come to their own conclusions – and then explain them. A role for casuistry is to develop any given individual's judgmental capacity – which means being able to arrive at and explain difficult decisions.

The method for developing such capacity is to work through cases, under instruction: in particular, to present one's holding as to what is, or was, the right thing to do; to provide a rationale for the holding, consistent with the moral tradition employing the casuistical practice; and then to deal with objections and rebuttals. (If you want to read a more expert and fuller account of casuistry, see, Jonsen and Toulmin[12] or make do with Wikipedia.)

The parallels between casuistry and case-method *legal* instruction are doubtlessly strong. You can easily imagine a case teacher asking whether you agree or disagree with a judge's holding in a case, and also whether you agree or disagree with the opinion rationalizing the judge's holding.

What about parallels between casuistry and case-method *management* instruction? A strong parallel is that management instruction trains judgment, using similar methods. The student has to work through cases, arriving at decisions (holdings) and explaining their rationale; *lots* of cases. Some parallels are not so straightforwardly neat. In casuistry, individuals need to explain their "holdings" to fellow members of the same *moral tradition*; in management, individuals need to explain their "holdings" to fellow members of the same *professional practice*. In casuistry, the issues are about dilemmas that arise because of *incompatible moral principles*; in management, issues that aren't easy to resolve for all sorts of reasons, including *goal ambiguity, unclear technology, uncertainty,* and *organizational politics*. Accordingly, it seems sound to conclude that professional practice is theorized in the Harvard tradition as involving "judgment" in arriving at decisions and "argumentation" in support of them, whatever else may be true of it.

This point may seem tediously made, but let me remind you that casuistry is not a property of *all* theorizations of management as a professional practice. It is Harvard-esque. For the *modern management school*, casuistry is not a guiding idea: its guiding idea – inspired by modern medicine – was to skillfully apply theory, or theory-based tools, to the issue at hand, to choose the best option for policy or action.

So, let's pick up the discussion of Moore, where we left off. Look at how he presented the case of the Town Librarian. Moore tracks the librarian's hypothetical reasoning toward a judgment about *whether* the Town Library's existing program/public service operation should be preserved or, instead, modified. To get a finer picture of Moore's idea of professional practice, we need to observe that a judgment as to whether to preserve or modify a public organization's program/public service operation is conditioned by a certain kind of instruction.

Specifically, this kind of instruction involves the use of a purposive theory of public management, according to which public organizations effectuate public value creation. This purposive theory doesn't *determine* the issue of whether to preserve or modify a public organization's program/public service operation: but, given the case facts, it would certainly *incline* a public manager against a decision in favor of preserving the status quo.

The Town Librarian and Latchkey Children case illustrates how Moore's theory of public management "works." Think of this theory as a functioning-whole, for which a serviceable but distant analogue is a machine – a simple one, with only two components. One machine-component is a purposive theory of public organizations; the other is a purposive theory of an individual's professional activity. In this simple machine, the two components are coupled, in that its purposive theory of public organizations serves as a reference point for an individual practitioner's thinking as it moves toward practical conclusions and, as well, as an idiom with which to formulate explanations for such conclusions, to be presented to fellow professional practitioners. *How* does this simple machine work? That's theorized in terms of how judgment works (which is to say, mainly in terms of philosophical theories of mind, rather than in terms of science of cognition), and in terms of how arguments persuade (which is to say, mainly in terms of rhetoric).

So, to restate the question that has now been discussed at some length, how is the idea of a public manager within Moore's purposive theory of public management related to the idea of a manager in purposive theories of business management? Based on what has been said so far, there's *similarity* in the main lines of theorization, in that professional activity is theorized along casuistical lines and as the "tradition" within which judgment and explanation flow is a purposive theory of a variant-form of enterprise. Alongside similarity is difference. The difference is in the specifics of the tradition: Moore's purposive theory of public organizations is not a replica of the purposive theory of business management; it is developed on the basis of a theorization of public programs and public institutions (as we shall see specifically in Chapter 4).

Having examined "public organizations" and "public managers," we're now at a stage where we can attempt to make sense of the third concept in Moore's purposive theory: strategic public management. As before, I ask – is this term a classificatory category? Of course not – how could it be? If it's not a classificatory category, then its meaning comes from how strategic public management relates to other ideas that we've been talking through, such as a purposive theory of public organizations. It's not exactly the same idea, because strategic public management theorizes public managers' professional activity, not just the effectuation of public value creation by public organizations. Strategic public management is not exactly the same idea as casuistical professional activity, either. If strategic public management were devoid of a purposive theory of public organizations, it would be oddly empty of substance, and it would be alien to the Harvard-esque tradition of management theorizing. So how should this problem of reference be solved? I would propose that we use "strategic public management" to refer to "the machine": a purposive theory of public management, consisting in a purposive theory of public organizations, coupled with a purposive theory of professional activity.

Now, let's solve another problem: labeling and presentation. For our intra-mural discussion, we can use the term "purposive theory." But it's not common. If you Google its word frequency, you can't even find it. If you Google the term, you'll find that it has had a meaning in the professional discipline of law, but not elsewhere. In extramural discussions, you might instead refer to strategic public management as a *theory of professional practice*, one that is specifically coupled with a theory of public organizations as effectuators of public value creation.

You may have noticed that the term "public managers" has slowly disappeared from the text, whereas "professional practitioners" has come to be used in its place. That's intentional, and I wish to explain why, in brief. It's a solution to a problem that I run into as a teacher of public management: it's devilishly hard to get students to read Moore's text with any depth. I attribute this problem, in part, to their understandable lack of familiarity with purposive theorizing involving both enterprises and professional activity. This pattern is prevalent among politi-cal scientists; I reckon a contributing cause is that analyzing "public managers" as a classificatory category falls well within their comfort zone. They fix their attention on what I think belongs in the background; what I want to see fixed upon escapes their grasp. From this standpoint, just reducing exposure to the term "public managers" should help.

There's another problem: Moore's purposive theory of professional practice is relevant to more actors than those who match the "definitional" and "typical" properties of public managers, in Moore's discussion of that matter. It's truly rel-evant to anyone who's engaged in professional activity involving public organiza-tions, while concerned to effectuate public value creation as they do so. These actors might be staff executives; they might be government auditors; they might be consultants. The list goes on.

The term "professional practitioners" is a good substitute for "public manag-ers." It's not an obscure term, like casuistry, or a high-register one, like effectuate. It's garden-variety. In fact, "professional practitioners" is the term Herbert Simon uses to refer to those who engage in problem-solving, whatever professional discipline they had been trained in. In that context, the term is used for people whether or not they belong to "hard" professions, such as medicine, law, archi-tecture, or accounting. I don't think that the shift from "public managers" to "professional practitioners" does violence to Moore's theory, even if all of the case studies in his book are about people whose roles matched the definitional properties of public managers.

I may be taking an extreme view, but I think that the idea of public managers in Moore's book was more an expository device than anything else. It made the discussion more concrete; it made the messages, and even some arguments, sticky. It was a powerful expository device: but it has gotten in the way of under-standing his argument.

By way of summary, let's try to visualize Moore's purposive theory of public management as a professional practice, with the aid of Figure 2.1. As you can see, the main elements of the diagram are (a) a purposive theory of public

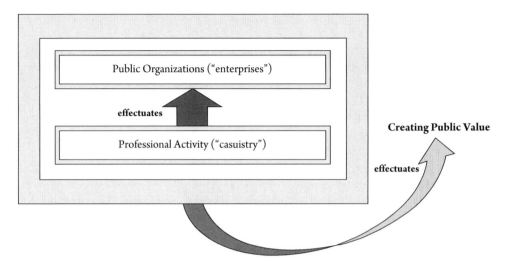

Figure 2.1 A model of Moore's purposive theory of public management as a professional practice

organizations and (b) a purposive theory of professional activity in relation to public organizations. I include the reference to "enterprises" in the upper rectangle to remind you that the term "public organizations" in Moore's text covers (a) public service operations and the programs they deliver, as well as (b) performance of public organizations' management function.

Let me now explain the arrows. One feature of Moore's theory of public management is that professional activity is theorized as being oriented to fulfilling public organizations' purposes, while another feature is that the purposive nature of public organizations is to effectuate public value creation. By compressing these two thoughts into one, you get the emblematic code-phrase that "public managers create public value." Accordingly, I put public organizations and professional activity together in a single box – for professional practice in public management – and then present both public organizations and professional activity as effectuating public value creation. This way, the structure of the theory is preserved, while aligning its presentation with the book's stickiest idea.

If you've read Moore's book, you might be wondering why I so far haven't dealt much, or at all, with many of the ideas that might have stuck with you, as in the case of the strategic triangle diagram, with the terms, value, support, and capacity, placed in one or another of its corners. The reason is that I've showcased the background or "meta" argument of Moore's book. The excuse is that, in my experience, you won't *understand* these sticky ideas, unless you have already learned how to fit them within Moore's overall purposive theory of public management; and, further, I submit that you won't be able to do *that*, unless you appreciate where the ideas came from.

You will see more of the "foreground" argument of Moore's theory of public management in Chapter 4. However, there's an important piece of unfinished business to take care of now. And that is to "rediscover" Herbert Simon's ideas as they relate to professional practice in settings that include enterprises like public organizations; the rationale for this excursion was explained in this chapter's introduction. Let's now proceed, beginning with the telling of the backstory to Simon's design-oriented theorization of professional practice in the context of organizations.

Discovering the backstory on Simon, design, and management

In 1949, Herbert Simon left his academic position at Illinois University of Technology in Chicago to join the faculty of the Graduate School of Industrial Administration (GSIA) of Carnegie Institute of Technology (later, Carnegie-Mellon University), in Pittsburgh, Pennsylvania.[13] His own move was part of a larger event. GSIA had also successfully recruited promising economists from the University of Chicago, who had been associated with its Cowles Commission for Research in Economics (as indeed Simon had been). The influx was due to GSIA's having signed up to embody and implement a new – "modern" – approach to the management discipline. The approach was positioned against two existing ones: a trade-school approach found on the undergraduate level in many universities, and the Harvard Business School approach at the graduate level. The "modern" approach to the management discipline was conceived and presented as being more scientific than its predecessors. A more specific, central idea was that management practice would come to derive from fundamental knowledge, scientifically discovered, by the sort of researchers GSIA was to appoint as faculty. Thus, Simon was present at the creation of a true modern management school.

The modern management school idea was deliberately constructed. A key source of the idea was the so-called modern *medical* school. This approach to the medicine discipline was embodied by Johns Hopkins University, in Baltimore, Maryland, considered to have been among the first research universities (on the German model) in the United States, along with the University of Chicago. Under the modern medical school, faculty would be recruited and promoted for their scientific research promise and achievements, while medical students would devote most of their first two years of study to acquiring medicine's fundamental scientific knowledge. Part of the idea was that a modern medical school would be good for the practice of medicine: medical advances would flow from medical research conducted scientifically; young doctors would be schooled in the most advanced medical knowledge and practices; and medical practice would inevitably improve as a result. These ideas had been developed around 1910, with support from the Ford Foundation. Beginning in the late 1940s, the same foundation encouraged using the modern medical school as a precedent for theorizing the management discipline and developing business schools along lines that resembled it.

Simon's relationship to GSIA and the modern management school was different from that of economist colleagues who had come there from the Cowles Commission. Simon did his doctorate in political science, working within the field of public administration, at the University of Chicago. During the depths of the Great Depression and during much of World War II, Simon worked in institutions that did practical public administration research, first in Chicago and then at the University of California, Berkeley. By the time he moved to GSIA from Illinois University of Technology, Simon had published "The proverbs of administration" in *Public Administration Review*,[14] and had completed what was later the first edition of *Administrative Behavior*.[15]

Simon's views on the management discipline were compatible with those of his GSIA colleagues in a number of regards. By looking back to "Proverbs of administration," you can suppose why. In that article, Simon sought to discredit the practical value of what he called classical administrative theory. In a line that stole the show, Simon stated that a fundamental problem with classical administrative theory is that it lacked theory. Simon critiqued classical administrative theory as peculiarly detached from properly theorized empirical realities of organizational phenomena, such as the way in which expertise channels decision-making, typically even more so than formal authority does. Simon complemented this critique of classical administrative theory by presenting an approach to diagnosing administrative problems, which he called administrative analysis. Simon indicated a direction for developing better theory that could be used for such analysis. This was the direction that he followed in developing organization theory along the lines of decision-making. So, for Simon, it was important to develop fundamental knowledge of organizations in order for both public administration and management to be disciplines worthy of the name.

The importance of developing fundamental knowledge for the management discipline was an idea Simon shared with his GSIA colleagues. Nevertheless, there was a difference in view. Simon's picture of management practice was different from that of using theory-based tools in making decisions about matters to do with a single functional area of management, like finance or marketing. His picture of management was closer to what was done by organizations in effectuating major accomplishments in the life of an organization or nation. From the standpoint of the 1950s, a recent case-in-point was the Manhattan Project, which had drawn together vast national resources and organized the U.S. effort to develop atomic weapons. The Manhattan Project later became a model for other organized efforts to develop solutions to major problems – in particular, for efforts organized by the RAND Corporation. Simon had first-hand experience with RAND projects in the national security field. A hallmark of such projects was that they involved people whose domains of expertise were dissimilar. From this perspective, management involves problem-solving, where problem-solving requires coordinating activity so that multiple domains of knowledge are brought to bear. That is a different perspective on the practice of management than applying theory-based tools in making decisions within a domain of an organization.

Pulling the threads of this story together, we can see that for Simon, professional practice in managing looks somewhat similar to creating artificial systems (including but not limited to those of a physical or digital character). The aspect of creating artificial systems of greatest relevance to management was organizing such efforts and (thereby) enabling the activities of analysis, synthesis, testing, evaluation, and decision-making. If management students were going to be able to contribute to this, they would have to know something about organizing, decision-making, and designing.

This seems like an important backstory to *Sciences of the Artificial*. That volume first came out in 1969, some years after Simon parted company with GSIA colleagues and became based in other parts of Carnegie-Mellon University, specifically its departments of psychology and computer science. In a way, he wanted engineers to be taught not only how to do the work of analysis and design of artificial systems (important as this was), but how to "manage" problem-solving, as well. What he wanted *managers* to be taught was not just how to make decisions within an organization's functional domains, but how to manage problem-solving, including in settings where the challenge is to create novel artificial systems, including those of a physical and digital character.

In Simon's purposive theory of artificial-system creation, the mechanism for creating artificial systems is a project. Just to accentuate its specific association with creating artificial systems, let's label this idea as a "design-project." At the point where a design-project is complete, systems are not yet in production, or operational. Design-projects are constituted by several functions: specifically, analysis, synthesis, testing, and evaluation (see Figure 2.2).

Figure 2.2 visualizes Simon's purposive theory of design-projects as a conceptual hierarchy. The functional elements of design-projects are represented by the five boxes arrayed along the hierarchy's base. Saying that these boxes represent functional elements means that each function needs to be performed to an adequate extent in effectuating a design-project's intent. The functions are evidently differentiated. The outcome of analyzing problems is a problem-structure and solution-structure; the outcome of synthesizing solutions is designs for artificial systems; the outcome of testing and evaluating solutions is information about the fit between the behavior of an artificial system and its intent. The outcome of evaluating alternatives is information about the relative merits of solutions that have eventuated from the upstream functions within design-projects. The outcome of selecting alternatives is a commitment to proceed with the downstream

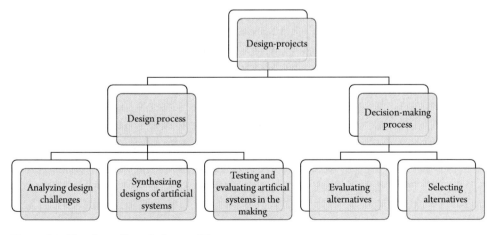

Figure 2.2 Visualizing Simon's theory of design-projects

realization of the artificial system that was designed upstream. The functional elements are not only differentiated; they are interdependent. Without synthesizing designs for artificial systems, there's nothing to test and evaluate. Without analyzing design challenges, there's not enough structure to a problem or solution for design synthesis. And so on.

Relative to these functional elements of design-projects, the middle level of the hierarchy is a higher-level break-down, consisting in the design process and decision-making process. Grouping the elemental functions in this way makes the point that the creation of novelty within enterprises and their organizations depends, in part, on performing functions that do not fall within Simon's concept of decision-making. Specifically, the creation of novelty depends on performing the function of design synthesis, which falls within Simon's concept of the design process. Stepping back from these details, the idea is that design-projects involve decision-making *and* designing as distinct, but interdependent functions, with their corresponding processes.

Chapter 5 of *Sciences of the Artificial*, when twinned with that volume's first chapter, promotes the idea that creation of novelty – specifically in respect to artificial systems – is critically important to organizations. That stance underwrites the importance of design-projects within organizations. Pushing the idea of design-projects, in turn, positions "designing" as an intrinsically important aspect of organizations. That is the take-away that has been picked up by a variety of fields of management, including information systems.

Taking into consideration the history of business schools recounted at the outset of the present chapter, Simon's Chapter 5 can be seen as a bid to reformulate purposive theories of management. In particular, it represents an attack on dominant ideas within the modern management school, which were drawn from the modern medical school. Creating novelty in artificial systems was not a central issue for mainstream thinking within the modern management school. The mainstream of the modern management school was focused on creating fundamental knowledge about finance, marketing, and operations – and translating such knowledge into tools to be used by managers skilled in their use as they make decisions within organizations. Accordingly, design-projects – and the sort of problem-solving they effectuate – were not of great interest or concern. History shows that Simon was keen to establish his contrasting ideas about management within the modern management school, to which he belonged when serving as a professor at Carnegie's Graduate School of Industrial Administration.

However, what this historical account doesn't elucidate is the relevance of the idea of design-projects for the Harvard version of the professional discipline of management. Within that tradition – a predecessor and rival to the modern management school – decision-making was theorized as a mechanism for performing the management function within enterprises (a perspective that was reinforced as HBS responded to its rival, around 1960). Management continued to be theorized as a judgmental process that is improvable through simulated experience with administrative situations, whereby students present rationales for specific choices and courses of action, in the face of critique through instruction.

Figure 2.3 Visualizing the Harvard tradition of purposive theorizing of enterprises and their management

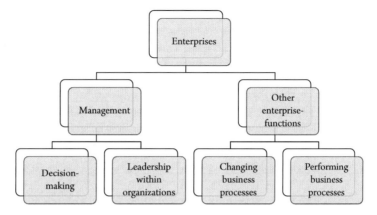

In addition, management was theorized as constituted by bringing about the adoption of decisions within an organization and the setting in motion of their follow-through, via what might be broadly labeled as leadership within organizations.

Figure 2.3 places these ideas in a scheme that situates the Harvard tradition within Fayol's purposive theory of enterprises. As discussed in Chapter 1, Fayol's theory held that the effectuation of enterprise-intent requires the performance of six enterprise-functions, namely, accounting, commercial, finance, management, security, and technical, in alphabetical order. The figure above groups all the enterprise-functions apart from management on the right hand-side. These enterprise-functions are depicted as being similar in that they are performed by businesses processes; in recognition of the fact that business processes undergo change in order to be adequate to their functions, an additional element is added, namely, "changing business processes."

Now let's consider Simon's Chapter 5 in relation to this Harvard-esque scheme. If we stick with the idea that design-projects are for creating novel artificial systems, then we should place design-projects squarely within the box for "changing business processes," on the basis that business processes are typically performed through use of artificial systems. However, we can take Simon's Chapter 5 to be relevant to the enterprise-function of management, as well, by seeing Simon as challenging the idea that management is decision-making plus leadership. Management itself involves designing, by this argument – even if management also involves decision-making and leadership. This interpretation is fair, as Simon published on creativity, an idea tied to design synthesis, but is not specific to creating novel artificial systems.

We can think of Simon's Chapter 5, having arisen as a strong dissent from the modern management school to which Simon institutionally belonged, as being a friendly amendment to the Harvard tradition, from which he was institutionally distant. To reiterate, this amendment involves seeing the enterprise-function of management as performed by the function of design synthesis, enabled by analysis of design challenges. An auxiliary amendment is that design-projects – with their interlocking design and decision-making processes – are mechanisms for performing the enterprise-function of management. This point is an amendment of the Harvard tradition as its stereotypical mechanism for performing the enterprise-function of management is what individual managers do within organizational settings. Design-projects are not theorized in this way: they are collective organizational phenomena. To think of design-projects in this way, this concept has to be reformulated to the extent that they are seen to create novelty in any form of purposeful phenomena within organizations, not just artificial (technical) systems. Plans and organizational arrangements are examples of the kind of novel, purposeful phenomena that eventuate from design-projects but don't fit the category of artificial systems. In sum, we can consider placing ideas that relate to design-projects, like design synthesis, as well as the idea of a design-project itself, inside an updated mainstream version of the Harvard tradition. If we do so, then we will recognize Simon's gift to the Harvard tradition of theorizing management.

Structuring design-oriented purposive theories of management and public management

I would now like to follow through on this line of thinking, to the point of formulating a design-oriented purposive theory of enterprises and their management, by unifying the Harvard tradition, on the one hand, with Simon's ideas about designing, decision-making, and design-projects, on the other. Among other things, doing so will elucidate the meaning of the book title, *Public Management as a Design-Oriented Professional Discipline*. In particular, it elucidates the idea of professional knowledge within this discipline, by pointing to the conceptual structure and origins of its intellectual foundation. Put directly, the unified Harvard-Simon conception of enterprises and their management constitutes the underlying intellectual foundation of professional knowledge within the professional discipline of public management, as it is constructed in this book. The adjective "design-oriented" is meant to dramatize this synthesis between the Harvard tradition and Simon's stance in *Sciences of the Artificial*. I will now present the synthesis, with the aid of Figure 2.4, and then move on to discuss it more fully, as a prelude to the rest of this book.

The official label for Figure 2.4 is "Fundamentals of design-oriented theories of enterprises and their management." That label is accurate, especially as it is faithful to Henri Fayol's theory of enterprises. While accurate, the label is unfortunately forgettable. To overcome this problem, we can refer to Figure 2.4 as the "the sandwich diagram" or "the SD," for short.

Let me walk you through the SD to pinpoint what it consists in. The top slice is concerned with enterprises in their totality and their constitutive functions. The bottom slice is concerned with the activities in which professional practitioners, including those labeled as managers, engage as they work within enterprise-organizations. The slice in the middle is concerned with design-projects and their constitutive processes of designing and decision-making. Each slice consists in a two-level conceptual hierarchy. Enterprise-functions are constitutive of enterprises, while the design process and the decision-making process are constitutive of design-projects. As for professional activities, the subordinate

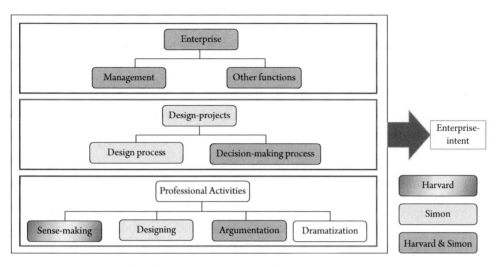

Figure 2.4 Fundamentals of design-oriented theories of enterprises and their management – the sandwich diagram

level elements are forms of professional activity, rather than a full set of constitutive functions.

I want to now make absolutely clear how this scheme relates to its origins. The top slice is due to Fayol's theory of enterprises, in which enterprise-intent is effectuated by performing six enterprise-functions, of which management is one. Fayol's theory runs through the Harvard tradition; in fact, one of the most famous conceptual schemes in that tradition – Porter's value-chain[16] – can be traced back to it. For his part, Simon didn't reference Fayol's theory of enterprises; indeed, his best-known early publication[17] was scathing in its critique of ideas about organizations that drew from Fayol's theory. Nevertheless, Simon's theorization of design-projects presumed that they were conducted within organizations and that those organizations effectuate enterprise-intent. For these reasons, I have coded all the elements of the top slice as originating from both Harvard and Simon.

The middle slice is due to Simon's theory of design-projects. However, that theory overlapped with the Harvard tradition, which came to theorize decision-making as the way in which the enterprise-function of management is performed within organizations. Thus, what's specifically tied to Simon's theory of design-projects is two ideas. One is the idea of design-projects itself, as an organizational mechanism for performing enterprise-functions. The other is the idea of the design process, with its constitutive functions of analyzing design challenges, synthesizing designs, and testing and evaluating designs. For these reasons, I have coded "design-projects" and "design process" as originating with Simon and "decision-making process" as originating from both Harvard and Simon.

As mentioned, the bottom slice theorizes what professional practitioners do when working within enterprises and their organizations. The Harvard tradition's pedagogy is known for emphasizing what I call the professional activities of sense-making and argumentation. They are integral to this tradition because managers have been depicted to play the role of making decisions in the face of circumstances that pose challenges to effectuating enterprise-intent. The Harvard theory of making decisions has origins in casuistry, as argued earlier. Casuistry consists in making sense of situational circumstances as they relate to a community's moral principles, deliberating about the proper course of action through the exercise of judgment, and providing an explicit rationale for the resulting decision through the exercise of the ability to formulate and state a sound practical argument. Accordingly, the ideas of "sense-making" and "argumentation" trace back to the Harvard tradition.

If you think about Simon's take on what professional practitioners do within enterprises and their organizations, you need to grasp the idea of designing. Don't be confused by the term "designing" showing up in the bottom slice, while the term "design-process" shows up in the middle slice. Designing is the profile of activity done by individuals in a dynamically stable context within an enterprise, a context that specifically includes a design-project in which numerous individuals participate. The designing/design-process distinction is just like the distinction within organization theory between thinking and communicating, on the one hand, and the decision-making process, on the other. As to what designing consists in as an activity, that's a long story: it's not particularly detailed in Simon's *Sciences of the Artificial*, as his main point is that professional practitioners need to learn to design, through forms of education that simulate experience, much as takes place in studio classes within professional training in architecture. For our immediate purposes, we can recognize, first, that "designing" is a form of professional activity within a design-oriented theory of enterprises and their management and that, second, this idea originates with Simon's *Sciences of the Artificial*.

Anything else said about the sandwich diagram's bottom slice is more footnote than main text. I'll make three such points. First, the idea of argumentation stems from both Harvard and Simon. For Simon, argumentation is something that professional practitioners do when participating in either the decision-making or design processes. Argumentation is part of communication within decision-making, and the same is true for communication in performing the analysis of design challenges and the testing and evaluation functions within design processes. (It's not true of synthesizing designs.) For this reason, argumentation is coded as Harvard and Simon. Second, I code "sense-making" as Harvard rather than Harvard and Simon, because this idea is much more explicit within the Harvard tradition, because of its connection with casuistry, than in Simon.

Third, I've introduced two concepts – professional activities and dramatization – that are intrinsic to the design-oriented theory of enterprises and their management but are not prominent bits of the vocabulary of either Simon or Harvard. Accordingly, both are left "uncoded" in the sandwich diagram. The term "professional activities" does no more than serve as umbrella term for all the items that are listed underneath it, a list that can be expanded to include other ideas like deliberation as well as another subordinate level of concepts. This term is more suitable than either "practices" or "skills." It's more suitable than "practices" because within a discussion of enterprises and organizations, the idea of practices connotes patterns of activity that have a basis in the organization itself. It's more suitable than "skills" because these professional activities, while skillful, are inherently social or interactive, whereas the idea of skills connotes dexterity in manipulating data, information, or other substances. The other reason to take care in labeling this collection of activities is that the idea of "skill" is more strongly linked to the modern management school than to the Harvard tradition: in the former, skill is what an individual does in using theory-based tools to reach a conclusion on what decision is optimal for performing an enterprise-function under particular conditions. Thus, I wish to downplay the vocabulary of skill, as the design-oriented theory here is taken to be a synthesis of Simon and Harvard, not of Simon and the modern management school.

Turning to "dramatization," this term is drawn from the work of Erving Goffman, the venerable north American sociologist who famously theorized social action and situations as if they are on-stage performances that sit alongside back-stage interactions among individuals who form teams. His famous book was *The Presentation of Self in Everyday Life*.[18] The idea belongs here for a couple of reasons. Dramatization refers to a professional ability that is cultivated through practice and instruction within the Harvard tradition. In that classroom, you need to be good at dramatizing both your arguments and yourself to earn a superior mark. Furthermore, we can see dramatization as contributing to a theory of leadership within organizations, an idea that helps to broaden out the Harvard tradition from its casuistical base, which is concerned with decision-making specifically and narrowly.

Now that I've taken you through a discussion of what the sandwich diagram consists in, let me remind you of what it is for. It is for creating a theory of enterprises and their management, one that distances itself from the modern management school, while improving the Harvard tradition. (Note: In my judgment, Simon can be used only to reformulate either the modern management school or the Harvard tradition: it doesn't have the historical heft or internal constitution to carry off being a theory of enterprises and their management, on its own – a point I come back to in Chapter 8.)

Conclusion

I have worked you through this long background argument for reasons having to do with the architectonics of this book on public management as a design-oriented professional discipline. One reason is that if public management is to be a professional discipline (an argument with reasons of its own), public management needs to expand and teach professional knowledge about public organizations and professional practice. If it is going to do that, then it needs to build up a purposive theory of public organizations and professional practice within them. A good precedent and point of departure for doing so is Moore's *Creating Public Value: Strategic Management in Government*, for reasons discussed earlier in this chapter and in the last one. However, there are issues to consider in choosing to make Moore's book a foundational work for purposive theorizing of public management. The issues arise because Moore's book thoroughly reflects the Harvard tradition, while the Harvard tradition has limitations even in the view of its sympathizers and adherents, like me. In my mind, the most effective way to set out reservations about the Harvard tradition – and to point toward ways of overcoming them – is to do the background work of synthesizing Harvard and Simon, to form the outlines and basic vocabulary of a design-oriented purposive theory of enterprises and professional practice within them.

This book shows a way to build up professional knowledge about public management, while providing something of an installed base of such knowledge itself. You will soon see how I draw on a variety of otherwise isolated works to create this base, when you get to Chapter 4, which is divided into sections about public organizations, design-projects, and professional activities. However, as a prior step, you're invited to listen in on a conversation about this aspect of public management as a design-oriented professional discipline, where Marshall is trying to bring along Nora, Olivier, and Petra, to a place where they can take it all in.

NOTES

1 Augier and March (2011).
2 Lynn (1996).
3 Simon (1996).
4 Van Aken (2004).
5 Moore (1995).
6 A precedent for using the word "effectuate" in this way is Sarasvathy (2008).
7 This statement is a case of "context channels activity, which eventuates in outcomes," which I take to be the conceptual structure of scenarios. See Chapter 3.
8 The background reference to this statement is Fauconnier and Turner (2002).
9 Texts like Moore's are not usually, if ever, presented as well-structured, purposive theories – for understandable reasons, considering their audiences. But suppose that this was something to be done. Formulating, or re-constructing, such theories in a structured way requires using tools of interpretation and some standards of presentation. Such tools and standards would constitute a patterned-language for theorizing purposeful phenomena. Use of such a patterned-language would enable a professional discipline's development. Statements like ones enumerated above exhibit such a patterned-language. More will be said along these lines as we progress.
10 Fayol (1919/1984).
11 Augier and March (2011: 152).
12 Jonsen and Toulmin (1988).
13 This section is based primarily on Augier and March (2011).
14 Simon (1946).
15 Simon (1947/1968).
16 Porter (1985).
17 Simon (1946).
18 Goffman (1959).

3
Understanding mechanism-intent thinking and analysis in public management

What is design-oriented public management? The line taken in this book is that design-oriented public management is a professional practice tied to a professional discipline, whose defining purposive, mechanism-intent phenomenon is public organizations. Moore's *Creating Public Value: Strategic Management in Government*[1] is the direct source of purposive theories of public organizations. His book is also the implied source of the idea that the professional practice of public management includes the professional activities of sense-making, designing, argumentation, and dramatization. Simon's *Sciences of the Artificial*[2] is the direct source of the idea of a professional discipline, as its associated professional practice, being defined by a kind of purposeful, mechanism-intent phenomenon: his term for such disciplines was sciences of the artificial. Simon is also the source of the idea that design-projects are mechanism-like aspects of enterprises that create novelty for their technical and other enterprise-functions, as well as the idea that design projects depend on practitioners engaging in the professional activity of designing.

A take-away from Chapter 2 is that a post-Moore, neo-Simonian synthesis is needed to boot-strap public management as a design-oriented professional discipline. The idea of public management being a professional discipline has been proposed before, in Lynn's *Public Management as Art, Science, and Profession;*[3] but Lynn's proposed content, as summarized in his concluding chapter, lies distant from what is here presented as the post-Moore, neo-Simonian synthesis.[4]

This take-away reinforces that of Chapter 1: specifically, it makes sense to establish first principles of public management as a professional discipline. The first principles are that public management, like any science of the artificial, is a two-fold enterprise of teaching-and-learning for professional practice and discipline-development. The teaching-and-learning enterprise's conceptual design includes the interrelated functions of acquiring professional knowledge, improving professional abilities, and strengthening professional competence. The discipline-development enterprise's conceptual design includes the interrelated functions of strengthening disciplinary identity, expanding professional knowledge, and faculty development.

In this chapter, several ideas will be added to the post-Moore, neo-Simonian synthesis about public organizations; these include "forward engineering" (specifically, conceptual and embodiment designs); "reverse engineering" (specifically, redocumentation and design discovery); and "processual sociology" (specifically, scenario-processes with context-activity-outcome dynamics). While all three ideas have some affinity to Simon's *Sciences of the Artificial* and Moore's *Creating Public Value*, none of them can be found there. Thus, this book goes beyond connecting the dots of the two "traditions" represented by Simon and Moore.

The chapter will illustrate my observation that the ideas of forward engineering, reverse engineering, and processual sociology are disjointed in public management, as they are in surrounding fields of inquiry. Forward-engineering is evident in discussions of policy analysis,[5] strategic planning,[6] and rhetoric.[7] Reverse-engineering is evident in discussions of evaluation research methods.[8] Processual sociology is evident in organization studies[9] and research on policy processes.[10] Their combination is not unprecedented, as it can be discerned in Simon's *Sciences of the Artificial*,[11] in Mashaw's *Bureaucratic Justice*,[12] Wilson's *Bureaucracy*,[13] publications by Bardach,[14] Tendler's *Good Government in the Tropics*,[15] Barzelay and Campbell's *Preparing for the Future*,[16] van Aken's account of management as a design science,[17] and Patton's account of developmental evaluation.[18] But you have to know what you're looking for.

This chapter unifies the disjointed ideas of forward-engineering, reverse-engineering, and processual sociology by developing the idea of "mechanism-intent thinking and analysis," specifically about public organizations. If you Google "mechanism-intent thinking and analysis," you won't find anything. Are there synonyms? Mechanism-intent thinking and analysis could be called instrumental thinking, but that's essentially a way to position it in purposive theories of decision-making.[19] It could be called functional-teleological thinking, but that's essentially a way to position the idea in philosophy.[20] It could be called purposeful thinking, but that would associate the idea exclusively with forward-engineering,[21] as well as program planning.[22] It could be called design-thinking, but that term is also exclusive to forward-engineering, and it references a specific school of thought about designing as a professional activity in enterprises.[23]

It feels odd that there's a need for this new term, "mechanism-intent thinking and analysis." However, it's needed for purposes of this book. In fact, in writing it, I came to see that *mechanism-intent thinking and analysis is a golden thread that can be used to weave together design-oriented problem-solving, design-rediscovery through design-focused case studies, and purposive theorizing about public organizations, design-projects, and professional activities.*

Finding the golden thread was a drawn-out, messy enterprise. I can speed up the process for you, but you're unlikely to understand it without experiencing some of its messiness. In this chapter, I simulate that experience. The technique for doing so is the dialogue, an ancient device for argumentation and persuasion, with some additional story-like features to make it slightly entertaining. You know the scene: an institution where public management is taught within a degree program, and where public administration is taught as a discipline. You've met the characters in the story – Marshall, Nora, Olivier, and Petra – back in Chapter 1. You know the plot: they are forming, storming, and norming. You know the teleology: they will end up performing, much to the satisfaction of Alicia, Ben, Claire, Dimitrios, Eva, and other students who choose to take "the course."

By now, you will certainly have gathered how the story relates to this book as a whole. "The course" is plainly a metaphor for public management as a design-oriented professional practice, tied to a professional discipline. Almost as plainly, the teaching-team meetings are a metaphor for the discipline-development enterprise within it. Specifically, the teaching meetings are a metaphor for the faculty development function. As anyone like Marshall will know, the teaching team meetings reflect the reality that public management doesn't train its own PhDs, and that many deans and directors find it optimal to hire practitioners to teach the subject. Accordingly, Nora is an assistant professor trained in political science; Olivier is a PhD student in public administration who hasn't had a doctoral course that covers management and/or public management; and Petra is a practitioner. You won't mistake the take-away from this chapter: Faculty development has to be done for public management to be a design-oriented professional discipline, while reading this book should be part of the embodiment design for performing this function.

The show begins after the teaching team meeting participants have settled into their chairs and have exchanged all appropriate pleasantries. They are once again discussing the content of the initial session of "the course."

Mechanism-intent thinking and analysis illustrated: the conceptual design of the course

Marshall: In teaching the course, I think it's important that we are all on the same page. Tell me your questions about the introductory video that students are supposed to view before they come to class.

Nora: Why do you introduce the course by presenting what you say is its "conceptual design"?[24]

Marshall: Let's be clear what enterprise-functions within the course are performed by this video. In Fayol's terms, the two enterprise-functions are commercial and technical.[25] In respect to the commercial function, the intended outcome of viewing the video is for students to decide to take the course. In respect to the technical function, the intended outcome of viewing the video is receptivity and alertness to the course content. Do you follow?

Nora: Yes, what you say is consistent with what we discussed in our previous teaching team meeting. However, you've introduced some new language, that of "intended outcome." I'd like to make sure that I understand that term, now that you've introduced it.

Marshall: Shall I do that now?

Nora: Yes, as long as it doesn't hamper your answering my original question.

Marshall: It won't, as clarifying what is an intended outcome will help to clarify what is a conceptual design, and that will help to answer your original question.

Nora: Then, go ahead.

Marshall: I first have a question for you. What's an outcome?

Nora: It's the state of affairs that exists when an event or process has run its course.[26]

Marshall: Good, can we agree to say that a scenario-outcome is a state of affairs that exists when the activities within a scenario-process have ceased?

Nora: Yes. I like the fact that you make clear that the concepts of activities and outcomes are part of the idea of a scenario-process. But it would be handy to have a more compressed way of stating this idea.

Marshall: How about: Within a scenario-process, scenario-outcomes eventuate from scenario-activities.

Nora: That is more compressed. But you've introduced another term! Eventuate.

Marshall: It's true, but it helps with the compression you asked for. All it means, really, is that there's a relation between activities and outcomes within a scenario-process. The relation is between activity that can change conditions, on the one hand, and a state of conditions that exists when the activity ceases, on the other. The relation between activity and outcome can also be seen as being similar to the relation between causes and effects.

Nora: What would be the effect caused by scenario-activity?

Marshall: You could say that the effect is the occurrence of terminal conditions in the spatial and temporal location where the scenario-process takes place.

Nora: Out of curiosity, does this concept of a scenario-process have a specific source?

Marshall: The prime source for me is Andrew Abbott: especially some of the essays in his 2001 book, *Time Matters*,[27] and his 2016 book, *Processual Sociology*.[28] In economics, a well-known source was Thomas Schelling, particularly his book, *Micromotives and Macrobehavior*,[29] which I read in graduate school. But if you're asking what is the ultimate source of the concept of scenario-process, I would defer to cognitive scientists, like Lakoff and Johnson, who argue that our conceptual systems are embodied within us and originate in direct experience. By this account, we all learned the concept of scenario-process as infants, particularly when we started to crawl about, with a destination in mind.[30] As for the idea that concepts like "eventuate" can be used to compress a number of distinct and more basic relations among concepts – such as "before and after" and "cause and effect" – I'd point you to Fauconnier and Turner's book, *The Way We Think*.[31] If you'd like to see how scenario-processes are theorized in philosophy, I'd recommend Nicholas Rescher's *Process Metaphysics*.[32]

Nora: Thanks for all that, Marshall. I didn't quite realize there's so much theoretical background to the idea of a scenario-process, but I probably shouldn't be surprised.

Marshall: Are you ready for me to discuss the idea of an intended outcome?

Nora: Yes.

Marshall: The term "intended" is a verbal marker for the idea that the scenario-process under examination is purposeful.

Nora: Yes, I get that. Didn't the video say something along the lines that scenario-processes are mechanism-like aspects of enterprises?

Marshall: Correct, but it would be helpful now to bring in an idea about designing and designs. As a scenario-activity, designing eventuates in representations of mechanism-intent phenomena.[33] Intended outcomes are features of such representations. Specifically, they are features of representations of mechanism-like aspects of such phenomena, provided that such aspects are conceived of as scenario-processes. Even more specifically, intended outcomes are representations of the outcome conditions of scenario-processes, that is, the states of conditions that eventuate from scenario-activities.

Nora: Does this mean that intended outcomes are features of the conceptual design of mechanism-intent phenomena, generally, and of enterprises, in particular?

Marshall: If you want to introduce intended outcomes in a representation that is meant to be a conceptual design, then that's fine – but conceptual designs don't need to specify intended outcomes of mechanism-like scenario-processes.

Nora: It sounds like a conceptual design is a flexible concept.

Marshall: Well, I don't know if the concept is flexible. What I do know is that conceptual designs are mechanism-like phenomena within design-projects. They perform functions. One function is analogous to the commercial function: here, the role of a conceptual design is to secure client approval of what the designer proposes. Another function is analogous to the technical function: here, the role of a conceptual design is to channel the activity of formulating an embodiment design for the same mechanism-intent phenomenon being created. It's a matter of designer judgment whether to include the intended outcomes of mechanism-like scenario processes within the conceptual design; the alternative is to stick with a higher-level representation and specify those intended outcomes in the course of formulating the embodiment design. So, I'd say that a conceptual design isn't a flexible concept, but it's a concept that fits well with design-projects being a kind of mechanism-intent phenomena.

Nora: So, are you saying that intended outcomes of scenario processes might or might not be specified within a conceptual design, but they must be specified within an embodiment design?

Marshall: You're asking me for a purposive theory of design-projects, Nora. Speaking for myself, I absolutely agree with the first part of this statement; and I have a pro-attitude toward the second part. However, I can imagine a situation where a designer, when presenting an embodiment design, would rather specify scenario-context and scenario-activities, rather than their outcomes. You could imagine this being the case in a design for judicial proceedings,[34] and in some educational settings.

Nora: Let me restate, then: A mechanism-intent phenomenon's scenario-processes may or may not be specified within a conceptual design, but no representation is rightly considered as an embodiment design unless it includes some specification of its mechanism-like scenario-processes.

Marshall: Nora, I think we're now in a position to discuss your original question: Why do you introduce the course by presenting what you say is its "conceptual design"?

Nora: Yes, I think so.

Marshall: The conceptual design diagram is a feature of the introductory video, which performs the course-enterprise's commercial and technical functions. The conceptual design diagram is apt for performing the commercial function, for the reason that it provides a comprehensive, holistic representation of the course, without overloading the viewer with information. That combination of properties is conducive for students deliberating over what optional courses would best be assembled into their overall degree program. Content-wise, the diagram serves as a "prop" in a show that fosters the impression that the professor put in a lot of thought in planning the course, and it establishes an expectation that the course is well-designed and fit for purpose.[35]

Nora: I see this, and I like the idea that the diagram is a prop in a show, as well as the idea that conceptual designs are inherently comprehensive and compact, qualities that are helpful to client deliberation. Do you want to add anything?

Marshall: Just the obvious, really. The conceptual design diagram is aligned with performing the constitutive technical function of expanding students' professional knowledge. Specifically, students will see that frameworks for representing artificial-systems-in-the-making can be used to represent enterprises that are being presented to their stakeholders, provided that the frameworks recruit the sort of mechanism-intent theorizing of enterprises that was pioneered by Henri Fayol. Students may also draw the inference that acquiring professional knowledge about designing, as well as acquiring ideas for mechanism-intent theorizing of enterprises, may assist in strengthening their professional practice within enterprises.

Nora: Thanks, Marshall, I'm satisfied, and I am also conscious that others will have their own issues to raise.

Seeing clearly the profile of mechanism-intent thinking

Petra: To be honest, I feel ambivalent about the ideas that you and Nora have been discussing over the course of the meeting today.

Marshall: Perhaps you like some of these ideas, but don't care for others. Is that the situation, Petra?

Petra: I like the ideas about designing. They are quite popular today, and I have always seen myself as being more creative than some of my professional colleagues. I guess it's just that I wonder if I am having to change my vocabulary to conform to your language, rather than for any other reason, Marshall. It all makes me feel as though what I do know from experience isn't going to be valued in the course.

Marshall: It's not the first time I've heard comments like that, Petra. They've been voiced by participants on executive programs, on numerous occasions. Is there a specific route of entry into this discussion you think would be most helpful to follow?

Petra: Perhaps we could start from the ideas that I do know and then you can show me what's better about the ideas and vocabulary you use and want to teach.

Marshall: That would be fine. What ideas are you most comfortable with?

Petra: I'm comfortable with ideas around program design, planning, and evaluation.

Marshall: Okay, do you have in mind frameworks like program results chains?

Petra: Yes, I've worked with that framework before. Am I to think that you don't like it?

Marshall: I'm ambivalent.

Petra: Then we're even! Seriously, tell me the specifics of your attitude and why.

Marshall: My first reservation is tied to the observation that program results chains are representations of programs, rather than of public organizations. From the perspective of purposive theories of public organizations, program results chains are not actually comprehensive, at least as they are stereotypically elaborated: their scope is often limited to the technical function of public organizations; the management function falls outside of scope. As a public management person, it seems to me that it's important to engage in mechanism-intent thinking about performing the management function.

Petra: That's fair enough.

Marshall: Good. My second reservation, Petra, is that the idea of program results chain is a bit of a muddle when it comes to representing the mechanism-like aspects of programs. As you know, the categories are inputs, activities, outputs, and outcomes. As I read this, I see the idea of a conversion process quite clearly. The idea of a conversion process is one where process-inputs *feed* process-activity, which then *yields* process-outputs. But then I see the term, "outcomes." The concept of outcomes is part of the idea of a scenario-process. The idea of a scenario-process is one where scenario-process-context *channels* scenario-process-activity, which *eventuates* in scenario-process-outcomes. Part of my reservation is that it doesn't make sense to see outputs as the source of outcomes. There is no process relation between outputs and outcomes (although there can be a process relation involving multiple conversion processes and multiple scenario-processes). So, you do have to wonder what's going on.

Petra: What are you thinking?

Marshall: What I think is going on here is that a program results chain is a strange combination of what a designer would see as a program's conceptual and embodiment designs. The relation between input-activity-output seems like an embodiment design, with the mechanism-like aspect of the enterprise being a conversion process. However, the comparative relation between outputs and outcomes is trying to do the representational work of a conceptual design, whereby the yielding of outputs represents the functional composition of the enterprise, while outcomes represent program-intent. A consequence is that there's a lack of clarity about the embodiment design, that is, what a program consists in and how it works, as it's not clear where outcomes come from. Meanwhile, the utility of working with the conceptual versus embodiment design distinction and relation is lost: for instance, the functional fit between them is presumed, not subject to critical thinking. The whole construct reminds me of the old joke that a camel is a horse designed by a committee. I much prefer the clarity of my approach, which tracks the conceptual versus embodiment design distinction and that sees mechanism-like aspects of enterprises – the embodiment design – as processes, whether scenario-processes or conversion processes (though mainly the former).

Petra: As I think about what we've just been discussing, I'm now intrigued by the possibility that frameworks from the field of design will provide more connectivity and coherence among the ideas that I've used for program planning and evaluation. So, you've definitely begun to neutralize my earlier ambivalence. I think it would really help now to have a good illustration of the use of these frameworks from the field of design.

Marshall: How about we illustrate them with our course? Specifically, how about we illustrate it with the course introductory video?

Petra: That should work.

Marshall: Good – so the course is the overall mechanism-intent phenomenon; it's analogous to an enterprise. Let us focus on the course introductory video as a mechanism-like aspect of the course, which figures in the lead up to the first class as well as a reference within it.

Petra: I get that. It was a take-away from your discussion with Nora.

Mechanism-intent analysis: realistic evaluation versus reverse engineering

Marshall: There are three essential questions to ask of any mechanism-like aspect of a mechanism-intent phenomenon. First, what is it *for*? Second, what does it *consist in*? Third, how does it *work*?

Petra: Those questions make intuitive sense to me, but you probably have a specific source from which they come.

Marshall: Actually, the idea comes from reverse engineering. You know that idea, right?

Petra: Of course, I have come across it, but I couldn't define it off the top of my head.

Marshall: Then Google it.

(The meeting goes quiet as Petra, Olivier and Nora all search with their smartphones.)

Petra: Wikipedia defines reverse engineering as the process by which a man-made object is deconstructed to reveal its designs or to extract knowledge from the object.[36]

Olivier: Lower down in the Wikipedia entry it says that reverse engineering is the process of analyzing a subject system to identify the system's components and their interrelationships and to create representations of the system in another form or at a higher level of abstraction. The source here was the Institute of Electrical and Electronics Engineers.

Marshall: From the context, it seems like they have in mind reverse engineering of a software system, but they've used the term "subject system" to be generic.

Olivier: Further down, it says that reverse engineering involves both redocumentation and design recovery. Redocumentation is creating a new representation of the computer code so that it is easier to understand, while design discovery is the using of reasoning from general knowledge, or personal experience of the product, in order to fully understand the product functionality.

Marshall: Petra, do you see how these ideas about reverse engineering relate to the three questions about mechanism-intent phenomena?

Petra: I see that what they call the "subject system" is what you call the mechanism-like aspect of a mechanism-intent phenomenon. I think they may have the better term!

Marshall: Perhaps they do, but I don't want to imply that all mechanism-like aspects of mechanism-intent phenomena are closely analogous to technical systems: many of those I have in mind have emergent properties. But as long as that's understood, I'm happy for you to use the term "subject system." Do you see any other connections, Petra?

Petra: Yes, I see a connection between the idea of "redocumentation" and your second question about a subject system, namely, "what does it consist in"?

Marshall: I agree. So, what does the course introductory video consist in?

Petra: Viewed holistically, the course introductory video consists in a fully scripted performance, presented in a video format. Analytically, the scripted performance consists in spoken text and in a diagram representing the course's conceptual design. In reverse engineering terms, the spoken text and the diagram are system components.

Marshall: Right! And to push the analogy with reverse engineering and redocumentation further, what's the interrelation among the system components?

Petra: It's simple: the spoken text includes your discussion of the diagram.

Marshall: Right again! Now, could you focus on the diagram and break this component down further?

Petra: Sure. It consists in a collection of shapes and text elements that's about the functional composition of the course, as well as in a collection of text elements about the course's intent. I can also break down the functional composition of the course further. It consists in three boxes, labeled, respectively, as expanding professional knowledge, improving professional abilities, and strengthening professional competence. Situated between these boxes are arrows, alongside the word "enables."

Marshall: Thanks, Petra. I appreciate that your redocumentation was entirely descriptive: you didn't make any claims about how these "signs" – whether shapes or text – were intended to be meaningful to a viewer. You stuck to redocumentation, and avoided design discovery.

Petra: I'm wondering if you have some terms we could use to refer differentially to the short and long answers to the redocumentation question.

Marshall: That would be useful. What terms come to mind for you?

Petra: The short answer is a "high-level representation"; the long-answer is a "granular representation."

Marshall: I think that those terms work well, at least for someone who knows a bit about system design or reverse engineering.

Petra: These are common terms in my professional circles.

Marshall: Keep the distinction in mind: I plan to use it later. For now, let's revisit the idea of design discovery. Olivier, could you repeat the definition?

Olivier: Design discovery is the using of reasoning from general knowledge, or personal experience of the product, in order to fully understand the product functionality.

Marshall: Let me reword this definition to make the idea clearer. Design discovery is a process for understanding the functionality of a subject system. That understanding eventuates from reasoning. The reasoning relates facts about what the subject system consists in, to statements about what the subject system is for. The reasoning process involves general knowledge, or what we in social science call "theory," in combination with inferential moves, or what many philosophers call induction.[37]

Nora: Marshall, these reverse engineering terms are completely new to me, but now I think I am beginning to understand the ideas of redocumentation and design discovery. In social science terms, can we say that redocumentation is descriptive, while design discovery is explanatory?

Marshall: Nice point, Nora. Your suggestion that redocumentation is similar to description, on the one hand, and that design discovery is similar to explanation, on the other, is cogent.[38]

Petra: Marshall, was your answer to Nora's question anything different than "yes"?

Marshall: My answer was "yes," but that doesn't mean that design discovery and social science explanation are so closely analogous that there's no distinction to be made at all between them.

Petra: Nora, is that what you understood Marshall to be saying?

Nora: I do now. But what I don't know is what distinction is to be made between design discovery and social science explanation. What is it, Marshall?

Marshall: Let me start with the similarity. Design discovery involves explaining selected facts about a subject system that come from doing redocumentation. If a subject system is described as a scenario-process, then the selected facts are going to be its trajectory and/or outcome. Now for the difference. Design discovery explains functionality: that concept *relates to* a scenario-process, but it isn't identical to it. Functionality is an assessment of the adequacy of a scenario-process (or of a subject system more generally) relative to a mechanism-intent phenomenon's conceptual design and, especially, the aspect of intent. So, in understanding a subject system's functionality, you are both explaining and assessing it. You *explain* a scenario-process' trajectory and/or outcomes – and you *assess* its adequacy relative to intent. In sum, design discovery depends on explanation, but it also depends on mechanism-intent thinking.

Petra: I think I understand the idea now. What's called the "subject system" in reverse engineering is called the "evaluand" in evaluation research,[39] where the goal is to learn how things work.

Nora: Is Petra right about that, Marshall?

Marshall: Yes. There's a much-cited book by Pawson and Tilley, entitled *Realistic Evaluation*.[40] It argued that the goal of program evaluation research is exactly as Petra said.

Olivier: We read that book in our evaluation research methods course. One of the main things I remember about it is the equation, $C + M = O$, where O stands for a program's outcome. The idea was the outcomes depend on mechanisms and context.

Petra: I remember hearing about C + M = O in a short course on evaluation. I didn't know who came up with it. Marshall, can we say that C + M = O is an approach to design rediscovery?
Marshall: Yes, Petra.
Petra: Plain "yes"? No "if, ands, or buts"?

(Nora and Olivier laugh out loud.)

Marshall: I can add a "because." We can say that C + M = O is an approach to design rediscovery, because it is a model of a subject system and because it outlines an explanatory argument in which outcomes are the argument's *explanandum*.
Nora: Petra, be careful what you wish for.

(Marshall and Petra now laugh out loud.)

Petra: I certainly didn't wish for Latin. What's an *explanandum?*
Nora: It just means "the conditions that are to be explained by an explanatory argument."
Olivier: Is an *explanandum* a dependent variable?
Nora: Yes, if you're talking about variable-centered research designs. But the *explananda* within case-oriented research designs aren't theorized as variables, so they can't be dependent variables. In other words, all dependent variables are *explananda*, but not all *explananda* are dependent variables.
Olivier: Can you give us any references on this?
Nora: The book I remember is Charles Ragin's *The Comparative Method.*[41]
Marshall: Good going, Nora. There are also good discussions of this idea in Andrew Abbott's *Time Matters*[42] and in Howard Becker's *Tricks of the Trade.*[43] Petra, if you're interested, I'd recommend Robert Stake's books, both the *Art of Case Study Research*[44] and *Qualitative Research: Studying How Things Work.*[45] Stake writes for a broader audience than academic researchers in political science, sociology, and anthropology.
Petra: Thanks, Marshall, that's considerate. I'll add Stake's books to my ever-growing reading list. Getting back to C + M = O, can I take it that it's the right approach to design rediscovery?
Marshall: It's a good point of entry into a discussion of approaches to design discovery, because it has the same goal as design discovery and because so many people in the evaluation field know about it. But I think it's flawed.
Petra: Great. The one thing I felt I knew about design rediscovery turns out to be flawed. You've made my day, Marshall.
Olivier: Actually, I always felt a sense of unease about C + M = O, although their case illustrations made it seem okay. So, maybe it *is* flawed, somehow.
Nora: Marshall, what's your version of C + M = O?
Marshall: The short answer is C + M = O in Pawson and Tilley's approach represents what I've been calling the mechanism-like aspect of a mechanism-intent phenomenon, which, in turn, I have been theorizing as scenario-processes. So, C + M = O is a scenario-process, within my design-oriented or mechanism-intent thinking approach to public organizations and public management.
Petra: Are you saying that your approach is different because it involves mecha-

nism-intent thinking, whereas Pawson and Tilley's approach didn't? Or are you saying that your approach is different because it is about public organizations, rather than public programs?

Marshall: More the former than the latter but both are at play. There's mechanism-intent thinking in Pawson and Tilley, but it's not as thorough-going as what you see in our course. Pawson and Tilley don't embed their discussions in the literature on engineering design. They do so in a line of philosophy known as critical realism, which made sense given what they were up against.

Petra: I'm still not absolutely clear about what's different about your approach, Marshall.

Marshall: I think it will be clearer once you see that my approach involves several small differences, which in combination makes for a bigger difference. And I think the best way forward is to complete the illustration that you asked for, when we started going down this path of discussion in today's meeting.

Petra: I'm all ears.

Mechanism-intent analysis illustrated: the course introductory video

Marshall: Right, let's first take stock of where we are. What you like to call the "subject system" is the course introductory video. We agree that this subject system is a scenario-process, whose overall profile is that of viewing a performance presented in a video format. We agree that we want to consider three questions about the subject system: what the video is for; what it consists in ("redocumentation"); and how it works ("design rediscovery"). We agree that, within the course, the subject system performs two of Fayol's enterprise-functions: commercial and technical; that's what it is for, in broad functional terms. We agree that you provided *two* good answers in redocumenting the subject system: one, a high-level representation, limited to the spoken text and conceptual design diagram and their interrelation; the other, a granular representation, focusing on the shapes and text in the diagram and their configuration. We agree that answering the third question involves explanation of *explananda*, which would normally be the trajectory and/or outcome of the scenario-process; however, we also agree that the choice of *explananda* has to be based on mechanism-intent thinking about the relation between the scenario-process, on the one hand, and the commercial and technical functions that the video is designed to perform, on the other.

Petra: Put that way, Marshall, we have already covered a lot of ground and are on the same page.

Marshall: Now, we also have some loose ends in our discussion so far. One is about a feature of mechanism-intent thinking, namely the distinction between a mechanism-intent phenomenon's conceptual design and its embodiment design. Another is about how to explain the *explananda* that have been chosen, when it comes to answering the question of how the subject system works, if its mechanism-like aspect is theorized as a scenario-process.

Petra: Yeah, I remember the distinction between a conceptual design and an embodiment design, from an earlier discussion, but I'm not sure I got my head around it yet. And the second issue is one that I thought that Pawson and Tilley had addressed, as Olivier also had thought.

Marshall: Do you see why the conceptual design versus embodiment design distinction is important, Petra?

Petra: I grasp why it's important to define the conceptual design when you're doing forward engineering: you want to make sure that you achieve great clarity about the intent of the mechanism-intent phenomenon you're creating, and you want to make explicit your general lines of mechanism-thinking about how to effectuate such intent. Armed with a conceptual design, you're in a position to design a technical system for implementing it – and evaluate alternatives, in making a decision. The same argument holds when the conceptual design is implemented by scenario-processes.

Marshall: Splendid! I'm pleased you've picked up on the fact that the conceptual versus embodiment design distinction originated in professional discussions of forward engineering. Do you think the distinction has a role in reverse-engineering, too?

Petra: I'm not sure, except for the fact that reverse-engineering isn't an end in itself: it's meant to be a basis for forward-engineering.

Marshall: That's the big picture, yes. I'd say that a useful outcome of reverse engineering is a high-level characterization of a mechanism-intent phenomenon, with a clear conceptual design, alongside a more detailed characterization of the same mechanism-intent phenomenon. The high-level one will be most useful early in a design-project: it will help in deciding whether the subject system is a good precedent for the mechanism-intent phenomenon to be created, and it will be useful in building up analogies between the subject system and the one to be created, as the design-project proceeds.

Petra: I can see that reverse- and forward-engineering would ideally work together like that.

Marshall: So, we now have the idea, from reverse engineering, of what a subject system is *for*; what it *consists in*; and *how* it works; and we have the idea from forward engineering, that conceptual designs have different roles in a design-project than do embodiment designs.

Petra: Yes, we do have those ideas, Marshall. And what are you going to do with them?

Marshall: I am going to combine them into a unified whole – something that Pawson and Tilley didn't attempt.

Petra: Will you illustrate this grand synthesis with the mundane example of the course introductory video?

Marshall: Indeed, I will.

(Marshall pulls out a sheet of paper from a plastic document wallet and sets it on the table, so that Petra, Nora, and Olivier can see it (Table 3.1).)

Marshall: I call this table a mechanism-intent analysis of the course introductory video. It consists in a 2 x 3 matrix. As you can see, the columns reference the forward-engineering distinction between conceptual and embodiment designs,

Table 3.1 Mechanism-intent analysis of the course introductory video

	Conceptual design	Embodiment design
What's it for?	• Perform the course's commercial function (outcome: decisions to take the course) • Perform the course's technical function (outcome: receptivity to the course content)	(No different from cell to left)

What does it consist in?	• Projection of the conceptual design diagram	• Conceptual design diagram features:
		  – Functional composition (3-functions) and (3-fold) enabling relations, with vocabulary drawn from realm of professional education
		  – Main intent and side-benefits, tied to public management as professional practice and discipline
		  – Effectuation relation

	• Spoken text	• Spoken text features include vocabulary of mechanism-intent thinking, enterprises, features, effectuation of intent
How does it work?	• Frame activation (evokes the frame of a show) • Frame alignment (the video is evidently meant to introduce the course, during the 'shopping' phase of course selection, within a setting of education for professional practice) • Cultural authority of established professors (important for credibility of ideas that differentiate course from stereotypes of management courses)	• Meaning of "functions" grows out of cultural background about "management" courses • Meaning of ideas is conveyed through visual markers of relations among concepts, such as between functions and between functional composition and intent • Meaning of ideas is conveyed through the labeling of relationships, with the vocabulary of enabling and effectuation • Ideas are presented with historical references and disciplined style

while the rows reference the reverse-engineering distinctions among the questions: what is the subject system for, what does it consist in ("redocumentation"), and how does it work ("design rediscovery"). I've filled in the cells with content that is specific to the course introductory video.

(Marshall looks to see how Petra, Nora, and Olivier react to the table.)

Petra: That seems interesting. Maybe we should all comment on this.
Olivier: I like the title of the table: mechanism-intent analysis of the course

introductory video. In this context, it suggests that mechanism-intent analysis has a role in both reverse- and forward-engineering. That seems to make sense, for your design-oriented approach to public management, Marshall.

Marshall: Yes, if you try to do forward-engineering without having done mechanism-analysis of a subject-system, you can't learn from experience – and, more importantly, you can't readily use what you've learned from experience to solve problems in public organizations, or other enterprises, at least via design-projects.

Petra: That's actually a cool point: I suspect I'll remember it, and tell others about it.

Nora: How did you get the idea for this table, Marshall?

Marshall: Truth be told, the precedent for it is a table that comes at the end of Chapter 7 of Michael Barzelay's new book, the one I talked about in our last meeting. The table presents the analysis of what he calls a design-focused case study. Specifically, the case is one of an international cooperation project between a donor country and a partner organization in a developing country. I liked the idea of the table, and I was looking for a way to introduce it into today's meeting.

Nora: You really need to get us those page proofs, Marshall.

Olivier: Yeah, Nora's right. Looking at this table, I'm not entirely clear why there's nothing in the upper-right-hand cell.

Marshall: That's because an embodiment design doesn't add clarity about the intent of the mechanism-intent phenomenon you're creating; that's entirely the role of the conceptual design. Olivier, it's simply down to the meaning of these concepts.

Nora: As I look at the table's second row, the relation between the cells seems to be consistent with what Petra said earlier on. The cell on the left is the high-level representation, while the cell on the right is the granular representation.

Marshall: That's correct. What this means is that the conceptual versus embodiment design distinction is no different from the high-level versus granular distinction, when it comes to the second row, which is about redocumentation, in reverse-engineering terms.

Nora: So, it looks like you're stretching the concept of "conceptual design" as you create the grand synthesis of mechanism-intent thinking, so that it spans forward- and reverse-engineering.

Marshall: That's correct. That is what I think Barzelay was doing in Chapter 7 of his book.

Petra: I think I'm beginning to see the potential value of this grand synthesis, Marshall.

Nora: I want to make sure I understand the bottom row, about how it works. What do you have in mind as outcomes?

Marshall: The meaning of the course introductory video to the students.

Nora: Fine, now I'm interested in the terms "frame activation" and "frame alignment."

Petra: If I may interject, do these terms signify *explananda*, or something else?

Nora: They are not *explananda*: they do the explaining of them. They fall under the concept of *explanans*.

Petra: I now know what to talk about at dinner tonight with my kids.

Olivier: What sort of *explanans* are "frame activation" and "frame alignment"?

Nora: I'll give it a shot, as I recognize these terms from the social movements literature, and specifically from a book entitled, *Dynamics of Contention*, by a distinguished gang of political sociologists, Doug McAdam, Sidney Tarrow, and Charles Tilly.[46] They present *explanans* like these as social mechanisms.

Marshall: Exactly. Social mechanisms are non-lawlike theories about social processes and the conditions that result from them. As theories, they involve descriptive and causal idealization. They often go together with descriptive idealizations where reality is represented as social processes, with flows of action and interaction being integral. Lines of action and actor beliefs are typically seen as reciprocally related – something that is definitely true of frame activation and frame alignment. Causation is taken to be emergent rather than deterministic.

Olivier: I keep coming across the idea of social mechanisms, but I hadn't seen this compact definition of them before. Did you take it from *Dynamics of Contention*?

Marshall: Yes, but I have other sources, too, including one that was published a few years before *Dynamics of Contention*, in 1998. It was an edited book, entitled *Social Mechanisms: An Analytical Approach to Social Theory.*[47] In what I just said I added the line about theories involving both descriptive and causal idealization, going hand in hand. I took that idea, which is called construct idealization, from some of the chapters in an edited book that came out in 1999, entitled *Models as Mediators: Perspectives on Natural and Social Science.*[48]

Olivier: These books haven't been on our reading lists in public administration.

Nora: I didn't know about these references, either.

Marshall: I'm not surprised. From the perspective of sociology, contemporary public administration and political science are both a bit insular. Frankly, it's a bit of an accident that I know this literature. I was luckily put onto it by a senior colleague, a sociologist interested in management, at the end of the last century, just as these books were being published.

Olivier: Is there anything in public administration that reflects these ideas?

Marshall: Certainly. You can read a review of this work in Chapter 6 of Barzelay's book, in a dialogue format. It's funny, because that chapter has the same feel as the discussions we've been having together in our own meeting!

Petra: That's hilarious. I think I'll read that.

Marshall: Great. I actually think it will help you make sense of what we've been discussing. For one thing, it tries to clarify terminological confusions in this design-oriented approach to public management. Specifically, it shows how to integrate the vocabulary of mechanism-intent analysis with the vocabulary of social mechanisms, where the latter is used in understanding the causal properties of scenario-processes and in explaining their trajectories and outcomes in empirical cases of subject systems. And then you can see how these ideas are applied to an actual design-focused case study, about the international cooperation project I mentioned a moment ago.

Petra: Then maybe we should all read those chapters before spending time discussing the bottom row of the 2 x 3 matrix that analyses the introductory course video?

Nora: I think Petra is right.

Marshall: Okay, I'm fine with that. Petra, how would you like to achieve closure to the discussion of these matters today? After all, you kicked it off.

Petra: I'd like for each of us to say something about what we understood and what we still want to understand better. And then maybe you can comment on what Nora, Olivier, and I said.

Marshall: Good suggestion; let's do that, and then we can call it a day.

Nora: I like Petra's sense of good meeting process, but I don't think we have time left in this meeting for the three of us to do this.

Marshall: You're probably right, Nora. Let's make sure we get the full benefit of Petra's perspective. So, with Olivier's permission, Petra, give us your thinking, without worrying about stepping on anybody's time.

Summing up

Petra: I'm game: here it goes. What I understand from the course introductory video and from our discussions in our two teaching team meetings so far, is that we are engaging with an unusual – and possibly unique – approach to public management. I understand that the course we are teaching provides a window on that approach, probably not the totality of it, but an essential aspect of it. I understand that the conceptual design of the course – as diagrammed – is emblematic of the approach. Along those lines, I understand that the intent of this approach to public management includes strengthening the practice of public management, specifically in relation to undertaking design-projects as well as in performing the management function of enterprises that we can call public organizations. I understand that what's called the side-benefit in that diagram – strengthening the identity of public management as a professional practice, tied to a professional discipline – is more than a side-benefit, when it comes to the approach to public management overall. I understand that strengthening professional competence is a function to be performed by the course, and that performing this function is held to depend on improving the students' professional abilities and expanding their professional knowledge.

Marshall: You're on a roll, Petra. Keep going.

Petra: I understand that professional abilities are not unlike skills, but they aren't skills in using established tools for making decisions about enterprises within organizations. I understand that the course highlights professional abilities that have been theorized in different fields, like psychology, design studies, philosophy, and sociology. I understand that professional competence depends on the abilities called sense-making, designing, argumentation, and dramatization. I understand also that professional knowledge and professional practice both involve mechanism-intent thinking. I understand that mechanism-intent thinking is core to public management as a design-oriented professional practice. I understand that mechanism-intent thinking has a long history in the field of management and in human culture. I understand that we need to find a way to bring mechanism-intent thinking to life for our students. Finally, I understand that the way our course is introduced – by presenting the mechanism-intent thinking behind the course design – is a way to bring this way of thinking to life, as well as to motivate students to decide to take the course.

Marshall: You nailed it, Petra. How about what you still want to understand?

Petra: There are things that I want students to understand that I am already beginning to understand, and there are things I want to understand that I'm just beginning to become aware of.

Marshall: What do you have on these two lists, by way of an indication?

Petra: On the first, I'd like the students to understand the vocabulary of mechanism-intent thinking about enterprises and, specifically, public organizations. On the second, I'd like to understand how to explain how enterprises work, using the idea that scenario-processes are mechanism-like aspects of them.

Nora: Marshall, do you want to say anything about how you're going to get students to understand mechanism-intent thinking?

Marshall: There's really two ways. The main way is through immersion. They just keep seeing it, no matter where they look. They'll see it in the introductory course video. They'll see it when I lecture about the readings in the course, as I present them in these terms. They'll see it when they use the discussion questions in preparing for class. They'll see it in using the guides to doing their writing assignments. The secondary way is to make the vocabulary of mechanism-intent thinking and analysis explicit. What I've done in the past is to tell the students that there's a pattern language of mechanism-intent thinking and analysis, and they might want to keep it in mind as they try to make sense of everything they are reading and doing in the course.

Nora: Pattern language?

Marshall: I took the term from the title of a book on designing,[49] but the authors use the term in a different way. I prefer to say pattern language, rather than "standard vocabulary," because I don't think professional practice requires using the terminology of the pattern language. But I do think there needs to be a mechanism-intent pattern to the ideas that practitioners use in their professional life.

Petra: Can you illustrate the pattern language of mechanism intent thinking and analysis?

Marshall: Yes. Let's begin with two statements:

- Humans and organizations create, use, and improve purposeful, or mechanism-intent, phenomena.
- Enterprises are a kind of purposeful phenomena, in relation to which public organizations are a sub-type.

Petra: So far, so good.

Marshall: I'm now going to give you a string of statements about an enterprise's conceptual design:

- An enterprise's conceptual design is a representation of thinking about enterprise-intent and about the effectuation of enterprise-intent through the performance of enterprise-functions.
- Effectuating enterprise-intent depends on performing enterprise-functions; equivalently, functions *effectuate* intent.
- How well one enterprise-function is performed can depend on how well other enterprise-functions are performed; equivalently, functions *enable* functions.
- How well an enterprise's functions are performed depends on how its management function is performed.

Petra: I like those short-hand phrases: within an enterprise's conceptual design, functions *effectuate* intent, and functions *enable* functions. I recognize this part of the pattern language from the diagram on the course's conceptual design. I'm not sure whether I want to use the term "effectuate" outside our course, but I am happy to see it used intramurally. There must be more to the pattern language, Marshall, so please continue.

Marshall: I'm now going to give you a pattern language about an enterprise's embodiment design, while elaborating it through use of ideas taken from both forward engineering and processual sociology, beginning with three basic statements:

- An enterprise's conceptual design *is implemented by* its embodiment design.
- An enterprise's embodiment design *is constituted by* its scenario-processes.
- Scenario-processes are mechanism-like aspects of enterprises.

Petra: That's *so* clear. Please continue.

Marshall: By all means. You'll recall that reverse engineering an enterprise consists in redocumentation, together with design discovery. So, here is a string of statements about redocumenting enterprises:

- Redocumenting an enterprise consists in describing its scenario-processes and connections among them.
- A scenario-process consists in events that begin with initial conditions and end with outcome conditions; the difference between them is change; the similarity between them is continuity.
- A scenario-process is an event-like process that consists in activity, its context, and its outcome.

Petra: I'm tracking this, Marshall. I do now see how scenario-processes are mechanism-like aspects of enterprises, and that's what's redocumented in reverse-engineering.

Olivier: If I can jump in, I think I now better grasp the concept of a scenario-process. As a scenario, it's like an event with a pattern. As a process, it's a relation of activity, context, and outcome within events. You can place the accent on either process, or on events, but it's the same idea overall.

Nora: That's quite subtle, Olivier. It helps me to relate ideas about process within policy process theories, with ideas about case studies in historically-oriented political science.

Marshall: I agree fully with Nora on that, Olivier.

Petra: Can you please give us your pattern language around design rediscovery, Marshall?

Marshall: Here is a string of three statements about that:

- Rediscovering a design within an enterprise consists in explaining the outcomes of its scenario-processes and assessing the functional fit between scenario-processes and the enterprise's conceptual design.
- An explanation of a scenario-process' outcome involves relations among scenario-activity, scenario-context, and scenario-outcome.
- An explanation of a scenario-process' outcome includes some construct (and causal) idealization of how scenario-context *channels* scenario-activities and how scenario-activities *eventuate* in scenario-outcomes.

Petra: I like those short-hand phrases: within an enterprise's embodiment design, context *channels* activity, and activity *eventuates in* outcomes.

Nora: I like these phrases, too. But how would you justify using the terms "channels" and "eventuates" here, Marshall?

Marshall: I could cite some precedents for my choice of words,[50] but that would divert attention from the main issue, which is about how explanation works within case-oriented research and processual sociology. I see them as placeholders for more substantive ideas about the causal properties of the context-activity relation, on the one hand, and of the activity-outcome relation, on the other. The place occupied by "context channels activity" and that of "activity eventuates in outcomes" can be filled, for instance, by ideas related to social mechanisms. For example, in the mechanism-intent analysis of the course introductory video, the "context channels activity" placeholder was replaced with frame-activation, while the "activity eventuates in outcome" placeholder was replaced with frame-alignment.

Olivier: Is it fair to ask what is your precedent for using the term "placeholder," Marshall?

Marshall: Surely it is! The placeholder idea – and the phrasing – comes from philosophy of science. Specifically, it comes from the philosophy of biology. The title of the book that I am referring to is *In Search of Mechanisms: Discoveries Across the Life Sciences*.[51]

Olivier: That's not what I expected to hear.

Nora: As a matter of fact, I once heard a philosopher of science say that biology has come to be the queen of the sciences, and I have been given the impression that the social mechanism literature in social science has consciously emulated biological system research. So, Marshall's finding a precedent in the philosophy of biology is actually not hugely surprising to me.

Marshall: It's also true, Nora, that ideas about reverse engineering emulate ideas in biological system research.[52] Some philosophers have traced this connection back to Aristotle.[53]

Petra: I feel we're in an airplane that just ascended from 15,000 feet to 40,000 feet in 20 seconds. Can we get back closer to Earth now?

Marshall: Yes, that would be a good idea, as we only have use of this meeting room for another two minutes.

Nora: I think a take-away from this meeting is that because there's so much going on in this idea of design-oriented public management, some of it will have to remain behind the scenes for our students.

Marshall: I agree with that! Along these lines, we also need to think more about how to position the very idea of a pattern language of mechanism-intent thinking and analysis. My main pedagogical idea, though, as I said earlier, is that we should immerse students in it, rather than tell them how to swim, from the edge of the pool. Coming to think of it, one way to immerse them in mechanism-intent thinking about public management is to have them read Chapter 4 of *Public Management as a Design-Oriented Professional Discipline*.

Petra: Should we read that chapter of Barzelay's book ourselves before our next meeting, then discuss that idea?

Marshall: That's a fine proposal, Petra. I will get you the material before the end of the day.

Petra: Good meeting, Marshall. Thanks, everybody.

NOTES

1 Moore (1995).
2 Simon (1996).
3 Lynn (1996).
4 For an extended discussion of this point, read Chapter 8. For a quick encounter with it, browse the Glossary.
5 Majone (1989), Dunn (2015), Colebatch (2002).
6 Bryson (2018).
7 Simons (2001), Kaufer and Butler (1996).
8 Pawson and Tilley (1997).
9 Vaughan (2005).
10 Barzelay and Gallego (2010).
11 Simon (1996).
12 Mashaw (1981).
13 Wilson (1989).
14 Bardach (1998, 2004).
15 Tendler (1997).
16 Barzelay and Campbell (2003).
17 Van Aken (2004).
18 Patton (2011).
19 Vickers (1965/1983).
20 Ariew and Perlman (2002).
21 Pahl and Beitz (1999).
22 Funnell and Rogers (2011).
23 Brown (2009).
24 The idea of a conceptual design is discussed in Cross (2008). Cross attributes the idea to Pahl and Beitz (1999), who draw on German traditions of engineering design. Cross says that a conceptual design establishes function structures and suitable solution principles, which are combined into concept variants. As for an embodiment design, "starting from the concept, the designer forms and develops a product or system in accordance with technical and economic considerations" (Cross 2008: 36).
25 Fayol (1919/1984). The full list of enterprise-functions in Fayol's purposive theory of enterprises is technical, commercial, finance, accounting, and security.

26 Among many sources, see Abbott (2016), especially the chapter on outcomes, which was originally published as Abbott (2005).
27 Abbott (2001). The best single source on this perspective is the chapter in this collection entitled "From causes to events." It was previously published as Abbott (1992).
28 Abbott (2016).
29 Schelling (1978).
30 Lakoff and Johnson (1980, 1999).
31 Fauconnier and Turner (2002).
32 Rescher (1996).
33 Goel (1995).
34 Mashaw (1981).
35 On dramatization, rhetoric, and stage-management, see Goffman (1959) and Hilgartner (2000).
36 Wikipedia, "Reverse Engineering" https://en.wikipedia.org/wiki/Reverse_engineering (Accessed: December 20, 2018).
37 Baggini and Fosl (2003: 8).
38 On the idea of cogency, within argumentation theory, see, Rehg (2009).
39 *Evaluand*, a generic term coined by Michael Scriven, may apply to any object of an evaluation. It may be a person, program, idea, policy, product, object, performance, or any other entity being evaluated. Encylopedia of Evaluation. http://methods.sagepub.com/reference/encyclopedia-of-evaluation/n178.xml (Accessed: December 19, 2018).
40 Pawson and Tilley (1997).
41 Ragin (1987).
42 Abbott (2001).
43 Becker (1997).
44 Stake (1995).
45 Stake (2010).
46 McAdam, Tarrow, and Tilly (2001).
47 Hedström and Swedberg (1998).
48 Morgan and Morrison (1999).
49 Alexander, Ishikawa, and Silverstein (1977).
50 A precedent for context channeling activity is Lahlou (2017). A precedent for "activity eventuating in outcomes" is Abbott (2001).
51 Craver and Darden (2013). I'm grateful to Professor Alan Love of the University of Minnesota's Philosophy Department for this reference.
52 Wimsatt (1997).
53 Ariew and Perlman (2002).

4

Theories of public organizations, design-projects, and professional activities: a Public Management Gallery tour

If you were to sign up to a course with the theme of design-oriented public management, you would correctly expect to work on projects. In compensation, you'd hope for a short reading list. In this respect, you might be in for a surprise.

Glancing through the reading list, you see a blur of titles. *Creating Public Value*; *Preparing for the Future*; *Strategic Planning for Public and Non-Profit Organizations*; *The Science of Design: Creating the Artificial*; *Problem-Solving in Organizations*; *Schemas in Problem-Solving*; *The Nature of Design*; *Why?*, *The Presentation of Self in Everyday Life*; and those are just the starred readings. It doesn't help that most of the authors' names are unfamiliar: Moore, Bryson, Simon, van Aken and Berends, Barzelay and Campbell, Marshall, Cross, Tilly, and Goffman. Why so many readings, many not specific to public management? How is this going to work? Is it too late to shop for another course?

Why so many readings? There are two reasons. One is to demonstrate that public management is a discipline, with authors and readings that everyone who's educated in it should know. The other – more important – reason is that design-oriented professional practice is both a creativity-dependent and thinking-intensive phenomenon. Research on designing, and on inventive problem-solving generally, is clear that creativity involves generative, critical thinking about the purposeful phenomena with which professional practice is concerned. In a professional discipline, generative, critical thinking is developed through successive encounters with theories (and other forms of ideas) about such purposeful phenomena. If you're taking a course on design-oriented public management, you're going to encounter such theories. And as there are multiple purposeful phenomena in public management, your reading list will be longer than you might hope.

Why are many readings not relevant exclusively to public management as a professional practice? The reason is that there's a lot to this professional practice that is no less relevant to other areas of professional practice. What purposeful phenomena are specific to public management? Public organizations. What purposeful phenomena are common to public management and other areas of professional practice? One answer is problem-solving and design-projects. A further answer is professional activities, including sense-making, designing, argumentation, and dramatization.

The reading list for a design-oriented public management course is challenging not only because of its substantial size. The challenge is heightened because it's taxing to read literature from multiple fields, such as public management, management, problem-solving, cognitive science, designing, and social theory. Each has its own specialized vocabulary about the phenomena it focuses on – and there is more than one way to theorize purposeful phenomena in the first place. And, as if that's not enough, studying these ideas is not just a matter of learning them: it's a matter of examining them critically, with a view to how they could be creatively used within professional practice – including those projects that you'll also spend time on in your course. Getting through the reading list is an even bigger ask than it may seem at first.

How is this going to work? This chapter addresses that all-important question. Before I explain how, let me tell you a story. A few years ago, as the academic year was about to begin, I ran into a colleague of mine in the main lobby of our building, as we waited for the lift. Professor Chrisanthi Avergou was just back from sabbatical; and, intriguingly, she was looking forward to returning to teach her core course on the information systems master's degree. She told me, to my surprise, that she had used some of her sabbatical to write and record videos about some of the extensive theoretical material in her course, and she was hoping that viewing the videos would help students engage with that material, also saving time for critical discussion of it during class.

Eventually I followed suit in my own course on public management by scripting and recording lecture material about some work of Herbert Simon and Mark Moore, among others. I intended for this material to be used both inside and outside my LSE courses. However, it took me a while to come up with the concept for the collection of videos that I planned to do. What finally came to mind was that our field needed an *anthology* of classic writings. But I feared that the terminology of an anthology of readings would spoil the (admittedly inflated) idea that the videos were a cutting-edge innovation. So, I needed to work on the concept.

Several years earlier, during a getaway weekend in Berlin, I had visited the Bauhaus Archives, a museum about the celebrated Bauhaus School, which existed in Germany from 1929 to 1933. As is well-known, Bauhaus is considered a primary source of the very idea of "design" – an idea that encompassed architecture, industrial product design, graphic design, and fashion design.[1] The School's leadership and faculty included the most prominent architects and artists of the time in central Europe, including Walter Gropius, Johannes Itten, Wassily Kandinsky, Paul Klee, László Moholy-Nagy, Hannes Meyer, and Ludwig Mies van der Rohe. As for the Bauhaus Archives, the museum exhibition mainly consisted in displays about these individuals, their work, their positions in relation to contentious issues within and outside the School, and their ideas about designing and education for it. What brought all of this information to life was the audio-guide, which was exceptionally well-scripted and pleasantly spoken. The whole visit to the Bauhaus Archives made a big impression on me.

It was about a year later that I started to script and record videos about public management authors and their works. The first video I made was about Herbert Simon and his reputation-making 1946 article on "The proverbs of administration." I introduced Simon, identified the issues that he raised in this piece, stated his claims, and presented his argument. I went on to critique the piece as well – arguing that he broke some rules of proper argumentation. After I released the video, I remember explaining to a colleague that it was sort of like a segment of the audio-guide I had listened to while visiting the Bauhaus Archive. Some months later, I built on that idea. I decided that public management needed something like a Bauhaus archive museum, and that a collection of my videos could serve as a virtual one. So, I conjured up the idea that I was creating a Public Management Gallery, consisting of a collection of related displays and audio guide segments about our field's leading lights, past and contemporary. The entire suite of videos would be called the Public Management Gallery Tour. I had my concept, and a narrative line about it.

Figure 4.1 The Public Management Gallery

This chapter is a visit to the fictional Public Management Gallery. The Gallery is divided into three floors, with each floor exhibiting theorizing about the purposeful phenomena involved in public management practice: public organizations, design-projects, and professional activities, respectively. Each floor of the Gallery consists in a few displays, each about the purposive theorizing in one publication. Each display is accompanied by an audio-guide presentation about that publication.

In relation to the teaching-and-learning enterprise within the professional discipline of public management, this chapter's specific role is to introduce you to the purposeful, mechanism-intent phenomena with which public management is concerned and, more specifically, to how they have been theorized. These purposive theories are meant to be critically examined, as part of the teaching-and-learning enterprise. They are also meant to be used in channeling a generative, critical-thinking process in an educational setting. Let the show begin.

Entering the Public Management Gallery space and meeting the curator

You and a companion have made your way to the Public Management Gallery, walking to the entrance on the upper level. You continue into the exhibition's anteroom. On one wall is a word cloud image.

You settle your earbud headphones into place and touch the audio guide's icon for the play command. What you hear is as follows.

Welcome to the Public Management Gallery and to this audio-guide for your self-guided tour. My name is Michael Barzelay. While you're visiting the Public Management Gallery, I'll be your host. Let me briefly introduce myself. I'm from the USA. I consider my home to be Connecticut, although I haven't lived there during the past 35 years. I've been involved academically with

Figure 4.2 The Public Management Gallery word cloud

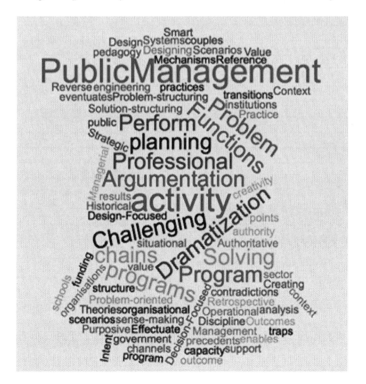

public management since 1980. At the time I was a student on Yale's public and private management master's degree, in its School of Management. When I did my PhD in political science, I didn't have anything to do with public management. I took my qualifying exams in contemporary analytic political theory, international relations, and comparative West European politics. My dissertation was a case study about sector-specific policy-making in politicized market economies; my supervisor was Charles E. Lindblom. In 1985, after finishing my PhD, I became an assistant professor at Harvard's Kennedy School of Government; part of the deal was that I was going to teach public management, which I did, for ten years. I moved to London School of Economics and Political Science (LSE) after that long period. I've taught public management to students on degrees all across the LSE. I've also practiced public management in a way, when I headed LSE's Department of Management for a few years. I've been the co-editor of the academic journal, *Governance*. I've done a lot of consulting and I collaborate with a government-based school of public administration in Latin America. That's me.

My role in the Public Management Gallery is as the founding curator. I founded the Gallery to pursue my passion of fostering a reality where public management is a design-oriented professional discipline. There's a lot packed into this statement, more than I can discuss in this audio guide. If you're really interested, read my book, *Public Management as a Design-Oriented Professional Discipline*, which is in stock at the Gallery bookstore.

The exhibition is laid out on three floors. Each floor's gallery space will feature authors and the purposive theories that they presented in their publications. Each floor is themed. The upper floor, where you are standing now, is about purposive theorizing of public organizations. The mezzanine floor, just below, is centered on design-projects. The lower floor is centered on the professional activities of sense-making, designing, argumentation, and dramatization. Now, if you will, please proceed into the Gallery proper and focus your attention on the first display area.

You now leave the Gallery's anteroom, turn a corner and enter the Public Organizations exhibition. The first exhibition room is bright and airy, thanks to being on the upper floor. Off to the left, a clutch of people is seated on cushioned benches, listening to the Gallery Tour audio guide on their own smartphones.

You spot an empty space on the front bench, move expeditiously toward it, excuse yourself to your soon-to-be-neighbors, sit down, and advance the audio guide to the next recording segment. Without a wait, the curator's voice is heard again.

Listening to purposive theories of public organizations: Moore's *Creating Public Value*

This exhibition room is devoted to one of the most well-known academic theorists of the professional practice of public management – Mark Moore. He has been a professor at Harvard University for his entire academic career, mainly based in the Kennedy School of Government. For quite a stretch of time – something like 15 years – Moore was effectively in charge of public management teaching within that school. He chaired and taught in executive programs, shaped the master's curriculum, sponsored the writing of dozens of teaching case studies, influenced faculty hiring (including my own appointment there), and wrote a book about public management, entitled *Creating Public Value: Strategic Management in Government*. The book took almost 15 years to write, and it was published in 1995 by Harvard University Press.[2] It was presented as being emblematic of the Kennedy School's approach to public management, and that was how it has largely been read. It "stands for" an approach to public management, just as much as it advances particular lines of argument.

It would be uncharitable to suggest that this book is best known for its title. But there's enough truth in this statement to make the title a point of entry into a discussion of the book. The first thing you'll notice about the title is that it has two parts. Typically, you can't reverse the order of a book's main title and subtitle and have it make just as much sense. Moore's book is definitely atypical in this way, among many others.

To understand the relation between the two parts of the title, you need a little background. Specifically, you need to know about the sources of the ideas of "creating value" and "strategic management," referenced in the main title and sub-title, respectively. The proximate source was Harvard Business School. The proximity was partly geographic: if you look on Google Maps, you'll find the distance between those schools is 750 meters (or a half-mile in local terms), thanks to there being a bridge across the Charles River. There was also an institutional connection: some professors at Harvard Business School (HBS) had been involved in curriculum development and teaching about public management during the late 1970s and early 1980s, as was Moore, when he was still a youthful faculty member. In crossing The River, the business school professors brought along the HBS case method pedagogy, as well as the idea of strategic management. The idea of "creating value" was also part of the HBS lexicon, though that idea gained much greater currency as the 1980s progressed, for a raft of reasons, including the growing prominence of Michael Porter and his approach to business strategy.[3]

To understand the idea of strategic management in government, you need to know about the precedent idea of strategic management in big companies.[4] The roots of this idea can be found in a most famous theorization of enterprises and their management, which was published around the time of World War I, by Henri Fayol.[5] In its English translation, it was titled *General and Industrial Management*. Fayol's theory was about enterprises, a *kind* of purposeful phenomenon. It wasn't about organizations as a kind of empirical phenomenon; and it wasn't about specific enterprises. It was a purposive theory of commercial enterprises as a type.

Fayol's theory had some of the same form as systems or functional biology, invented by Aristotle.[6] Fayol theorized enterprises as being functionally invariant, just as is the case for biological theories of human organisms; our bodies are uniform in performing such functions as respiration and circulation, for example. Under Fayol's purposive theory of enterprises, these phenomena are

Mark H. Moore

CREATING PUBLIC VALUE
STRATEGIC MANAGEMENT IN GOVERNMENT

1995   Harvard Kennedy School   Moore

Source: *Creating Public Value: Strategic Management in Government* by Mark H. Moore, Cambridge, MA: Harvard University Press, © 1995 by the President and Fellows of Harvard College. (Book jacket image reprinted with permission.)

Figure 4.3 The Public Management Gallery display on Mark Moore and *Creating Public Value*

uniform in that enterprises can't survive or thrive without performing six functions: in alphabetical order, these functions are accounting, commercial, finance, management, security, and technical. Without performing the technical function, an enterprise wouldn't be able to offer products for sale. Without performing the commercial function, an enterprise wouldn't sell its products. Without performing the security function, an enterprise would lose control of what it owns. Without management, the enterprise would lack organization, direction, and coordination. Fayol went on to discuss the management function in detail; how it enables the other enterprise-functions; and, most of all, how it can be performed by the activities of professional practitioners working in directive roles in commercial business organizations.

In form, "strategic management" is basically the same as Fayol's theory of enterprises. It's a purposive theory. Enterprises are the purposeful phenomenon. Performing enterprise functions is necessary to effectuate enterprise-intent. Management is an enterprise-function that enables all other enterprise-functions to be performed. The most important aspects of the management function are performed through the activities of executives, particularly those holding positions located within an organization's "strategic apex."[7] By the early 1960s, other layers of argument had been added to Fayol's purposive theory of enterprises to form "strategic management." These layers included developments in the field of management (such as the work of Chester Barnard[8]) and in the social scientific study of decision-making in organizations (such as the work of Herbert Simon and James G. March[9]). But the form didn't substantially change.

Let's use this historical account to get a feel for *Creating Public Value: Strategic Management in Government.* Both Fayol's enterprises and Moore's public organizations are theorized as effectuating enterprise-intent. In Moore's book, the *substance* of enterprise-intent is labeled as public value. The content of this idea draws on political theory. Moore holds that public value consists in the realization of political aspirations for aggregate social conditions. He also holds that the restriction of liberty through the exercise of public authority cuts in the opposite direction.

While the argument about the *substance* of enterprise-intent draws on political theory, the argument about the *effectuation* of enterprise-intent draws on legal and empirical theorizing about state authority and institutions. A feature of this line of argumentation is that the use of public authority requires legitimacy, while the use of public money requires political support. Another feature of this argument about the effectuation of enterprise-intent is that program delivery – the analogue to the technical function in Fayol's theory – needs to be performed.

Moore brings these lines of discussion together, to answer the question of what's required for a public organization to effectuate public value, in Chapter 3, where he presents the idea of a "strategic triangle." Its corners represent the ideas of value, legitimacy and support, and operational capacity. Value refers to the substance of public value. The related ideas of legitimacy and support have already been mentioned. Operational capacity is what is required to deliver programs. Thus, public value is effectuated by (a) performing the program delivery function and (b) the legitimacy and support of the public organization and/or program.

Moore's theory of professional practice by public managers hangs off his purposive theory of public organizations. A public manager should think deeply about enterprise-intent, in public value terms, and a public manager should think and act imaginatively and deliberatively about how public value is to be effectuated. When doing that, the contributing factors of operational capacity, on the one hand, and legitimacy and support on the other, deserve utmost attention. That is the overarching idea of strategic management in government, in a nutshell.

Moore works out implications of these ideas for the professional practice of public managers, in the form of guidelines and frameworks. For example, Moore provides guidelines for dramatizing a public organization: the guidelines involve the presentation of an organization's mission. As another example, Moore lays out multiple, contrasting profiles of a public manager's engagement with a public organization's authorizing environment; the profiles include bureaucratic entrepreneurship, policy development, and negotiation. In later chapters, where the focus is on innovation and operational capacity, Moore echoes Fayol's ideas about planning and controlling, two constitutive functions of management in his purposive theory of enterprises.

All that said, many of the implications take the form of case commentaries. That's a hallmark of a Harvard tradition of management theorizing; it has an important history of its own, in law school education and in a form of moral theorizing called casuistry.

Moore's book makes good reading. The first chapter is about a Town Librarian who thinks imaginatively and deliberatively about how to effectuate public value, taking into account an observed shift in patterns in library usage, especially during the after-school hours. Chapter 3 presents the strategic triangle and the guidelines about dramatizing a public organization through the formulation of statements of its mission. And, if you want to know more about Moore's book, and its relation to management theory, then have a look at Chapter 2 of *my* book, *Public Management as a Design-Oriented Professional Discipline.*

I would now invite you to move forward to visit the second display on this level of the Public Management Gallery. It's about another purposive theory of public organization, and it features another famous professor of public management. I hope you can find a spot on the bench in front of that display, as I have a lot to say about it.

Listening to purposive theories of public organizations: Bryson's *Strategic Planning for Public and Nonprofit Organizations*

The professor featured here is John Bryson. If you're involved with the field of public management as an academic, then you're sure to be very familiar with Bryson's ample and influential scholarship. If you're involved with public management as a professional practitioner, you're very likely to have come across –

Humphrey School of Public Affairs
University of Minnesota

Bryson

Source: *Strategic Planning for Public and Nonprofit Organizations*, by John M. Bryson, © 2018 by John Wiley & Sons. (Book jacket image reprinted with permission.)

Figure 4.4 The Public Management Gallery display on John Bryson and *Strategic Planning*

and even used – one or more of the five editions of Bryson's major statement about strategic planning.

The main title of this book is *Strategic Planning for Public and Nonprofit Organizations*. The cover of the fifth and most recent edition – published in 2018 – is featured in the display in front of you.

Bryson is McKnight Presidential Professor of Planning and Public Affairs at the University of Minnesota, based in the Hubert Humphrey School of Public Affairs. He has been on the Humphrey School faculty for decades, and twice serviced as Associate Dean. He is a prolific researcher and well-regarded (and liked!) academic leader in the field of public management.

The main title indicates that Bryson's book is a purposive theory of two different forms of enterprises: public organizations and nonprofit organizations. It focuses on strategic planning. So, let's start there. Bryson defines strategic planning as follows: "Strategic planning helps produce fundamental decisions and actions that shape and guide what the organization is, what it does, and why it does it."

Let's clarify what this statement means by asking what strategic planning is for, what it consists in, and how it works. Those are questions to ask about purposeful phenomena like strategic planning.

What strategic planning *is for* is indicated by the book's sub-title: strengthening and sustaining organizational achievement. That's Bryson's way of phrasing the idea of "effectuating enterprise-intent," language that I introduced in likening Moore's book to Fayol's purposive theory of enterprises. It may be worth pointing out that Bryson's preface mentions several terms that relate to the idea of organizational achievement: fulfilling missions, meeting mandates, satisfying constituents, and creating public value.

We can be a bit more specific about what strategic planning is for, if we liken Bryson's purposive theory of public organizations to Fayol's purposive theory of enterprises, with some depth. Remember that within Fayol's theory, enterprises can't survive or thrive without performing six functions: accounting, commercial, finance, management, security, and technical. Remember that without management, the enterprise would lack organization, direction, and coordination. Consider that without the management function being performed adequately, the other enterprise-functions will suffer, altogether undercutting the prospect of effectuating enterprise-intent.

Now recall that strategic planning, under Bryson's definition, "shapes and guides" the public organization. That phrasing suggests that the idea of "strategic planning" in Bryson's purposive theory of public organizations is closely related to the idea of "performing the management function" in Fayol's purposive theory of enterprises. This relationship between ideas can be stated more precisely. *Strategic planning is for performing the enterprise-function of management in public organizations*, which, in turn, enables the performance of other enterprise-functions, which, in turn, strengthens and sustains the achievement of public organizations.

Let's sharpen up this idea by next answering the question of what strategic planning *consists in*. Recall that Bryson's definition states that "strategic planning helps produce fundamental decisions." That statement suggests that strategic planning is a decision-making process. Put in terms of mechanism-intent thinking and analysis of enterprises, strategic planning is a *scenario-process* within organizations, whose *profile* is that of decision-making. By definition, scenario-processes eventuate in outcomes. Thus, strategic planning *eventuates in* decisions about the enterprise.

More can be said about what strategic planning *consists in*. But before breaking this idea down further, let's consider the third question: how does strategic planning work? It's a more interesting and potentially fruitful question to examine, compared to the questions of what strategic planning is for, and what does it consist in.

You can't expect that you'll get a sharp answer to that question from a definitional statement. But there are hints in Bryson's definition of strategic planning, which, as you will recall is that: "Strategic planning helps produce *fundamental* decisions and *actions that shape* and guide what *the organization* is, what it does, and why it does it" (emphasis added). We've already established that strategic planning *is for* performing the management function; so the question is *how* it does that. *How* do *decisions* that eventuate from strategic planning *shape the organization*? The answer to this is that they give rise to "actions" that change how the public organization's enterprise-functions – such as the technical or security functions – are performed. Fine, but how do decisions that eventuate from strategic planning *lead to* such actions and their downstream effects? That's a question that Bryson's definition of strategic planning can't answer: but there's nevertheless a hint in the term *"fundamental* decisions." The hint is that strategic planning works when participants in the organization believe that the *decisions* eventuating from strategic planning truly address the enterprise's *fundamental* issues.

Let's summarize where we have been before adding more depth to this account of Bryson's purposive theory of strategic planning for public organizations. Strategic planning *is for* performing a public organization's management function, which means that it is for enabling the performance of all enterprise-functions, which means it is for effectuating sustained organizational achievement. Strategic planning *consists in* scenario-processes within organizations, whose profile is that of decision-making. Strategic planning *works* by generating actions that change how enterprise-functions are performed.

There's much to be added to this summary. We have time for only one further step in this direction. In the preface to the fifth edition of his book, Bryson states that "strategic planning at its best makes extensive use of analysis and synthesis in deliberative settings to help leaders and managers successfully address the major challenges that their organization (or other entity) faces" (p. xvi). This statement implies that if strategic planning is to work, its scenario-processes need to include a phase that eventuates in a decision identifying the enterprise's major challenges. It also implies that the decision-making process has to be deliberative: a characteristic that – as a matter of sociological theory – grows out of its activity and its context.

There's a second implication of the idea that "strategic planning at its best makes extensive use of analysis and synthesis in deliberative settings." *Analysis* and *synthesis* are defining ideas in purposive theories of *designing*. In those theories, analysis enables synthesis, and synthesis eventuates in designs, that is, representations of objects. In the context of strategic planning, designed objects could be representations of "major challenges" as well as of "fundamental decisions."

We should thus revisit the earlier definition of strategic planning, within Bryson's purposive theory of public organizations. Nothing changes in what strategic planning *is for*. But something changes in what strategic planning *consists in*. It consists in scenario-processes with *two* distinct profiles: *designing and decision-making*. If strategic planning is different in what it consists in, then it has to be different in how it works. And it works by designing *enabling* decision-making. As Bryson stated: "Strategic planning at its best *makes extensive use of analysis and synthesis* in deliberative settings to help leaders and managers successfully address the major challenges that their organization (or other entity) faces." Please bear this thought in mind when you go down to the Mezzanine level of the Gallery, which is about design-projects.

Bryson's book includes a wealth of frameworks and guidelines that elaborate this purposive theory of strategic planning and public organizations. The master guideline for strategic planning is the following 10-step approach:

1. Initiate and agree on a strategic planning process
2. Identify organizational mandates
3. Clarify organizational missions and values
4. Assess the external and internal environments to identify strengths, weaknesses, opportunities, and threats
5. Identify strategic issues facing the organization
6. Formulate strategies to manage the issues
7. Review and adopt the strategic plan or plans
8. Establish an effective organizational vision
9. Develop an effective implementation process
10. Reassess strategies and the strategic planning process.

The chapters in Bryson's book are organized around this master guideline. Each chapter provides specificity around how to perform a given step. In each case, the scenario-process is more detailed, in terms of its outcome, its activity, and in the tools that can be used to help produce the outcome. It's a very well structured and detailed purposive theory, making it quite useful.

This is probably as good a point as any to bring this audio-guide presentation on John Bryson and his strategic planning book to a close. You should now be able to tackle the task of reading and appreciating it as a purposive theory of strategic planning and public organizations. Besides that, you will now be able to compare, contrast, and integrate this purposive theory with Moore's. That will be good for your professional knowledge about public management, and it will be good for the professional discipline of public management. It's something you might do if you're taking a course on public management.

Before you head down to the mezzanine level for the continuation of the Gallery Tour, why don't you visit the café around the corner to the right. You can also re-charge your smartphone for the next leg of the Gallery Tour.

Listening to purposive theories of design-projects: Herbert Simon's *The Sciences of the Artificial*

Welcome to the Mezzanine Level of the Public Management Gallery. As you enter, take in a sweeping view of the three displays on design-projects that you will be viewing here:

Source: Simon, Herbert, *The Sciences of the Artificial*, third edition, [Cover], © 1996 Massachusetts Institute of Technology, published by the MIT Press. (Book jacket image reprinted with permission.)

Figure 4.5 Entering the exhibition section on design-projects

I'll be giving you a brief account of each one in this series of audio-guide segments. Together, they should give you a sense of the important role played by the idea of design-projects in purposive theorizing about public organizations and the professional practice of public management.

We begin with Herbert A. Simon and his book, *Sciences of the Artificial*.[10] There's a ton that you really ought to know about both. I will tell you as much as I can within the short period during which you will be comfortable standing in front of the display.

It's almost impossible to imagine that anyone who takes the time to visit the Public Management Gallery wouldn't recognize the name, Herbert A. Simon. Let me give you a test to see how much you already know. Here are some questions: state whether you think they are True or False.

First, Herbert Simon was awarded the Nobel Prize in Economic Sciences in 1978. True or False? True, you say? You are CORRECT!

Second, Herbert Simon was an economist. True or False? True, you say? WRONG! His PhD was in Political Science. For a while he taught in a business school. He was a professor of computer science and psychology. He was a lot of things, but an economist wasn't one of them.

Third, Simon was an organization scientist. True or False? True, you say? CORRECT! He devoted quite a lot of his work to understanding what favored and disfavored the making of intelligent decisions within organizations. And surely that work was theoretical in character. Not only did the work claim to be true of organizations generally and universally, but it also drew on theoretical ideas, from many sources, including philosophy and psychology.

Fourth, Simon proposed that the discipline of management be developed as a design science rather than as a professional practice. True or False? False, you say? CORRECT! Simon proposed that the discipline of management be developed as a professional practice, and that this should be done through rational inquiry about solving problems through the complementary activities of designing and decision-making, especially within organizational settings. Simon came up with the sticky label of "a science of design" to refer to such rational inquiry, which he hoped would play a role in the teaching and learning enterprise of the professional discipline of management, among others. But he didn't say that management itself should be a design science. Others have said Simon advocated that management become a design science, but that doesn't make it true.

Now, tally up your score. Of your four responses, three were correct. Overall, your responses show that you're quite well informed about Herbert Simon. And it's unlikely that your beliefs will go out of date, because Simon isn't with us any longer. Sure, you didn't get a perfect score. But the incorrect response was probably due to being primed to thinking that somebody who won the Nobel Prize in Economic Science was an economist. No worries: this just shows that your brain processes information like everyone else here in the Public Management Gallery. You can feel at home.

Let me remind you why Simon is here with us in the Public Management Gallery. Remember this image, from when you entered the building?

Well, you're now on the mezzanine floor. That suggests that Simon is here because he had something to say about design-projects. And so, let me now tell you why THAT is true and what you might want to remember about the relationship between design projects, on the one hand, and public organizations and professional activity, on the other.

Simon had something to say about design-projects in his book, *Sciences of the Artificial*, the third and final edition of which is pictured in the display. Where, specifically? Try the index. If you look through the index for "projects," you won't find any entry. So, try the entry for "design," then look for "projects" as a sub-entry. Find the sub-entries that begin with P. You find "problems, large-scale." And then "process of." Getting closer to "projects." But the next sub-entry is "representation of." It begins with R. So, perhaps the association between Simon and "design-projects" is just something in your curator's mind?

While I have encoded the term "design-projects" in the Public Management

Gallery Tour, I dare you to deny that this idea was central in the chapter of *Sciences of the Artificial*, entitled "The science of design: creating the artificial." In that chapter, Simon analyzes a scenario-process that eventuates in decisions that lead to – and structure – an artificial system's realization. All of the constitutive activities of the scenario-process are located within the same span of time. Some of the constitutive activities eventuate in more than one representation of an artificial system's design. Such designs channel other constitutive activities that eventuate in decisions. These two categories of activities – designing and decision-making – cease at some point, as when the organization is satisfied with the artificial system concerned and with the decisions made about it, or possibly for other reasons. This scenario-process is the concept that I label "design-projects." To invoke an old-fashioned American idiomatic expression, "if it looks like a duck and sounds like a duck, then it's a duck."

There are a couple of more substantive reasons why I feel confident about using this label. One is historical. A fairly recent book about the history of business schools in North America provided some detail about Simon's work and what influenced him.[11] To make a complex story simple, Simon's real-world analogue to the scenario-process just presented was projects he participated in, as an affiliate of RAND Corporation; and the mother of historical precedents for those projects was, in turn, the Manhattan Project, which eventuated in an artificial system for prosecuting World War II with U.S.-controlled atomic weapons. Augier and March also explain how Simon came to see "problem-solving" through collective generative and deliberative processes as being an essential form of organizational activity in business and other forms of enterprise. Accordingly, as a matter of history, Simon saw design-projects as being a universally key mechanism for effectuating enterprise intent – whatever words he used to communicate this view.

The other substantive reason is that the notion of design-projects provides a direction for purposive theorizing of public organizations and the professional practice of public management. It's a direction that is missing from mainstream theorizing of enterprises. As a matter of history, design-projects were not part of Fayol's purposive theorizing of an enterprise's management function, though, as an aside, he probably did think of projects as being mechanisms for an enterprise's technical function. The idea of design-projects is also marginal to purposive theorizing about public management. Specifically, the terminology of design-projects is missing from Moore's book: if you look in the index for either "design" or "projects," you'll come away without a reference. It's even marginal to the vocabulary of Bryson's book. There's no index entry for projects; and the most related sub-entry for strategic planning is "process." That suggests that even Bryson's purposive theorizing of public organizations didn't take full advantage of Simon's suggested direction for theorizing management. So, I state my case: design-projects have a major role to play in purposive theorizing of public organizations and public management; and time will tell if this direction for theorizing comes to pass, and how well it works.

If you'd like to know more about Simon's theorizing about design-projects, you have three options. One is to read Chapter 5 of *Sciences of the Artificial*.

A second is to read Chapter 2 of my book, *Public Management as a Design-Oriented Professional Discipline*. A third – the best option – is to read both.

Listening to purposive theories of design-projects: *Problem-Solving in Organizations*

This segment of the Gallery Tour is principally about Professor Joan van Aken, on the one hand, and the book, *Problem-Solving in Organizations,* on the other. On the display, you can see the book jacket of the third edition of this book, which I will refer to, for the sake of brevity, as *PSO*. Published by Cambridge University Press, *PSO* is co-authored by van Aken and Hans Berends,[12] whose handsome images are staring back at you from the display.

If I'm right, you're likely expecting me to explain why you've encountered van Aken and *Problem-Solving in Organizations*, spot in the middle of the Public Management Gallery Tour. Let me tell you a story.

I came across the first edition of *PSO* as a result of studying van Aken's articles that advanced the idea that management should be researched and taught as a design science.[13] I was impressed with what I read – and checked him out. I got hold of *PSO*. I discovered that the book was written not only as a synthesis of theorizing about problem-solving in organizations, but also as a guidebook for students on undergraduate business courses who have to complete a business project in their final year of study. It was written clearly and succinctly. I felt that my own students might like to read a number of the chapters. Besides that, I had been looking for a reading that would introduce my students to ideas about designing – one that wouldn't be about designing machines, products, and/or software. *PSO* ticked that box; indeed, it brought in ideas about designing in order to add some depth to ideas about problem-solving in organizations, which had otherwise tended to be indistinguishable from literature on decision-making. So, I assigned two of the early chapters of *PSO* for the second week of my course.

I was in for a surprise. My students didn't like *PSO*; they loved it. A week later, one student told me he used the material during a team exercise within a recruitment event for a consulting company. He was able to get the other team members to follow his lead. (Eventually he got the job, and LinkedIn tells me he's working for McKinsey.) I kept using the material, year after year. I have recommended it to other teachers, and everybody likes it (at least).

As I wrote my book, *Public Management as a Design-Oriented Professional Discipline*, I came up with the idea of a three-layered pattern of purposive theorizing and professional knowledge about public management, with the middle-layer being about design-projects, sandwiched between a layer above, for purposive theorizing about public organizations, and a layer below, for theorizing about professional activity. If the middle layer was going to be about design-projects, I needed material to represent purposive theorizing about them. That's the story.

Now the argument: The reason *PSO* has a place in the Gallery Tour is that it spells out a purposive theory of design-projects in a fuller way than Simon did. Indeed, *PSO* translates Simon's ideas into a theory of design *projects* and into a purposive theory of *enterprises*, while picking up on some of the history of thought of problem-solving.

Some of the early theorizations of problem-solving were formulated between the two world wars of the twentieth century, as part of an intellectual movement known as pragmatism. A major figure in this movement was John Dewey; his most famous statement about problem-solving was *The Public and its Problems*. Dewey's theorization of problem-solving was enormously influential, and it was elaborated by many leading mid-twentieth-century thinkers in sociology, law, political science, and economics at U.S. universities. The best known such thinkers include Herbert A. Simon, Harold Lasswell,[14] Albert O. Hirschman,[15] Charles E. Lindblom,[16] James G. March, and Aaron Wildavsky. They didn't agree with each other on everything, but their writings certainly added great intellectual depth to debates about the constitution and possibilities of problem-solving.

Van Aken and Berends' book, while reflecting the history of debates about problem-solving, provides a distinctive line of argument about professional practice in organizations. In summary form, their argument is that business projects are mechanisms to perform enterprise functions, while this type of mechanism is constituted, essentially, by a line of design activities. This line of activity eventuates in well-formed precursors to solved problems, consisting in object and realization designs. These precursors structure and/or feed other scenario-processes consisting in decision-making activities. Decision-making activities eventuate in decisions about preserving, modifying, or replacing mechanisms for performing an enterprise's functions; in substance, such decisions may involve adopting and implementing the object and realization designs that eventuated from the earlier business project.

In line with this sketch, *PSO* taps into the idea – immanent in Simon's main line of theorizing in *Sciences of the Artificial* – that purposeful phenomena, or solutions, within enterprises are artificial systems. You can see this slant in the way van Aken and Berends label the process-outcomes of problem-solving scenarios, specifically, "object designs" and "realization designs." An "object design" specifies a purposeful phenomenon as it is to exist at a later point, once the downstream activity of realization makes the object design fully real – but an object design is silent on specifics of the realization activity. Conversely, a "realization design" is silent on the object specification, but does specify the downstream plan in enough detail that the object design can be realized.

As you'll intuit immediately, the vocabulary of object and realization design is anchored in engineering and architecture; fabrication is a standard term for realization in engineering, while construction is a standard term for realization in architecture. Given this vocabulary, it makes sense for van Aken and Berends to theorize business projects as a cascade of activities that run from the upstream one of creating an object's conceptual design to a downstream one of creating an object's fully embodied design, with some intermediate stages between them. Most tellingly, van Aken and Berends employed the concept of business projects to transfer to the field of management a purposive theory of problem solving in engineering and architecture, according to which creating solutions consists in a multi-stage, cumulative activity, where each stage leading to an object and realization design involves a specific type of progression, demanding a specific frame of mind and intermediate goal. It is for this reason it's correct to say that van Aken and Berends offer a Simon-esque, design-oriented theorization of professional practice within organizations.

That's probably all you need to be told about van Aken and Berends' *Problem-solving in Organizations*, for the purposes of your visit to the Public Management Gallery. When you exit the exhibition, you can flip through a copy of the book, if you have time to visit the ground floor Gallery bookstore and café. If you have time for a tall coffee, grab hold of the book and work your way through Chapter 3. Don't forget to look at the handy diagrams.

Would you now please meet me at the next display.

Listening to purposive theories of design-projects: *Preparing for the Future*

The main title of the book featured here is *Preparing for the Future: Strategic Planning in the U.S. Air Force*, which was published by Brookings Institution Press. Given that this book is about strategic planning, you might wonder whether you've been surreptitiously tele-transported from the mezzanine to the upper floor, where the exhibits on works about public organizations are located. Don't worry; nothing of the sort has happened. *Preparing for the Future* could properly have been displayed there; but what I have to say about it targets the design-project layer of public management purposive theorizing.

If you haven't yet looked closely at the display, you might be expecting a presentation of the book's two authors, along with some fanfare. However, fanfare would be unseemly, as one of the co-authors of *Preparing for the Future* is yours truly. I am happy to introduce my co-author, Colin Campbell. When the book project began, back around 1998, Colin was a professor and director of Georgetown University's public policy school, in Washington, D.C. By the time we finished he was a professor of political science at University of British Columbia, from which he retired some years ago.

The book's topical focus was on mechanism-intent theorizing of public organizations. The term "strategic planning" was a reference to such theorizing. A question we considered was what strategic planning is for. In line with Fayol and Bryson, we took strategic planning as being *for* performance of a public organization's management function. We formulated a specific line of purposive theorizing about the role of the management function, a precedent for which was a line of argumentation in a popular management book, entitled *Competing for the Future*.[17] We modified the argument, modestly, to cohere with purposive theorizing of public organizations.

The question of what strategic planning consisted in was pursued in an empirical, exploratory way, through reporting, analysis, and commentary on a raft of strategic planning cases that occurred within the U.S. Air Force (USAF) during a six-year period. One such case ran from mid-1995 through the end of 1996; one of its outcomes was an officially approved formulation of a USAF strategic vision, entitled *Global Engagement*. Another case ran from 1997 through 1999;

one of the outcomes of this case of the U.S. Air Force Futures Games was a strategic planning directorate presentation to the Air Staff senior leadership on the insights, issues, and recommendations arising from the futures games. A third case was the source of a successor Air Force strategic vision, entitled *Global Vigilance, Reach, and Power*, completed in 2000. The book not only analyzed each case, but also compared them as part of an effort to add some depth to purposive theorizing about strategic planning as a mechanism to perform the management function in public organizations.

The case analysis and commentary established a few directions for my own theorizing of public management, which I have pursued since then. The direction I will pinpoint here is to theorize episodic strategic planning efforts, like the Air Force cases, as mechanisms to perform the management function in public organizations – and to theorize such mechanisms, in turn, as design-projects. To be honest, the process by which I pursued this direction of theorizing was through teaching, as these Air Force cases became staples of all of my courses. I think the first time I framed these cases as "strategic planning projects" was when I was teaching executive short courses for the Australia and New Zealand School of Government (ANZSOG), more than a decade ago. This direction of theorizing, involving a dialogue between "ideas" and "cases," continued, and it wasn't long before I was using van Aken and Berends' book as a theoretical reading to go alongside the Air Force cases. It's been that way ever since.

You'll remember from what I said about *PSO* that design-projects are usefully theorized as scenario-processes; this framing was pursued in analyzing the case studies of strategic planning in the USAF, both in the book and in case teaching. That is, the "cases" have been analyzed as *design-project-type scenario-processes*. This framing carries a number of conceptual implications, such as:

- Strategic planning efforts are episodes understood as projects;
- Strategic planning projects are mechanisms to perform a public organization's management function in specific respects;
- Strategic planning activities are constituted by sequences of professional activity on the part of many actors, participating on the basis of their role in the organization or some other identity within the situation at hand;
- A strategic planning project's final "object-designs" are commonly labeled as strategic plans;
- Initial conditions of strategic planning projects reflect how legacies of previous strategic planning projects relate to the way the launch of their successors is stage-managed;
- Dynamically-stable contexts of strategic planning projects include the organization's formal role system; the persona that top organizational leaders establish in relation to the specific strategic planning project; the way milestone and gateway reviews have been programmed; and the project's official narrative;
- Some of the constitutive activities of strategic planning projects have more in common with archetypes of designing, while other such activities have more in common with archetypes of decision-making;

- How designing and decision-making come to be concatenated has substantial implications for the content and significance of the object-designs/strategic plans that eventuate from strategic planning projects; and
- Presentational drawings of strategy content are intermediate outcomes of strategic planning projects; how top organizational leaders respond to them has a significant modifying effect on project's dynamically-stable context and, consequently, on strategic planning projects' outcomes and legacies.

Admittedly, this nine-fold set of bullet points is extensive and densely written. Relax, you will be allowed to leave the Gallery even if you can't recite them. What's really important is the impression that this material leaves, so, if you don't mind, let me suggest some impressions of this display, and the mezzanine floor as a whole, that you might want to take away with you.

First, purposive theorizing about public management is well served by focusing specifically on design-projects as a mechanism for performing enterprise functions in public organizations – not least, for performing the management function. (Caveat: don't be tricked into thinking that design-projects are exclusively constituted by design activity, when the concatenation between design- and decision-making activity is key to how they work.)

Second, purposive theorizing of design-projects benefits from creative, critical thinking – and from analyzing empirical cases, for the same reasons why the same ingredients are beneficial for non-purposive, contemplative theorizing of phenomena as you encounter in social science research. Creative, critical thinking is a many-faceted process, but it does include formulating analogies among structures of ideas. As illustrated by the discussion of *Preparing for the Future*, fruitful analogies can be developed by seeing strategic planning and the creation of artificial systems as similar processes with qualitatively different outcomes. Likewise, you can see the benefit of analogies between design-projects and significant events in the unfolding history of a public organization.

Finally, I hope that you can see why purposive theorizing about public management needs to tap into two historical traditions of management as a professional discipline: the one represented by Moore (and also Bryson) and the one represented by Simon (and also van Aken and Berends). By this point in the Gallery Tour, you should be able to comprehend the attempt to blend these two traditions in forming the design-oriented professional discipline of public management.

If you will, now please make your way downstairs to the lower level of the Gallery, where you will be surrounded with theories about various forms of professional activity, all of which are crucial for public management as a professional practice, but none of which is unique to public management.

Introducing theories of four professional activities

Now that you've finished making your way downstairs, please take notice of the display welcoming you to the final portion of your tour of the Public Management Gallery. You saw the left-hand image as you entered the exhibit on the upper floor: it's here to remind you of the three-layer concept of purposive theorizing within the professional discipline of public management. If you look around, you'll also see some chairs; as this introduction to the lower floor of the Gallery will take a little time to present, you might want to relax your legs by sitting on one of them.

The aim of this part of the Gallery is to add depth to purposive theorizing of professional practice in public organizations. Accordingly, we must first ask what professional activities are *for*, and then turn to the question of what professional activities *consist in*. The idea of what professional activities are *for* is derived from the discussions of purposive theorizing of professional practice in public organizations that you heard while visiting the Gallery's upper and mezzanine floors. As such, there are two ways to present what they are for. One – keyed to the upper level – is that they are *for* performing enterprise functions of public organizations, including the management function. Another – keyed to the mezzanine – is that they are *for* effectuating design-projects. As for what professional activities consist in, the approach taken here is to see them as scenario-processes. As such, they consist in context-activity-outcome dynamics, just as Simon theorized design-projects. Professional activities should be theorized in a sufficiently granular way that professional practitioners in public organizations could easily recognize that they engage in them at work. In sum, professional activities are granular-scale scenario-processes whose context-activity-outcome dynamics effectuate design projects or otherwise contribute to performing a public organization's enterprise functions.

You might wonder why I didn't say that professional activities are compositional elements of the professional practice of public managers. After all, what unifies Mark Moore's theorization of public management is the idea of a public manager; and he theorizes this unifying idea by identifying a number of compositional elements, such as formulating a public organization's strategy, imagining how public value can be created, declaring a public organization's mission, engaging in political management, and managing trajectories in operational capacity. While that's all coherent in its own way, Moore's theorization is typically resisted by those who consider the idea of a public manager role as institutionally ill-fitting or culturally inappropriate. I wish for the purposive theory of professional practice in public organizations presented here to avoid this fate; and to that end, I have presented

The Public Management Gallery

Sense-Making   Designing   Argumentation   Dramatization

Four Theories of Professional Activity

Figure 4.6 Entering the exhibition section on professional activities

the idea of professional activities in ways that cohere and resonate with Herbert Simon's processual approach to theorizing professional practice, rather than in line with Moore's role-centered approach. Accordingly, as theorized here, professional practitioners in public organizations are designers and decision-makers; as such, they are problem-solvers. Being a problem-solver involves engagement across a spectrum of differentiated professional activities, every one of which involves lines of individual thinking and action, as well as episodes of interaction with others during unfolding events in local-present situations.

I've been using the plural term professional activities, without naming any specific variant of them. I think you can see why I did that, the main reason being that I decided to give absolute priority to preserving the Gallery's approach to purposive theorizing about professional practice in public organizations. An added reason is that any given list of variant forms of professional activity will displease pretty much everyone. I didn't want to make you feel that way, too soon. But I can't ask you to hang on any longer. So, here's the list:

- *Sense-making* in public organizations
- *Designing* in public organizations
- *Argumentation* in public organizations
- *Dramatization* in public organizations.

As you consider the list, please take into account what each and every one of these professional activities is *for*. The long-version is that they effectuate design-projects or otherwise contribute to performing a public organization's enterprise functions. We can also say that sense-making, designing, argumentation, and dramatization are *for* "problem-solving," in keeping the rhetoric of Simon's approach to theorizing professional practice. Having made this broad point, I'd like to suggest that problem-solving is effectuated by *combinations* of these professional activities. Put the other way around, these variant forms of professional activity contribute to problem-solving in distinct ways. Accordingly, the list should be evaluated as a totality, rather than item-by-item.

A reason for distinguishing designing from argumentation is that the literature on designing is separate from the literature on argumentation. Essentially, the literature on designing is about creating and representing purposeful phenomena for eventual realization and use, whereas the literature on argumentation is about thinking critically and communicating persuasively about issues to be resolved through individual or collective deliberation and choice. Making this delineation doesn't negate the fact that purposive theories of designing and argumentation share common roots, especially in the philosophy of Aristotle.[18] It does, however, reflect academic specialization within universities, with designing being theorized mainly in architecture departments and engineering faculties, and with argumentation being theorized mainly in humanities faculties, in philosophy or rhetoric departments, mainly (though not exclusively). Reflecting this pattern of specialization, the literatures on designing and argumentation are written for different audiences. However, both are relevant for theorizing professional activity within public organizations.

The background argument is Simon's theorization of problem-solving through design-projects, which held that problem-solving requires both (a) creating designs for purposeful phenomena and (b) making decisions, whether about the process of creating a purposeful phenomenon, or about the issue of whether to proceed to realize a design for one. It's obvious that the professional activity of designing is intrinsic to creating designs. Moreover, the idea that argumentation is intrinsic to decision-making in organizations is immediately apparent: that is how issues are tackled and how decisions are rationalized.

In theorizing sense-making, there's mileage to be gained in asking what it is *for* – and what it *consists in*. The professional activity of sense-making, like the two mentioned earlier, should be seen as being *for* problem-solving and, relatedly, *for* performing the enterprise functions of public organizations, including the management function. But sense-making can also be seen as an enabler of the professional activities of designing and argumentation. As an enabler, sense-making's role is to provide a starting point and ongoing context for these respective activities. To be enabling, sense-making must eventuate in a sense of situational orientation on the part of individual professional practitioners, as well as in some clarity about what ideas and observations are relevant to the professional activities of designing and argumentation, in the specific situation at hand. This way of theorizing sense-making is plainly built on the premise that neither designing nor argumentation can be done well without a sense of situational orientation and such clarity about relevance; and a further premise is that it takes – or should take – effort to establish these enabling conditions.

As for theorizing what sense-making *consists in*, one direction is to focus on cognitive process. Within this realm are many approaches and substantive theories. Some are more concerned with how individuals arrive at a situational understanding on the basis of direct experience, while others are more concerned with how individuals attend to, store, and retrieve information. In addition, the literature includes *purposive* theorizing of sense-making. Some of this literature is concerned with problem-solving *generally*, much as Herbert Simon was in much of his writing. Still, some purposive theorizing about sense-making is concerned with problem-solving in specific domains of professional practice. An example of sense-making practices in public management is stakeholder mapping, the outcome of which is insights on stakeholder power and interests. Thus, the literature that's pertinent to theorizing sense-making as a professional activity is extensive and varied, with some purposive theorizing being domain-independent (as in the literature on problem-solving), while other purposive theorizing is domain-specific, as in the case of stakeholder mapping and public management.

I'm now going to turn to the fourth item within the list of professional activities that make up professional practice in public organizations: dramatization. Dramatization might seem out of place here, for the reason that the other three ideas about professional activity clearly belong to the vocabulary of problem-solving. Nothing you've heard in listening to this audio-guide would have led you to anticipate coming across theories about dramaturgical activity. It's not that dramaturgical activity – for example, projecting character-roles and playing-through performance routines – didn't appear in Moore's book, or Bryson's, or mine. Indeed, the case studies and illustrative examples of these books are clearly made of dramaturgical stuff. What is true is that dramaturgical activity was invisible, because, while it was part of the *phenomenon* of professional practice, dramaturgical activity was not theorized. The thesis here is that existing theories of dramatization – such as Goffman's – should become just as prevalent within purposive theorizing of professional activity as are theories of sense-making, designing, and argumentation.

I'll discuss dramatization in mechanism-intent terms, focusing entirely on what it consists in. In *The Presentation of Self in Everyday Life*, Goffman[19] analogized social processes to staged dramatic performances, not just to such performances themselves, but also to what precedes them – such as scripting – and to what is their result. Dramatic performances are scenario-processes involving events within "local-present" situations. Both the context and outcomes of dramatic performances are theorized, broadly, as social realities – a fundamental social theory concept. Social realities include a complex of social relations among those involved in the same local-present situation. The activity within dramatic performances consists in lines of action by individuals, as experienced by anyone who witnesses or participates actively in them. Such lines of action, in turn, are constituted by sequences of acoustical and gestural moves. Outcomes of dramatic performances are either validations or shifts in the social reality of a local-present situation, or some combination of the two.

This statement is plainly minimalist: it doesn't include any of the nuanced elaborations that made Goffman's theoretical discussion so profound and influential. For example, it doesn't mention steps taken to set the scene of dramatic performances, let alone those taken in scripting them. It doesn't mention the emergent properties of dramatic performances, arising from the interplay of individuals and their actions within local-present situations. However, nothing stands in the way of bringing this richer Goffmanian theoretical account of dramatic performances into purposive theorizing about professional activity within public organizations.

It's about time to get up from your chair to move to the main part of the lower-floor Gallery exhibition. If you're getting anxious to complete the Gallery Tour, don't worry. Testing of the audio-guide has shown that visitors are satisfied without hearing too much about the specifics of the featured literature on professional activities. They come away from what you will now hear with enough insight about the literature to read further on their own. So, please move into the main room. The fact that there's no chairs or benches should assure you that you won't be there for long.

Exemplifying theories of professional activity

Four books are on display in this gallery space, as you can quickly observe by scanning the scene.

The book about sense-making is *Schemas in Problem-Solving*, by Sandra P. Marshall (1995), now an emeritus professor of psychology at San Diego State University in California. Marshall's book was first published in 1995 by

Sources:
Tilly, Charles, *Why?* [Cover]. © 2006 Princeton University Press. (Book jacket image reprinted with permission.)
Cross, Nigel, *Engineering Design Methods: Strategies for Product Design*, Fourth edition. [Cover] © 2008, John Wiley & Sons. (Book jacket image reprinted with permission.)

Figure 4.7 Four theories of professional activity in public organizations (sense-making, designing, argumentation, and dramatization)

Cambridge University Press and has recently been updated and reissued. The book builds on decades of theorizing about human cognition to provide a theory of how problem-solving activity is channeled by conceptual schemas; and it also discusses how such schemas undergo change in response to experience and reflection on it.

Marshall introduces her book by explaining that the word and the concept it reflects date back to the writings of the ancient Greek philosophers, noting that schema is a letter-for-letter transliteration of σχημα, which means form, shape, or figure. Marshall adds that, "almost every modern usage of schema draws upon a person's application of knowledge found in memory to make sense of some experience or event taking place in his or her world" (p. 8).

Marshall's theory of problem-solving includes four stages, which she refers to as functions, because they are intrinsic to how problem-solving works. The stages that relate to sense-making are identification and elaboration; the stages that relate to other aspects of problem-solving are planning and execution. In scenario-process terms, the outcome of identification is *recognition* of a situation, event, or experience, whereas the outcome of elaboration is *understanding* of what has come to be recognized. For identification, the schema/activity relation involves pattern recognition. This dynamic essentially involves assimilating a situation to one or more schema that have come to structure an individual's cognition. It is referred to as pattern recognition because schema consist in numerous linked elements and because no single condition within a situation, on its own, is the cause of the identification outcome. Once identification has been achieved, the elaboration stage kicks-off, with the situational frame resulting from the identification stage channeling the elaboration stage activity. Here, the schema used for identification helps an individual grasp how various conditions occurring or present in the situation are connected – constitutively, causally, or otherwise.

Marshall's book is evidently situated within the cognitive science literature. That categorization carries a few implications for purposive theorizing about sense-making. First, if you'd like to understand more about what schemas consist in – and how they function – the advice would be to read more within the cognitive science literature, specifically where schemas play a role. Some of that literature is written for a popular, educated audience, with noteworthy examples being Lakoff and Johnson's *Metaphors We Live By*,[20] Cialdini's *Pre-suasion*,[21] and Konnikova's *Mastermind: How to Think Like Sherlock Holmes*.[22] Some of the relevant cognitive science literature is written for a broad academic audience, with noteworthy examples being Murphy's *The Big Book of Concepts*[23] and Fauconnier and Turner's *The Way We Think*.[24] Second, you might want to read about sense-making from perspectives different from cognitive science. An exceptionally prominent source is Karl Weick, whose writings on sense-making began with his *Social Psychology of Organizing*.[25]

The book about designing is *Engineering Design Methods,* by Nigel Cross,[26] now an emeritus professor of design studies at The Open University in Britain and a seminal figure in the field of design studies in Europe and beyond. This book builds on more than a century of theorizing about product design, picking up on some classic German theorizing from the late nineteenth century. That said, the first chapter's inspiring and closely-reasoned discussion of problem-solving is not confined to the book topic. For this reason, it's well-suited to theorizing designing, when this scenario-process is understood as a professional activity that is *for* effectuating design projects and for problem-solving more generally.

Cross' first chapter includes a compact and clear discussion of the widely-held idea that, when a design-project begins, the problem to be solved is ill-defined. Clients don't know how to communicate what they want to the designers, if they even know what they want. At this early stage, designers don't know what constraints pose design restrictions or trade-offs. Cross adds to this picture of design-projects an element that is reminiscent of the idea of garbage-can decision-making, namely, that the situation within the design-project includes ideas about what the object or product should be. These ideas have come into the situation because some designer or the client has an inclination to push for them; whether these ideas are suitable as design solutions is another matter entirely. Cross' theory of the professional activity of designing acknowledges that design-projects have something in common with the organized anarchies of the garbage-can model of organizational choice: namely, solutions chase problems. This complication then sets the scene for the rest of Cross' purposive theorizing of designing.

The hallmark of the ensuing argument is that designing consists in two co-occurring scenario-processes, both involving the same people in the designer and client roles. The two scenario-processes are problem-structuring and solution-structuring. Oversimplifying, the outcome of problem-structuring is definitive client intent as it relates to the design-project, whereas solution-structuring eventuates in definitive designs for the object or product. The details of this argument are instructive – and should not be missed by anyone interested in critical, generative thinking about designing as a professional activity, no less in public organizations than elsewhere.

The book about argumentation is *Why? What Happens when People Give Reasons, and Why*, by Charles Tilly,[27] who passed away several years ago after a distinguished academic career in sociology, teaching mainly at the University of Michigan and Columbia University. As the title suggests, Tilly's book is not a work of professional philosophy. It examines argumentation – the giving of reasons – as a social process. Under Tilly's analysis, giving reasons is part-and-parcel of defining a person's social relations with others. While that reality pervades situations and events where reason-giving occurs, it's also the case that reason-giving takes different forms, depending on the specifics of the situation and event concerned. In filling out this theory, Tilly proposes a four-fold classification of forms of reason-giving: convention, coded arguments, technical arguments, and stories. Arguments about performing enterprise functions and effectuating design-projects, in particular, can be seen as combinations of coded and technical arguments as well as stories. They're all relevant to professional activity in public organizations.

Tilly's book is quite well-suited to being a point of departure in learning about the literature on argumentation for a few reasons. First, it's written from the standpoint of argumentation being *for* problem-solving, which is evident in the use of examples. Second, it sees argumentation as consisting in how people *represent* their thinking to others, which provides a way to theorize what argumentation consists in. Along these lines, the idea that argumentation consists in four distinct forms – convention, codes, technical arguments, and stories – provides some depth to the idea. The analysis and thoughtful commentary in the book would surely help a professional practitioner think generatively and critically about how to engage in argumentation as a professional activity within public organizations.

All that said, there's plenty of other works to read on argumentation. In public administration, you shouldn't miss Hood and Jackson's *Administrative Argument*.[28] In public policy, you should look into Majone's *Evidence, Argument and Persuasion in the Policy Process*[29] and Dunn's *Public Policy Analysis*.[30] Some of the literature on how to do academic writing is relevant. A good example is Booth, Colomb, and Williams, *The Craft of Research*.[31] And, of course, the philosophical literature on argumentation is as relevant as it is endless.

We conclude with Goffman's *Presentation of Self in Everyday Life*, the obvious choice for a purposive theory of dramatization, as was discussed while you were seated in the ante-room of this floor's exhibit. There isn't much more to say to recommend it, other than to mention its stratospheric Google citation count. Just go buy it in the Gallery bookstore. You can find it to the left of the Gallery Tour logo, mounted on the wall ahead.

Figure 4.8 Logo of the Public Management Gallery

This concludes the audio-guide presentation of the Public Management Gallery Tour. I trust that you've enjoyed your visit. I hope you'll return for a refresher in the weeks, months, and years ahead.

NOTES

1 For information about the Bauhaus Archive, view https://www.bauhaus.de/en/das_bauhaus/44_idee/ (Accessed April 26, 2019). For a history, see Droste (2011).
2 Moore (1995).
3 Porter's second major text – Porter (1985) – is more relevant than the first in this respect.
4 Rumelt, Schendel, and Teece (1994).
5 Fayol (1919/1984).
6 Ariew and Perlman (2002); Leroi (2014).
7 Mintzberg (1983).
8 Barnard (1938/1968), Guillén (1994), Williamson (1995).
9 Simon (1947/1968), March and Simon (1958), Perrow (1986).
10 Simon (1996).
11 Augier and March (2011).
12 Van Aken and Berends (2018).
13 The main one was van Aken (2004). I discuss it in Barzelay (2012).
14 Lasswell (1971).
15 Hirschman (1973, 1991).
16 Lindblom (1959, 1990).
17 Hamel and Prahalad (1995).
18 Ariew and Perlman (2002).
19 Goffman (1959).
20 Lakoff and Johnson (1980).
21 Cialdini (2016).

22 Konnikova (2013).
23 Murphy (2002).
24 Fauconnier and Turner (2002).
25 Weick (1979).
26 Cross (2008).
27 Tilly (2006).
28 Hood and Jackson (1991).
29 Majone (1989).
30 Dunn (2015).
31 Booth, Colomb, and Williams (2008).

5

Core knowledge in a professional discipline of public management

Marshall: We've decided to assign Chapter 4 of the book to students on the course. What questions do we want to ask students to be prepared to discuss in class?

Nora: We should probably start with concept identification questions.

Petra: That sounds like a good idea. We'll serve them up – then Marshall will have to answer them!

Marshall: Go for it.

Olivier: I've got an easy one. What's a public organization?

Nora: That's easy?

Marshall: I'll make it easy by dividing my response into two parts: what are public organizations for, and what do they consist in. Within purposive theorizing of the professional discipline of public management, public organizations are *for* creating public value. Public organizations *consist in* enterprise functions – not least, management and program delivery – and the mechanisms that perform them. Such mechanisms are theorized as processes, with the main form being scenario-processes. The outcomes of scenario-processes play pivotal roles in how mechanisms work in performing enterprise functions. Scenario-process outcomes eventuate from scenario-process activities. Such activities partly consist in the lines of action of individuals, as they interact with one another within contexts that reflect the outcome of earlier scenario-processes. Thus, public organizations are purposeful phenomena that effectuate the creation of public value through the performance of enterprise functions, which, in turn, is accomplished by a multitude of scenario-processes and their context-activity-outcome dynamics, within which individual lines of action have a significant role to play.

Petra: That's pretty abstract, Marshall, but I can see how it pulls together points that were made in different segments of the audio-guide presentation.

Nora: Doesn't this answer beg a lot of questions?

Marshall: Surely it does, but not just because it is abstract and brief. It's also because practical arguments like this are always incomplete, as Aristotle pointed out in his theory of rhetoric. But fire away if you want to pose questions that this particular statement begs.

Nora: You present the mechanisms within public organizations as scenario-processes, but indicate that scenario-processes aren't the only form of mecha-nism. I vaguely remember there being another form. What is it?

Olivier: It's a conversion-process. I remember that conversion-processes result in outputs, whereas scenario-processes result in outcomes. Also, conversion-process activities are fed by inputs, while scenario process activities are chan-neled by context.

Petra: I understand that these pure types of mechanisms can be combined – as when an operating IT system – a conversion-process – is part of a management control system – a scenario-process.

Nora: Let's move on. Here's another easy question: what's management?

Marshall: In keeping with classical purposive theorizing of enterprises, manage-ment is a function within public organizations. If this function is not adequately performed, then the effectuation of public value creation will be adversely affected. Deficits in the management function's performance ramify in the inad-equate performance of other functions, such as program delivery and system development. The issue, then, is what mechanisms perform the management function. Turning again to classical purposive theorizing of enterprises, an authoritative answer is planning, directing, coordinating, and controlling. These four mechanisms are alike in two ways: they have a role to play in performing the management function and they mainly consist in scenario-processes, with their particular context-activity-outcome dynamics. The lines of action of individuals are constitutive of scenario-process activity.

Petra: A lot of practitioners would say that planning, directing, coordinating, and controlling are management functions, but you refer to them as mecha-nisms. Since functions and mechanisms are not the same ideas, somebody has to be wrong. Am I right?

Marshall: It's a neat question. I'll take your word for it that it's common to say that planning, directing, coordinating, and controlling are functions. If you want to label planning, directing, coordinating, and controlling as functions, then please think of them as *constitutive* functions of the management function of public organizations. The idea that a given function has constitutive functions is not unknown to science; in anatomy, breathing is a constitutive function of res-piration. Similarly, the idea that functions have constitutive functions is also not unknown to engineering design, with constitutive functions typically labeled as sub-functions. But many professional practitioners of public management aren't familiar with models that present constitutive descriptions of natural and purposeful phenomena, and many aren't very practiced in mechanism-intent thinking. So, we face a challenge as educators. The imperfect solution is to stick to one basic vocabulary, specifically, my patterned language of purposive theoriz-ing. And in the pattern language, management (like respiration) is a function, whereas planning, directing, coordinating, and controlling (like breathing) are mechanisms. So, Petra, nobody's wrong, but rather we just don't have aligned vocabularies.

Petra: Isn't that a problem, Marshall?

Marshall: If you say so, it is. But break it down. One problem is that people may not know how to engage in mechanism-intent style purposive theorization of public organizations and professional practice. Here, the solution is show them how and why to do it. Another problem is that people may not know how to *use* purposive theorizing in professional practice. Here, the solution is to show them how to do *that*. The common solution to both parts of the problem is education. That overall solution implies that people like us should dramatize the design-oriented professional discipline of public management and our roles as educators, so we can teach them what they need to learn.

Petra: So, how can I explain the idea of management to someone who's confused about the vocabulary of function and mechanism?

Marshall: A professional practitioner needs to be able to present their thinking as to whether and how a specific public organization's mechanisms for performing the management function are adequate. As they present their thinking, they should identify what they consider to be the conceptual design of the management function, if they are focusing on it. In representing the management function's conceptual design, they might say that the planning function enables the directing function, which, in turn, enables the coordinating and controlling functions, and so on. As they present their thinking, they should also identify what they consider to be the management function's embodiment design. In representing the embodiment design, they should identify the mechanisms for performing management's constitutive functions. In explaining how the management function is actually performed, they should drill-down into the mechanisms' context-activity-outcome dynamics and/or their input-activity-output dynamics, and they should then make an argument about the functional relation between the embodiment design, fleshed out in these terms, and the management function's conceptual design, which is what an embodiment design effectuates.

Petra: And what would you say if people don't get this idea?

Marshall: Like any other educator, I would present an analogy. I have found that an anatomical analogy usually works well. I point out that the conceptual design of a living body includes respiration and its *constitutive* breathing *function*. This conceptual design is effectuated by a body's embodiment design, which consists in a *mechanism* for breathing. This mechanism includes the cyclical activities of inhaling and exhaling, each involving their inputs (i.e., gases contained in air) and outputs (e.g., retained oxygen and released carbon dioxide). I joke that it's great that your body's embodiment design is adequate to its conceptual design, because otherwise you wouldn't be able to take in my explanation. If I have time, I complement this line with an analogy involving a physical machine, specifically a jug whose conceptual design involves removal of unwanted dissolved elements from tap water prior to drinking it and whose embodiment design involves a downward flow of water through a filtering unit and then into a portable basin. I keep a Brita filter jug in my office for this purpose.

Petra: I'm satisfied, let's move on.

Olivier: I'm ready to move down to the mezzanine level of the Gallery: what's a design-project?

Marshall: A design-project is a mechanism to perform the enterprise functions of public organizations, whether the management function or otherwise.

A design-project consists in two, interlocking, scenario-processes: designing and decision-making. Both are needed if a public organization is going to solve a "new" problem, or solve an "old" problem in a novel manner. Without designing, nothing novel can be done; without decision-making, nothing will change in how the organization's functions are performed. Stated in systems terms, a design-project's scenario-processes are, in multiple ways, interlocking. For example, an intermediate outcome of decision-making is typically to initiate the front-end stage of a design-project. As another example, the intermediate outcomes of designing constitute the initial conditions of decision-making, as, for example, when decision-making takes the specific form of a milestone or gateway project review. The designing scenario-process ultimately eventuates in object designs and realization plans, while the decision-making scenario-process ultimately eventuates in authoritative instructions to implement the realization plans for the object design.

Nora: If you wanted to add just another level of detail to this answer, what would you say?

Marshall: Well, I would want to say more about the initiation of a project's front-end stage and about project reviews. I'd also want to say more about designing and decision-making viewed in isolation from one another, by adding depth to the discussion of their respective context-activity-outcome dynamics. In discussing designing, I'd want to draw on Nigel Cross' ideas about problem- and solution-structuring. In discussing decision-making, I'd want to draw on Sandra Marshall's ideas about sense-making, Charles Tilly's ideas about argumentation, and Erving Goffman's ideas about dramatization.

Olivier: Well, then, the obvious next concept to identify is professional activities.

Marshall: As a collection, professional activities are constitutive of mechanisms that effectuate design-projects or that otherwise perform enterprise functions of public organizations. Within this collection are the professional activities of sense-making, designing, argumentation, and dramatization. Each professional activity is a scenario-process. The activity aspect of such scenario-processes consists in interactions among individuals. These interactions are, in turn, constituted by individual lines of action. Such lines of action are constituted, in turn, by talk and gestural moves.

Olivier: Is it correct to say that professional activities are individual-level phenomena in public organizations?

Marshall: I understand why you might think so, given that individual lines of action are constitutive of the scenario-processes that I conceive as professional activities. The answer to your question is, nevertheless, no. Public organizations are theorized here as purposeful phenomena. In providing a purposive theory of public organizations, I draw on precedents in management thought,[1] program planning and evaluation,[2] functional biology,[3] engineering design,[4] processual sociology,[5] and process philosophy.[6] None of these precedents is closely aligned with the idea that social phenomena are best theorized as hierarchically-stratified systems.

Petra: You lost me with some of these theoretical references, Marshall. Let me ask a yes/no question: are professional activities what individuals do in public organizations?

Nora: Petra, if I can jump in, it's an understandable issue, but it's not a yes/no question. What individuals do *is* constitutive of professional activities; therefore, your statement is correct, but one could equally argue that professional activities consist in what goes on *among* individuals. Argumentation – representing ideas to others so that they understand and respond to them – is an inherently multi-person process. So is dramatization, for essentially the same reason. Designing is inherently multi-disciplinary and is therefore multi-person in nature. The only professional activity that might not be inherently multi-person is sense-making, but even here the scenario-process outcome in a public organization might be a declared, collective situational orientation. If these qualifications are important to emphasize, then I think that "no" is a better answer than "yes." Right, Marshall?

Marshall: Yes, Nora, except that if one says "no" to Petra's question, without having provided any background, the questioner will think you must be a pointy-head academic. This is not an impression we should leave.

Nora: How about we ask them to discuss the relationship between concepts?

Olivier: That's an idea. How about the relation between strategic planning and the strategic triangle?

Marshall: These ideas figure in purposive theorizing about public organizations, not least in the work of John Bryson and Mark Moore. As far as professional practice is concerned, strategic planning and the strategic triangle are both relevant to formulating conceptual designs for public organizations; specifically, they add depth to such representations as they concern the management function. Bryson presents strategic planning as being *for* making fundamental decisions about the future of public organizations. Moore presents the strategic triangle as being *for* creating and assessing a public organization's strategy. In line with mechanism-intent theorizing, strategic planning and the strategic triangle are compatible ideas about a public organization's management function: Creating and assessing a public organization's strategy *enables* making fundamental decisions about a public organization's future.

Let's add some depth to this purposive theorizing by sketching a generic embodiment design for performing the management function. As part of an embodiment design, strategic planning is a mechanism for performing the constitutive management functions of planning and directing. Following Bryson and, more so, Barzelay and Campbell, strategic planning – as a mechanism – is specifically a design-project. As such, strategic planning projects are constituted by the scenario-processes of designing and decision-making.

Designing and decision-making are interlocking mechanisms. The designing mechanism within strategic planning projects eventuates in (novel) objects, whereas the decision-making mechanism eventuates in (fresh) decisions. The objects may be labeled as visions, alternative futures, planning options, and the like. The decisions may be communicated in documentary form and/or dramatized through performances during stage-managed events.

An embodiment design for strategic planning projects would typically include multi-person activities. Such activities would typically occur within a dynamically stable (though not stationary) project context, an effect of which is to certify various participants as agents of the organization's strategic planning.

This sketch of the generic embodiment design of strategic planning projects can be made more granular – for example, by typifying the professional activities of sense-making, designing, and argumentation, as they relate to such projects.

Nora: Marshall, are you stopping there? I thought you were going to talk about how Moore's strategic triangle can be incorporated into strategic planning projects.

Marshall: I paused only to make sure that you all are actively listening. Clearly that's the case, at least with you, Nora.

Petra: Keep going, Marshall.

Marshall: Relating the strategic triangle to strategic planning is challenging because Moore's purposive theory of strategic management in government has almost none of the features of strategic planning as this idea was just sketched out. Nevertheless, we can spot two points of contact between strategic planning projects and the strategic triangle, working with the generic embodiment design sketched above.

First, we can place the strategic triangle within the designing part of strategic planning projects. As an established tool for generating novel strategic planning objects, the strategic triangle would channel the activity within the designing scenario-process. In Moore's terms, a "strategy" would be such an object. As such, the strategic triangle could give some specificity to the "content" of objects that eventuate from the designing scenario-process within strategic planning projects.

Second, we can place the strategic triangle within the professional activities "layer" of the generic embodiment design for strategic planning. It certainly can be used to channel sense-making, designing, argumentation, and dramatization activities. For instance, the triangle corners for "support" and "capacity" are plainly relevant for sense-making, while the triangle corners for "value" and "capacity" are plainly useful for designing. The triangle as a whole is undeniably useful for argumentation, as it can give structure to the giving of reasons about shifts in a public organization's strategy. And, if an audience knows about the strategic triangle, it can be a useful prop in a stage-managed dramatic presentation about a public organization's strategy.

Nora: That interpretation of Moore in relation to professional activities and strategic planning projects is actually quite cool, Marshall. It would be a good point to make in an exam. With that thought in mind, how would you conclude a short essay on strategic planning and the strategic triangle, if you were going for full marks?

Marshall: The challenge has been received, Nora. Here it goes: the intent of strategic planning projects is to make fundamental decisions about the future of a public organization. Strategic planning projects are mechanisms for performing a public organization's management function, especially its constitutive functions of planning and directing. The strategic triangle can surely be used to channel activities within the designing scenario-process of strategic planning projects; its use would be reflected in the objects that eventuate from such scenario processes. Depending on circumstances, the strategic triangle might also be used within the decision-making scenario-process of strategic planning projects. The idea of how the strategic triangle can be used in strategic planning can be fleshed out by adding specificity to the collection of professional activities within a generic embodiment design for strategic planning projects, where this collection consists in sense-making, designing, argumentation, and dramatization.

Nora: Well, I'll give you high marks for that, Marshall.

Olivier: I'd like to raise the bar even further by asking you to connect the dots between three ideas within the purposive theorizing about public management, one from each layer of the Gallery. The three are: management, designing, and dramatization.

Marshall: If you can connect the management and designing dots, Olivier, I'll be glad to connect those dots with dramatization.

Olivier: I'll give it a go, Marshall. As for management, it's a function within public organizations, considered as enterprises, in accord with Fayol's theorizing of enterprises in his classic book, *General and Industrial Management*. Public organizations, in turn, are for creating public value, in accord with Moore's well-established book, *Creating Public Value: Strategic Management in Government*.[7] Putting these points together, management is a critical function within public organizations for effectuating public value creation; this point is entirely clear in Bryson's *Strategic Planning for Public and Non-profit Organizations*,[8] as well as in publications of others in the field.

Marshall: So far so good, Olivier. Please continue.

Olivier: In accord with Simon's *Sciences of the Artificial*,[9] designing is *for* creating novel mechanisms in response to an enterprise's challenges. A mechanism for responding to such challenges is design-projects. Designing is a constitutive process within such mechanisms, as is decision-making. Designing eventuates in object designs; in concept, these outcomes are "novel mechanisms" that resolve an enterprise's challenges, provided that they come to be approved for realization and utilization.

Marshall: So, we now have a fix on two dots; can you now connect them up?

Olivier: These ideas connect in two ways. Let's take the case where the "object design" eventuating from a designing scenario-process is meant to perform a public organization's management function; illustrations are a modified management control system and a new strategic plan. Here, designing is a way to respond to the challenges of a public organization's management function.

Marshall: That's straightforward. Please continue.

Olivier: Let's take the case where a design-project's front-end stage has started; illustrations are beginnings of strategic planning projects, or beginnings of system development projects. According to van Aken, a design-project's front-end stage will have been preceded by its fuzzy front-end stage, during which a challenge had been recognized and decisions made, the effect of which was to both establish the context of the design-project and to set its activities in motion. What happened during the project's fuzzy front-end stage arguably performed the enterprise's management function.

Marshall: Nice distinction, Olivier. Nevertheless, I'll stick to your first case when trying to connect these dots to dramatization.

Olivier: That's fine.

Marshall: Does anyone want to say anything about the "dramatization" dot, before I start to make the connection?

Petra: Well, I think practitioners can immediately relate to the idea that putting on a show is a big part of any professional's work-life. It's what we do whenever we make a presentation or participate actively in a meeting. There's more to our practice than giving reasons for views on issues; we always have to foster impressions about who we are in the situation at hand and how we stand in relation to others who are there with us. Fostering the impressions we intend doesn't always work. But we have to try, for all sorts of reasons. Some of those reasons are obvious, like decisions aren't made on the basis of information and argument.

Marshall: I've also found that practitioners pick up on many of the ideas in Goffman's dramaturgical theory of social processes more readily – and acutely – than with many other theoretical ideas. With that in mind, would you like to make a dramatization dot connection, Petra?

Petra: Well, let's run with the idea that designing is a scenario-process, consisting in context-activity-outcome dynamics, where the activity includes analysis and synthesis and the outcome is an object design. And let's run with the idea that dramatization is a scenario-process, where the activity consists in performances and where the outcome is the audience's experience of a show. So, setting these ideas beside one another suggests that object designs and shows are analogous as they are both outcomes of a public organization's scenario-processes.

Marshall: I like the method, and I follow the reasoning. Why not push the object design-show analogy further, to see where it takes us.

Petra: A question to consider would then be: how are object designs similar to shows?

Marshall: That's a good step. And how are they similar?

Petra: They are both purposeful phenomena.

Marshall: Okay, but subordinating two ideas to the same broader category doesn't in itself say how they are similar.

Petra: True, but I've come to have ideas about what are purposeful phenomena: in particular, they are functioning wholes, whether they are physically or digitally embodied systems, or not. The idea that objects are functioning wholes is clearly conventional, and much the same is true of their representations, namely as object-designs. We don't normally refer to shows as functioning wholes, but we do speak of shows "holding together," or not, as the case may be. Aren't shows functioning wholes, even as they are experiential?

Nora: We know what fits together in an object: it's the features. What is it that holds together in a show?

Petra: The characters' performances.

Nora: What holds the performances together? It's not their physical organization!

Petra: The scene, the character-relationships, and the narrative arc of the show come to mind.

Nora: I'm now seeing the analogy. What do you want to do with it?

Petra: Well, we have the idea that designing eventuates in object-designs, can't we extend that idea to say that sometimes designing eventuates in shows, or designs for them?

Nora: Well, I see there's some concept resonance there. Do you have any illustrations to offer?

Petra: Well, how about a strategic planning project? Isn't the scenario-process outcome something like a show, constituted by performances by such character-roles as planners or project teams, put on for an audience of decision-makers?

Nora: That rings true. So what implications does that reasoning hold for theorizing design-projects in public organizations?

Petra: The implication is that the object-designs eventuating from designing within design-projects can be systems or shows. Thinking of design-project outcomes as shows will make *theories* of dramatization as relevant to professional practice as putting on performances is central to professional life.

Marshall: Petra, you've just put on a winning show! Love it!

(Nora and Olivier applaud.)

Marshall: You might wonder why this all sounds so original. The answer is that the Harvard approach to management didn't bring dramatization into its purposive theorizing, even as it was central to student life in a case-teaching tradition. Meanwhile, Simon's approach stuck with the idea that decision-making in organizations was about search for information, making arguments, and exercising decision-making authority. And further, Goffman's ideas were seen as mainly useful as ways to counter the Simon approach to decision-making, rather than as something that could be melded with his ideas about artificial phenomena and designing.

Olivier: Do you think we should sum up?

Petra: I think we should still stare at these ideas about management, designing, and dramatization as if they are a challenging work of art, at least for the time being.

Nora: I think Petra's right, Olivier.

Marshall: Thanks everyone; let's meet later this week to do some creative thinking about the role of case studies. . . .

NOTES

1 Fayol (1919/1984), Porter (1985), Goodman (2000), Sarasvathy (2008).
2 Pawson and Tilley (1997), Stake (2010), Funnell and Rogers (2011).
3 Craver and Darden (2013).
4 Simon (1996), Dym (1994), Cross (2008).
5 Abbott (2001, 2016).
6 Rescher (1996).
7 Moore (1995).
8 Bryson (2018).
9 Simon (1996).

6

Design-focused case studies in the professional discipline of public management

This book is centrally concerned with developing the professional discipline of public management. Part of developing any professional discipline is creating knowledge that can be used within professional practice. As theorized in this book, professional knowledge is an umbrella term for purposive theorizing and design-precedents. This book has focused on purposive theorizing until now; however, for the next two chapters, the focus will be on design-precedents and, in particular, on their formulation through design-focused case study research.

As design-focused case study research is a new term, it's useful to compare design-focused case studies with their stereotypical analogues in social science disciplines. The chief similarities between design-focused and stereotypical case studies are two-fold. First, their intent is to attain intellectual insight into theoretically-defined phenomena. Second, they consist in research projects, whose activities include topic-setting, issue-formulation, research design (including case-definition), analytical reporting, explanatory argumentation, and argumentation about theoretically-defined phenomena.

In comparison with stereotypical case studies, design-focused case studies are similar in that they feature argumentation about theoretically-defined phenomena. The difference is that the two kinds of case studies are concerned with different kinds of theoretically-defined phenomena. Whereas stereotypical case studies are concerned with theoretically-defined *empirical* phenomena, design-focused case studies are concerned with theoretically-defined *purposeful* phenomena. This difference relates to the disciplines within which case study research is done. Theoretically-defined empirical phenomena, like the price system or elections, are tied to *social science disciplines*, whereas theoretically-defined purposeful phenomena, like machines, buildings, business firms, or public organizations, are tied to *professional disciplines*.

Stereotypical case study research projects are mechanisms for creating social scientific knowledge within a social science discipline. By analogy, design-focused case study research projects are mechanisms for creating professional knowledge within a professional discipline. The comparison requires a closer look at this complex analogy. The analogy is a close one insofar as both social science and professional disciplines provide contexts for case study research projects: for instance, a researcher pursuing any variant of case study research thinks of the meaning of the project at every step, with a view to presenting the study in the "context of justification,"[1] whether in publications or in person. The demands for justification can also be substantively similar, even when a study's theoretically-defined phenomena relate to different forms of disciplines, as between social sciences and professional disciplines. Nevertheless, the analogy between design-focused and stereotypical case studies unravels to the degree that knowledge of purposeful phenomena differs from knowledge of theoretically-defined phenomena in the social sciences (a matter of some debate).

This chapter is designed to develop the idea of design-focused case studies, as it relates to the professional discipline of public management. For the most part, the chapter proceeds as if it's possible to talk intelligently about design-focused case studies without being much concerned about the strength or weakness of their analogy with stereotypical case studies. Proceeding this way makes sense for two pragmatic reasons. First, developing more definitive contrasts with stereotypical case studies will require much more discussion than can fit within this chapter, or this book. A reason for that view is that "stereotypical case studies" exhibit misplaced concreteness: their varieties are not as distinct as a rainbow's rays of color. Second, a key interest here is to see design-focused case studies as being different from *lesson-drawing* case studies, whether or not these are conducted and presented within a professional discipline.

In shifting the category comparison to these other case studies, the term "design-oriented" takes on a different meaning. That is, it doesn't mark the distinction between purposeful and empirical phenomena, because both lesson-drawing and design-focused case studies are about the former. What's different is the whole idea of how to study purposeful phenomena within a professional discipline. Design-focused case studies bring mechanism-intent style purposive theorizing to bear in conducting research; they ask questions like: what is the phenomenon for, what does it consist in, and how does it work. Lesson-drawing case studies[2] ask questions like: what happened, why did it happen, and how could a better result have been attained by following an existing professional theory of action in a more faithful and/or discriminating manner.

In pursuing questions about purposeful phenomena, design-focused case studies have something in common with lesson-drawing case studies. Both involve dialogues between cases and professional knowledge. But they have different lineage-based frames. Lesson-drawing case studies originate in casuistry,[3] where the aim was to refine the practical judgment of individuals belonging to the same moral community, as discussed in Chapter 2. This intellectual practice was eventually picked up in professional disciplines, like law and business administration, and adapted accordingly. Design-focused case studies originate in professional disciplines akin to what Herbert Simon termed sciences of the artificial, including architecture and engineering. This intellectual practice has also been picked up in other professional disciplines, including management and public administration; it's more evident in some areas within these disciplines – including operations management[4] – than others.

This chapter is designed to help you make sense of the idea of design-focused case studies in public management. It's a challenge, similar to helping you to make sense of the whole idea of public management as a design-focused professional discipline. As the challenge is similar, so is the mechanism for tackling it. In what follows, you will encounter – and hopefully follow – a long conversation about this topic, one between two characters: You and Me. The conversation covers a lot of ground, beginning with the very idea of case studies. It builds on my earlier stated position about the same concept, then labeled as extrapolation-oriented case studies (in following Eugene Bardach's lead). But it revises that position, by stressing the interplay between case study research and purposive theorizing within a professional discipline (here, public management), and by making a link between design-focused case study research about public organizations and design-precedents in fields like architecture.[5]

This chapter is something of a purposive theory of case studies within the professional discipline of public management. What it grossly lacks is a "design precedent" for doing such case studies. However, this deficit is addressed in Chapter 7, which reports a design-focused case study about a variant of public organizations, an international cooperation project. However imperfect it may be, the case study in the following chapter brings concreteness to the discussion of design-focused case studies; as such, the two chapters can just as profitably be read in reverse order as in the order in which they are actually presented.

The dialogue begins

You: What is a case study?

Me: Many theorists of case study research make claims about defining properties of case studies, but not everyone says the same thing.[6]

You: Doesn't everyone agree that case studies are a form of qualitative research?

Me: No. Some theorists of case studies say that case studies can be quantitative.[7]

You: Maybe we should make the question about what people agree case studies aren't. And what they agree on is that they aren't a basis for generalization. Right?

Me: It's true that you're not going to find much encouragement from the literature on case studies to use them to generalize about populations of entities. But that doesn't mean that everyone agrees that case studies can't be used instrumentally.

You: Instrumentally, in relation to what end?

Me: Many defenders of case studies in the social sciences argue that they are *for* theorizing kinds of social phenomena.

You: Who has made these arguments?

Me: Probably the most well-known book author about case study research is Robert K. Yin.[8] He said that, while case studies aren't suited to making statistical generalizations, they are suited to making analytic generalizations.

You: What's an analytical generalization?

Me: An analytical generalization is a research-supported statement about a kind of phenomenon, as long as the statement is not a generalization about a population of entities.

You: Is the term "analytical generalization" in common use?

Me: Yes, for those who have read Yin's book. But the terms used to refer to research-supported statements about a kind of phenomenon tend to be specific to substantive traditions of inquiry.

You: Say more.

Me: The label used in processual sociology is "processes."[9] The label used in historical sociology is "modest generalizations about historically-defined phenomena."[10]

You: What are examples of social processes?

Me: Group formation and disintegration, policy-making in government, and decision-making in organizations.

You: What are examples of historically-defined phenomena?

Me: Political revolutions, civil rights movements, and foreign policy crises.

You: What would be examples of authors and instrumental case studies, whether about processes or historically-defined phenomena?

Me: Albert Hirschman[11] theorized social-economic reform, using the country case of Chile. Theda Skocpol[12] theorized political revolutions, using the country cases of France, Russia, and Iran. Graham Allison[13] theorized foreign policy crisis decision-making, using the case of the Cuban Missile Crisis, while Alexander George did the same on the basis of multiple case studies. Diane Vaughan[14] theorized organizational decision-making cultures, first using the case of NASA and then using the case of U.S. air traffic control centers within the Federal Aviation Administration. Michael Barzelay and Raquel Gallego[15] theorized public management policy-making, using the country cases of the U.K., Australia, Germany, France, Spain, Mexico, and Brazil.

You: Would they all have said they were making analytical generalizations?

Me: No, they'd use the language of their intellectual traditions. Accordingly, we should formulate and use a vocabulary that is appropriate to our discipline.

You: Alright. Shall I suggest some terms?

Me: I'd be grateful.

You: Design-oriented professional discipline of public management, public organizations, purposive theorizing, enterprise functions, mechanism-intent thinking, design-projects, sense-making, designing, argumentation, and dramatization. I realize it's a long list, and it doesn't provide an obvious label for "making analytic generalizations" from case studies.

Me: That's true. But there are some hooks here.

You: Other than public management and public organizations?

Me: Yes, purposive theorizing, mechanism-intent thinking, design-projects, and designing, for starters.

You: The only hook I see here is purposive theorizing, because of the word association between "theorizing" and "analytical generalizations."

Me: Let's work with that. If case study research in social science eventuates in analytical generalizations, then case study research in the professional discipline of public management eventuates in purposive theorizing. Purposive theorizing is a form of analytical generalizations, which is concerned with creating purposeful phenomena. Can you make some other connections?

You: I know that purposive theorizing is supposed to channel the professional activity of designing, which is supposed to effectuate the designing scenario-process within design-projects. And I know that purposive theorizing is more useful to designing when it involves mechanism-intent thinking.

Me: Purposive theorizing establishes a kind of lineage of thinking about what public organizations are for, what they consist in, and what makes them work. It establishes mechanism-intent thinking as a style of purposive theorizing. But purposive theorizing does not provide a sufficient "context" for channeling the professional activity of designing. Something big is missing.

You: What's that?

Me: In a word, design-precedents.

You: What are those?

Me: A design-precedent is an account of an actually or historically existing purposeful phenomenon that addresses what it's for, what it consists in, and how it works in effectuating what it's for. Such accounts result from research within professional disciplines, whether arts of design or (to the extent they are different) sciences of the artificial. Such accounts are communicated with the intent of being available for adoption as reference points in design-projects.

You: That sounds like an interesting idea. Did you make up this term, or did somebody else do that?

Me: I came across the term in a book by the architect, Bryan Lawson, entitled *What Designers Know*.[16] I have my notes on the relevant passages here on my tablet. Would you like me to read them out to you?

You: I'm all ears.

Me: Lawson wrote that, "Designers commonly and frequently make great use of what they often refer to as precedent. Precedents are often either whole or partial pieces of designs that the designer is aware of. . . . Precedent is seen by designers as an important part of their knowledge upon which they are able to draw in a 'designerly way'. . . . The early modern movement [in design] was a period in which precedent played an unusually minor role in what was thought to be a logical functionalist process. . . . The post-modern world of design has rejected such a view. . . . Precedent is such a vital, central, crucial feature of the design process that it plays a central role in all design education" (p. 96).

You: Is Lawson's view considered idiosyncratic in his field, whatever that is?

Me: Lawson is a professor of architecture and this book, like his others, fits within the literature on design studies. Ask any architect whether the precedent is important to their professional practice and the response will be unequivocally "yes."

You: I wonder why this idea of design-precedent didn't show up in this book before now.

Me: If it was going to come up, it would have done so in connection with Simon's idea of design-projects. But it didn't.

You: Why not?

Me: The whole issue of learning from experience wasn't central to Simon's scholarship; that was a major theme in the work of his one-time collaborator, James G. March.[17] Simon is known for thinking that "domain knowledge" would channel analysis in designing – and that analysis would somehow channel synthesis.[18] Simon didn't think of "domain knowledge" as consisting in design-precedents. I can't say what all the reasons for this were.

You: Okay, so what's the relationship between purposive theorizing and design-precedents?

Me: Would you want to take a crack at answering that question yourself?

You: Purposive theorizing and design-precedents are similar in what they are *for*. What they are mainly *for* is channeling the professional activity of designing.

Me: And how are purposive theorizing and design-precedents different from each other?

You: I could use some help on this question.

Me: Fair enough. The principal role of purposive theorizing is to provide an approach to problem- and solution-structuring, while the principal role of design-precedents is to use experience as a basis for solution-structuring. Accordingly, they play complementary roles in designing.

You: Alright, then, purposive theorizing and design-precedents have distinct, complementary roles in designing. Would you say that they have different sources, as well?

Me: I'd prefer to respond to a more precise question, which compares the two.

You: Fine, if that's the way you want to be! Could I ask whether you would agree that purposive theorizing comes from critical engagement with past theorizing, while, by contrast, design-precedents come from case studies?

Me: It's a well-put question.

You: I know. And the answer is?

Me: I'd agree with both claims in your statement, but I would caution against the possible implication that case studies have no role to play in purposive theorizing. And I would also point out that, within professional disciplines like public management, purposive theorizing has a role to play in case study research, especially in framing the topic.

You: As to the unstated implication: I wouldn't have thought of denying that case studies have a role in debating approaches to public management.

Me: We are definitely on the same page. Incidentally, how do you think we should tell others about what we have been discussing here? How should we label case studies that are meant to become design-precedents, at least in part?

You: I presume you've thought about this before. What labels have you tried out?

Me: There was a time when I used the term "extrapolation-oriented case research." It's in the title of my 2007 article on the topic we're discussing now.[19]

You: Why would you have used *that* term?

Me: I was building on Eugene Bardach's 2003 presidential address at the Association of Public Policy and Management (APPAM), entitled "The Extrapolation Problem."[20]

You: And you don't use that term any longer?

Me: Correct. Not enough people have read Bardach's APPAM presidential address or my article building on it, for the term to bring instant meaning. Besides, I had become disenchanted with Bardach's presidential address for its sketchy treatment of designing, and I wanted to use the design studies literature – which I had come across after writing my 2007 piece – much more fully and explicitly.

You: So, what came next?

Me: At a workshop that I organized in 2015, I used the term "design-precedent case studies."

You: And how did that go?

Me: All of my workshop guests were very polite. Nobody complained. Afterwards, however, one of the attendees – who worked at the General Accountability Office (GAO) – told me that "design-precedent case studies" just wouldn't work, for the simple reason that, as nobody in my audience would know what a design-precedent is, they wouldn't begin to imagine what a design-precedent case study would be.

You: That participant seems to have been rather direct; perhaps it's because he worked at the GAO.

Me: The other explanation is that he's my cousin.

You: So where did you go from there?

Me: I gave a paper presentation in 2016 during a panel at the International Public Policy Association (IPPA) conference at the National University of Singapore's LKY School of Public Policy. I used the term "design-focused case study." Judging from the discussants' comments and other feedback, the audience seemed to like it.

You: I'm not surprised. The term isn't perplexing like design-precedent case studies. People will want to learn more about design-focused case studies. So, changing "precedent" to "focused" seemed to do the trick!

Me: I'm sticking with "design-focused case studies."

You: Can you point to examples of them?

Me: Do you remember visiting the mezzanine level of the Public Management Gallery?

You: Of course. I remember the displays on Simon's *Sciences of the Artificial*,[21] van Aken and Berends' *Problem-Solving in Organizations*,[22] and Barzelay and Campbell's *Preparing for the Future: Strategic Planning in the U.S. Air Force*.[23]

Me: *Preparing for the Future* contains design-focused case studies, although the term does not appear there; it was published back in 2003.

You: Any other examples?

Me: From my own research, yes. My study of the management system within the Brazil in Action program.

You: How about anybody else's work?

Me: When I introduce design-focused case studies in teaching, I typically use work by the late Judith Tendler of MIT. The case was about a massive state-wide rural primary health program, known as the Health Agents Program, that was created and operated in the Brazilian northeastern state of Ceará, back in the 1980s. The publications were an article in *World Development*, co-authored by Sara Freedheim,[24] and a chapter in Tendler's *Good Government in the Tropics*.[25] The case study showed that the Health Agents Program was successful, even though (and in some ways, *because*) it consisted in organizational arrangements that deviated from the incumbent theories of organization design in government, based on rent-seeking theories. Drawing on what the authors called the industrial performance literature, the case study also examined how the Health Workers Program neutralized dilemmas that were characteristic of mass social programs in settings where populations were hard to reach, public financial resources were limited, and mayors operated clientelistic networks.

You: That sounds like an interesting study. What was the take-away lesson?

Me: Why do you think it offered one?

You: It would seem to be a natural expectation of a case study about management.

Me: That is true.

You: Are you saying that design-focused case studies do not offer take-away lessons?

Me: I am saying that insofar as design-focused case studies offer design-precedents, they do not offer take-away lessons. Insofar as design-focused case studies do offer take-away lessons, then they are engaging in purposive theorizing.

You: How would you go about dissociating the idea of a design-precedent from the idea of a lesson?

Me: To dissociate design-precedents from lessons, we need to uncover why the idea that case studies are for lesson-drawing is so natural.

You: It's so natural to me, I don't think I can help much in that.

Me: A standard way to de-naturalize an association is to provide some history. In this situation, history would be about the discipline of management. Do you remember the discussion of the Harvard approach and the Fayolian background, in Chapter 2?

You: Vaguely. I remember that funny word, casuistry.

Me: Recall that casuistry is a method of practical argumentation within a moral community, one that involves wrestling with decision dilemmas.[26] The method uses a form of the case method to train people in developing their faculty of judgment and their ability to provide reasons for their decisions, when they face decision dilemmas.

You: How is that relevant here?

Me: It's only relevant as background. The more directly relevant history is the idea of decision-making, which is taken to be the principal mechanism for performing an enterprise's management function.

You: That sounds natural, but I guess it's something we have to critically examine.

Me: Yes, what does decision-making in organizations consist in?

You: Well, I'd guess some mixture of thinking and communicating, within a context where roles are differentiated organizationally.

Me: Good. Now how do thinking and communicating fit together into a single human practice?

You: Is that where casuistry comes back in?

Me: Yes, in that casuistry is a method of practical argumentation that consists in both thinking and communicating.

You: Has anyone made the case that practical argumentation is a key activity within decision-making in organizations?

Me: Yes, Charles Perrow[27] interpreted March and Simon's original work on organization theory, back in the late 1950s,[28] precisely along these lines, in a chapter entitled "Neo-Weberian synthesis" in his *Complex Organizations: A Critical Essay*.

You: Alright, but what's the connection between decision-making and practical argumentation, on the one hand, and "lessons" and cases, on the other?

Me: Cases are typically presented as the basis for lessons. Decision-making and purposive theorizing are also straightforwardly connected. Purposive theorizing channels decision-making activity in organizations. Purposive theorizing is a main source of explicit premises in practical argumentation. Connecting the dots: cases are a basis for lessons that endorse or critique the purposive theorizing, which, in turn, channels decision-making in organizations.

You: So, this is why people would think that case studies would always offer a take-away lesson?

Me: It's an important part of the story, yes.

You: So, are you against presenting take-away lessons from design-focused case studies?

Me: I've learned not to be.

You: Learned?

Me: Yes, from referee comments on design-focused case studies that I've submitted for publication. So now I try to meet that expectation, and then try to exceed it by also providing design-precedents.

You: Why aren't referees satisfied with case studies that present design-precedents?

Me: Because they believe, or pre-suppose, that decision-making effectuates the management function of enterprises. They subscribe to March and Simon's organization theory; they have not taken fully on board Simon's theory of design-projects and his associated argument about sciences of the artificial, that, by contrast, design-projects, with their irreducible element of designing, effectuates the management of enterprises. If they did, and if they were aware of the centrality of the idea of design-precedent within the literature on design studies, matters could be different.

You: That sounds like a deep problem. How can it be tackled?

Me: For me, it has been by writing *Public Management as a Design-Oriented Professional Discipline*.

You: Has anyone else tried to tackle this problem, in public management?

Me: Yes, Eugene Bardach, an outstanding professor of public policy at Berkeley. His first explicit attempt to do so was back in 1993, in a commentary piece within a symposium section of an issue of the *Journal of Policy Analysis and Management*.[29] It was entitled, "Comment: the problem of best-practice research."

You: Did Bardach come out as for, or against, best practice research?

Me: Bardach agreed with the idea of what best practice research would be for, but he had strong reservations about what best practice research consisted in. He didn't think it worked, the way it was usually done. He made his argument by reconstructing a case study publication that he admired, indicating how it could exemplify the sort of best practice research he thought ought to be done.

You: Oh, what case study publication was that?

Me: It was a book entitled, *Breaking Through Bureaucracy: A New Vision for Managing in Government*, published in 1992 by University of California Press.[30]

You: I think I've heard of the title before. Who wrote it?

Me: Me.

You: I should have known.

Me: Obviously.

You: What did you think of Bardach's "Comment"?

Me: I liked it very much, and I still do.

You: What did you like most?

Me: I liked the fact that he set the question of how to analyze practices within a public organization in such a way as to reveal how they work as functioning wholes and how they relate to generic challenges that are not specific to time and place. Eventually I came to see that Bardach was onto something important – so much so that it would change how I do my teaching and research.

You: When was that?

Me: An important milestone was the publication of Bardach's presidential address to the Association of Public Policy Analysis and Management in 2003, entitled, "The extrapolation problem." It was published in 2004.[31] It is an inspiring piece. I've used it in my teaching routinely since then. It's the reading my former students say they remember most. Some of these students say they re-read it every six months not to forget it.

You: That's impressive. What was the beautiful idea?

Me: Start with the overall issue, which is a practical question. If you're a professional practitioner in Jefferson County and you're asked to look into how a given program works in Washington County as a step toward solving a problem in your county, what approach would you take?

You: What's the answer to this practical question?

Me: The answer was presented in two parts: what shouldn't be your approach, and what should be. You shouldn't just describe the observable features of a program in a "source site," like Washington County, because that description – even if detailed – will give you no more than a superficial understanding of how the program works there. You should seek insight into what causes the program's attractive characteristics in the source site. As you seek such insight, remember that you can only infer causes. You need theory to infer causes. You can get insight into how a program works in a source site by formulating an explanatory argument in which behavioral and/or social mechanisms play causal roles.

You: So, what are you supposed to do with this insight when it comes time to replicate the source site program in Jefferson County?

Me: Replicate social mechanisms; adapt features.

You: That's concise!

Me: Yes, that is how a student of mine expressed the take-away message. What do you understand it to mean, based on what we have been discussing here?

You: I gather that Bardach's message is partly a negative one: don't replicate features. I take that to mean that there's no reason for Jefferson County to copy Washington County's program, even if Jefferson County wants to replicate it.

Me: You'd have some reason to replicate a feature if you have reason to think that it plays a causal role in Washington County's program.

You: But I thought that features don't play causal roles, only mechanisms do.

Me: Wrong! That's a misunderstanding of mechanism-based explanation. In general, actually existing conditions do play causal roles in social entities and processes, but you need theory to gain insight into how.

You: Oh, I guess I was getting confused by this mixing of vocabulary from social scientific explanation and from the arts of design. I feel a little embarrassed.

Me: Don't be. Let's get back to the idea of replicating mechanisms, while adapting features. What does it mean to adapt a feature?

You: It seems like it means that you should introduce program features in Jefferson County that are similar but not identical to those in Washington County.

Me: Similar in what way?

You: I guess that they should be similar in their effects, even if they are dissimilar in what they consist in.

Me: Good! But "similarity in effect" is not like similarity in object characteristics, like color.

You: What would you call two features that have different object characteristics, but are exactly the same in their effects within a purposeful phenomenon?

Me: I'd call them functional equivalents. And it's not just me who would use that term! The underlying idea is that of equifinality. You can get the same effects with different features. It's an important principle to consider when you're designing.

You: So what does Bardach mean by "adapt features"?

Me: You tell me.

You: If you have reason not to replicate a feature observed in Washington County's program – say for reasons of cost or acceptability – then specify a different feature in Jefferson County, provided that this different feature will be functionally similar.

Me: And what would make a different feature similar in a functional way?

You: It would have to play a similar causal role.

Me: Can you be more specific?

You: It would combine with a behavioral and/or social mechanism to produce a similar or identical effect.

Me: That's the general idea, yes. So restate the argument, please.

You: It's often infeasible, or unacceptable, for a source site's program features to be copied in a target site. Therefore, don't try to replicate program features. Take a different approach. Consider the principle of equifinality: you can attain functional equivalence without object equivalence. You can't apply this principle, however, without understanding how the program works within the source site. Fortunately, you can gain insight into *how* a program has worked, by studying how features "combine" with behavioral and/or social mechanisms. When designing a program for a target site, work with the idea of creating a different combination of features and social mechanisms than in the source site, but with the social mechanisms being the same in the target site as in the source site. In a phrase: replicate social mechanisms; adapt features.

Me: Well done! Is there anything you think about Bardach's position that ought to be clarified?

You: I have some doubts about the idea that programs consist in features and social mechanisms and also about the idea that attractive program characteristics are due to how features and social mechanisms are combined.

Me: Fine, but first tell me what you find unproblematic, so we can pinpoint the issue.

You: Sure. I'm ok with the idea that programs consist in a multiplicity of features. I'm ok with the idea that some features are functionally and causally linked to others. Therefore, I'm ok with the idea that programs consist in combinations of features, because that statement sums up the two previous ones. But I don't know if I understand the idea of combinations of mechanisms.

Me: I can illustrate the idea with the case of a simple machine and its physical mechanisms.

You: What machine is that?

Me: A water filter jug. One physical mechanism is surface tension in liquids, specifically water. That mechanism plays a causal role in the movement of water from a tap into the jug's filter, keeping the surrounding area dry. Another physical mechanism is gravity. That mechanism plays a causal role in the downward movement of the water through the filter and into the basin, yielding filtered water ready for pouring into a container for drinking. The water jug works because of the combination of the physical mechanisms of surface tension and gravity.

You: Neat example. How do you explain that the idea of combinations of mechanisms applies outside the world of machines.

Me: If you want to read a thoughtful discussion about combinations of mechanisms in social explanation, I would point you to Diego Gambetta's chapter in an edited book with the title *Social Mechanisms: An Analytical Approach to Social Theory.*[32]

You: I think it's time to discuss the relation between features and behavioral and/or social mechanisms, particularly now that we realize that saying they "combine" is not very helpful. Did Bardach make clear what he saw as the condition-theory relation?

Me: Well, the piece was a bit brief on this issue, as it was essentially the text of his APPAM presidential address. But you could read an article entitled, "Learning from second-hand experience: methodology for extrapolation-oriented case research," published in *Governance* in 2007.[33]

You: Would you recommend that?

Me: I think it's a good piece, but I am biased.

You: How so?

Me: I wrote it.

You: And you're still happy with it, so many years later?

Me: I still find a lot to agree with. And I'm pleased that it's been cited a fair amount and that it has helped to spark interest in the discussion you and I are having now.

You: What do you agree with, and what are your reservations now?

Me: The main thing I did was to try to push Bardach's ideas about what programs consist in a bit further, by blending them with some basic theoretical ideas of processual sociology. Bardach's ideas included program features and behavioral and/or social mechanisms. Processual sociology's vocabulary includes context, activity, and social mechanisms.

You: Tell me a little more about how context, activity, and social mechanisms fit together in processual sociology.

Me: Activity is what individuals, collective actors, and machines do. Activity is temporally and spatially located. Activity consists in lines of action.

You: What does activity affect?

Me: Activity affects conditions in social entities and processes.

You: Are there patterns in activity and its effects on social entities and processes?

Me: We have a vocabulary to speak of such patterns, with scenario-processes being one term. Scenario-processes are constituted by activity. Scenario-processes eventuate in scenario-outcomes. Scenario-outcomes are reflections of the effect of scenario-activity on social entities and processes.

You: Is this vocabulary specific to "processual sociology"?

Me: No. Processual sociology takes process philosophy and adds the vocabulary of spatio-temporal location, actors, context, and events.[34] It also adds mechanisms,[35] but that's not unique to processual sociology either. It's been emphasized even more so in analytical social theory.[36] For present purposes, however, we can identify social mechanisms with processual sociology.

You: Can we return to the blend of language from design and processual sociology? How do you put them together?

Me: In the *Governance* article in 2007, I stated that activity within a program is influenced by process design features and process context factors. Both can be initial conditions and both can be conditions that are present during a stream of activity. The idea was that programs are constituted by process design features on purpose, while process context factors are present for other reasons.

You: Is it true that process context factors can be constitutive of a program, even when they are not there on purpose?

Me: Great question. I'm going to say "yes" to make the point that many of the conditions that are constitutive of a program or other purposeful phenomenon are (metaphorically) assembled rather than custom-made. Shifting metaphors, a given purposeful phenomenon is inevitably located within some socio-ecological context, and some of the conditions in that context will be part of the phenomenon. Take the machine example of the filtered water jug. A process context factor would be having potable water on tap, whereas a process design feature would be the handle on the jug.

You: So, the take-away here is that in processual sociology, scenario-outcomes eventuate from a combination of context and activity, while in public management, scenario-outcomes eventuate from a combination of process design features and process context factors, on the one hand, and activity, on the other.

Me: Good. Stated differently, the main idea is that processual sociology provides an intellectual tradition for theorizing a social phenomenon's context-activity-outcome dynamics, for the sake of advancing the discipline of sociology. The same intellectual tradition can be used to theorize purposeful phenomena that relate to public organizations, including programs. A step toward using that tradition to theorize purposeful phenomena is to adjust the vocabulary, with the idea of "context" in processual sociology being considered analogous to the idea of process context factors and process design features in public management.

You: Could you clear up something for me? Earlier in the book, you wrote about mechanisms as playing intent-fulfilling roles in an enterprise. As you've presented Bardach and processual sociology, mechanisms seem to be theories that are applied in understanding how a purposeful phenomenon works. I find it confusing to hear the term mechanisms being used in these two ways. Please help.

Me: You should mainly think of mechanisms as playing intent-fulfilling roles in an enterprise. As you do so, you will be engaging in purposive theorizing, in a mechanism-intent style. Within this style, there's merit in theorizing mechanisms as scenario-processes, with characteristic dynamics in relations among context, activity, and outcome. Now, in order to do mechanism-intent thinking well, you need to be able to think creatively and critically about context-activity-outcome dynamics. Social science theorizing about social mechanisms is helpful for that, even though such theorizing is usually geared to answering disciplinary questions in sociology.

You: That seems clear enough. Sociological theories of social processes involving social mechanisms are to be used to supplement mechanism-intent style, purposive theorizing about purposeful phenomena.

Me: That's the point. Social mechanisms analysis contributes to purposive theorizing along mechanism-intent lines and to case study research to create design-precedents.

You: It seems we still have a long way to go in this conversation.

Me: Yes, indeed! There are vistas that we haven't explored and loose-ends we haven't tied up. What do you think would be most helpful to you at this point?

You: It would be really helpful to have an example that truly illustrates what you would now consider to be a "report" on a true design-focused case study.

Me: I co-authored one over the past few years, specifically so that it would play such a role in this book.

You: Where can I find it?

Me: In the next chapter.

NOTES

1 Ravetz (1971).
2 González Asis and Woolcock (2015).
3 Jonsen and Toulmin (1988).
4 Hopp and Spearman (1996).
5 Lawson (2004).
6 Stake (1995), Ragin and Becker (1992).
7 For example, Ragin (1987).
8 Yin (2014).
9 Abbott (2001, 2004); Becker (1997).
10 Ragin (1987).
11 Hirschman (1973).
12 Skocpol (1979).
13 Allison (1971).

14 Vaughan (2005).
15 Barzelay and Gallego (2010).
16 Lawson (2004).
17 See March (2010), Levitt and March (1988), March, Sproull, and Tamuz (1991).
18 Dym (1994).
19 Barzelay (2007).
20 Bardach (2004).
21 Simon (1996).
22 Van Aken and Berends (2018).
23 Barzelay and Campbell (2003).
24 Tendler and Freedheim (1994).
25 Tendler (1997).
26 Jonsen and Toulmin (1988).
27 Perrow (1986).
28 March and Simon (1958).
29 Bardach (1994).
30 Barzelay (1992).
31 Bardach (2004).
32 Hedström and Swedberg (1998).
33 Barzelay (2007).
34 Abbott (2001, 2016).
35 McAdam, Tarrow, and Tilly (2001).
36 Hedström (2005).

7

Managing international cooperation projects for organizational capacity-building: a design-focused case study of the Egypt–Japan University of Science and Technology*

A mainstream view about development is that becoming a successful society depends on strengthening a society's organizations. This claim is not as banal as it may appear out of context. Fifteen years ago, this idea was put forward in challenging mainstream development thinking, which had held that economic progress depended on solving technical challenges – for example, in expanding irrigation and treating disease – on monumental scales and diverse circumstances. This earlier paradigmatic belief was put into question on the basis that succeeding in solving technical challenges on the scale required depended on factors that were organizational and administrative in kind: factors such as marshalling stable political support within the governmental system, the structuring of careers, and the efficient management of resources. This line of argument was summed up in terms of organizational capability being a fundamental enabling factor in development. The view that organizational capability is important to successful societies and their development has become self-evident, but is no less significant for that.[1]

The debate just summarized was instigated, transpired, and resolved in the institutional realm of development cooperation.[2] Given this context, the debate's resolution implied that building organizational capacity ought to become part of the intent of international cooperation projects whose mechanism-features include technical assistance. This implication was rationally straightforward; its further practical implications have been less so.

Over the past decade, experience has been gained with international

* Written with Masakatsu Okumoto and Hideki Watanabe.

cooperation projects that make organizational capacity development central to their intent. By way of illustration, Japan's institutions and instruments for international cooperation have been used in projects to strengthen the higher education sectors of partner countries, especially in the realm of technology and engineering; and those efforts have included the intent of building organizational capacity in universities.[3] A specific illustration of Japan's organization-strengthening higher education projects led to the founding and successful startup of a stand-alone university specializing in engineering research and postgraduate education in Egypt. These experiences are among those that offer the prospect of bringing to light the implications of a policy stance in favor of including organizational capacity development in the function and specific intent of international cooperation projects.

Turning this prospect of deeper understanding into reality involves research. A suitable form of research about international cooperation projects is the case study. This chapter reports on a research case study in which the empirical phenomenon includes Japan's support for establishing the Egypt–Japan University of Science and Technology (E-JUST). The support from Japan was orchestrated by the Japan International Cooperation Agency (JICA). Its partners in Japan included Tokyo Institute of Technology, Waseda University, Kyoto University, Kyushu University and Ritsumeikan University. The partner in Egypt was E-JUST and its sponsors in the Ministry of Higher Education and the Ministry of Planning and International Cooperation. As an empirical phenomenon, the establishment of E-JUST was a lengthy episode in which the process was first formalized in 2006. The implementation phase of Japan's project to support E-JUST's establishment began in 2009. The university has been up and running – though in provisional facilities – since 2010. The E-JUST–JICA–Japanese universities partnership remains intact and operating nearly a decade after its inception.

In broad terms, the aim of the case study is to clarify the implications of including organizational capacity-building within the intent of international cooperation projects. However, as "clarify the implications" is not itself a clear idea, somewhat more needs to be said by way of preliminaries to this chapter's report on the E-JUST case study.

The intent of the chapter is to advance professional knowledge about organization-strengthening international cooperation projects. As a general matter, professional knowledge is rational, empirically-grounded argumentation about purposeful phenomena.[4] In intent, professional knowledge has intelligence-value at the point where professional practitioners encounter situations that require problem-solving in the service of better realization of intent.[5]

Advancing professional knowledge about purposeful phenomena has much in common with research conducted in social scientific disciplines.[6] For example, theorizing is involved in advancing either disciplinary or professional knowledge. Some of the same aspirational standards apply: such as closely integrating ideas recruited from differing sources and keeping track of how lines of argument run from theory to case analysis and back again to theory. Another similarity between advancing disciplinary and professional knowledge is that explanatory research arguments about cases need to engage with ideas about causation that have clear meanings within identifiable traditions of social science research.[7]

Nevertheless, there are some dissimilarities, as well, because, unlike disciplinary knowledge, professional knowledge is meant to have intelligence-value in the professional practice of problem-solving. Accordingly, theorizing about purposeful phenomena includes arguments about mainstream or alternative doctrines about intent, function, and design. Another difference is that case analyses can have intelligence-value, without them being used to make empirical generalizations, *as cases*, provided they are well-theorized and well-argued.

This chapter reports on the case study of the Egypt–Japan University of Science and Technology. It introduces the empirical phenomenon of E-JUST's coming to be established with Japanese support and partnership. It develops a direction for purposive theorizing about such projects. It provides a detailed analysis of a feature of this project – known as the Strategic TV Conference. This case-within-the-case is offered up as a design-precedent[8] that might be considered when partners in an international cooperation project become concerned about how deficits in organizational capability will be a limiting factor on their project's success, where the intent includes but is not limited to organization-strengthening.

Establishing E-JUST: the empirical phenomenon (2006–2009)

From the beginning of 2005, Japanese and Egyptian government officials engaged in increasingly serious bi-lateral diplomatic discussions over Japan's prospective support for planning and establishing a research-intensive technological university in Egypt. In March 2006, the Government of Egypt and the Government of Japan announced that plans were afoot to establish such a university, namely, the Egypt–Japan University of Science and Technology (E-JUST). In substance, the idea of E-JUST included adapting what was seen from Egypt as Japan's successful model of post-graduate technological education and engineering research. The Japanese model included "lab-based education." The idea that E-JUST would include the Japanese learning system for engineering meant that the project would have to involve Japan's universities.

The mechanism that the Japanese government would use in supporting E-JUST's establishment was a technical cooperation project. Accordingly, the Japan International Cooperation Agency (JICA), the government's executive arm for Japanese Official Development Assistance, took the lead on behalf of the Japanese Government in 2006. Not much later, Egypt's minister of higher education set up a formal Advisory Committee on the Establishment of the Egypt–Japan University of Science and Technology.

When this advisory committee was formed in 2006, Professor Ahmed Abou-Ismail of Assiut University, in Upper Egypt, became its secretary-general. Unusually for Egyptian engineering academics, Abou-Ismail had earned his doctorate in Japan, at Tokyo Tech. Another committee member was Professor Ahmed B. Khairy. At the time, Professor Khairy was on leave from the faculty of engineering of Alexandria University, serving in Cairo as a First Undersecretary of the Ministry of Higher Education, overseeing cultural affairs and scholarships for the country's entire higher education system. In parallel, Khairy was involved in reforming Egypt's Academy of Science and Technology.

In addition to Abou-Ismail and Khairy, the Advisory Committee's membership included other engineering professors in Egypt. Two of them were early-career engineering academics who had earned their PhDs outside Egypt: Dr. Amr El Tawil and Dr. Ahmed El Mahdy. Both had returned to Egypt to join the engineering faculty at Alexandria University. Furthermore, the Advisory Committee included a few industrialists, including Engineer Amir Wassef, owner of Unitel, as E-JUST was envisioned to collaborate with Egyptian firms in engineering design projects.

The true kick-off event for joint project preparation was a three-day conference held in Tokyo in mid-April 2007. The conference included site visits to Tokyo Tech and Waseda University. The meeting's immediate product was a "results of discussions" report. It led off with a list of envisioned core attributes of E-JUST: being a governmental university based on the spirit of partnership between Egypt and Japan; being a research-oriented and graduate-focused university; and having the Japanese way of problem-based education and laboratory-based research. The report was specific about the target areas for developing research and graduate education: by way of illustration, these included micro mechatronics, robotics and medical robots in one area; and electronic and digital communication engineering and network security, in another area. The report took a firm view that the best location for E-JUST and its campus would be near Alexandria, in New Borg Al-Arab City, in an area that included a cluster of technology-oriented companies and that was anchored by the region's new airport.

It took time for the next major steps to ensue. In February 2008, the Director General of the Ministry of Foreign Affairs convened a meeting with the presidents of 12 leading Japanese universities, formally requesting that they participate in the E-JUST endeavor as part of the Japanese University Supporting Consortium (JSUC) for E-JUST. In April representatives from these universities, the MOFA and JICA visited Egypt to conduct a first project preparatory mission. In July 2008, Egypt's Ministry of Higher Education announced the formation of an Executive Committee for the project to establish E-JUST. The role of advisory committee secretary-general was supplanted by the role of committee chairman. Professor Khairy was appointed to this role.

By August 2008, the planning work for E-JUST by the Joint Preliminary Study Team was well advanced. The draft Record of Discussions outlined the responsibilities of the Egyptian government, which included the provision of Egyptian administrative personnel. It also defined the measures to be taken by JICA, such as dispatching Japanese experts to Egypt, providing the machinery and equipment for the new university, and training the Egyptian personnel in Japan.[9] The draft Record of Discussions also included a master plan and a Project Design Matrix (PDM), a comprehensive document that specified the main goals, indicators and means of verification. In September 2008, the Egyptian Cabinet formally approved the establishment of E-JUST. In October 2008, a ceremony was held in Tokyo to celebrate the signature of the final Record of Discussions.

At the point where the technical assistance project was approved, the blueprint for E-JUST's formal organization was elaborately detailed for academic staff and their grouping into departments and larger units engaged in education and research. In comparison to the institutional blueprint for E-JUST's "operating core" and "middle line,"[10] the one for its "superstructure" was sketchy, with only two definite features. First, the strategic apex would consist in the role of university president. Second, there would be a management board known as the university council, headed by the university president. There was no plan to form a major unit of the superstructure headed by an administrative professional called the university's "secretary-general," a standard organizational feature of Egypt's public universities. The secretary-general role's absence from the institutional blueprint reflected the advisory committee's wider view that E-JUST should *not* replicate patterns of governance found in the country's public universities.

During early 2009, E-JUST's superstructure consisted in an acting university council, headed by Professor Khairy as its chairman. The acting-status was to persist until the envisioned Board of Trustees for E-JUST was put into place and began to function. The acting university council was organized into committees, along the same lines as the sub-committees of the executive committee. There was also considerable continuity in personnel.

During the first half of 2009, JICA's support for E-JUST's establishment transitioned from the task of project preparation to that of project implementation. The E-JUST start-up team included JICA's own newly formed project team. As presented, the team leader's role was to be the chief adviser to the chairman of the acting university council. The individual chosen for the role was Dr. Tsunoda, who was to be dispatched to Egypt as a long-term expert.

In June 2009, a project monitoring mission was dispatched by JICA Headquarters to Alexandria, at the six-month milestone point. The mission was carried out by a two-person team: the head of the higher education team in JICA's Human Resource Development Department, Mr. Ko Goto, and Professor Chitoshi Miki. The mission took place in the face of strong signals that it was impractical to start-up E-JUST's educational activities beginning in September 2009. In the course of the review, acting university council members pointed to urgency in resolving a range of issues, in order for the university to begin operations and get on its feet as an institution. The main issues included: staffing of core subject teaching, policy and procedures for selecting academic staff selection on a merit basis; financial plans, both short- and medium-term; recruitment and selection of staff for non-academic roles; and selection of Board of Trustees members and plans for its organizing meeting.

During the review, Dr. Tsunoda took the view that more needed to be done by the Japanese partners to support E-JUST's acting university council. More specifically, he proposed the establishment of a meeting system for coordination, involving JICA, the Japanese universities active in both JSUC and the technical assistance project, and the members of E-JUST's acting University council. This suggestion was favorably received by Professor Miki and Mr. Goto. It was recognized that if Japanese universities were to be involved in the meeting system, their consortium for E-JUST would need to establish a specific working group for this purpose. Following the review, Professor Miki took this forward with his JSUC colleagues. Shortly thereafter, a plan for holding coordination meetings by teleconference on a regular, monthly basis was proposed to Professor Khairy, as chairman of E-JUST's acting university council; he accepted the proposal.

The first meeting was held in October 2009, under the chairmanship of Shuji Hashimoto, by then Provost of Waseda University. As for E-JUST, the participant-members included the acting University Council. Participants from JICA's Human Resource Development Department included the E-JUST project team members stationed in Alexandria and Higher Education team members based in Tokyo. JSUC was represented by its five-member Strategic Working Group, including Professor Hashimoto and Professor Miki. The Coordination Meeting – later called the Strategic TV Conference – thus had full coverage of the E-JUST superstructure, the JSUC Strategic Working Group, and the JICA E-JUST team.

The monthly meeting cycle came to exhibit a stable pattern (see Figure 7.1). Before the TV Conference, SWG members, JICA and E-JUST had a pre-meeting and confirmed the agenda. When they held the conference, starting from the confirmation of the minutes of the previous meeting, the discussion proceeded through topics and issues according to the agenda. The conference acted to assign tasks for follow-up in a future meeting. After the meeting, the points of the discussion were documented and confirmed among participants.

The first meeting discussed the formation of nine working groups, established

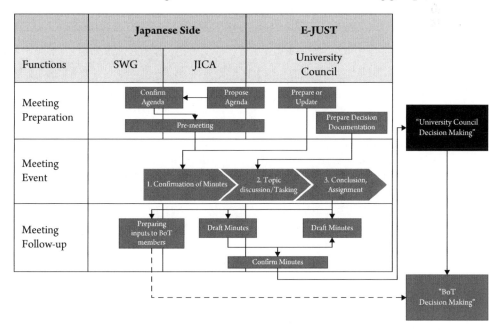

Figure 7.1 Swim lane diagram of the Japan–E-JUST Strategic TV Conference

on an interim basis, for the Soft-Opening phase. In addition, some issues for university management, such as setting up acting University Council, organizational chart and financial plan of 2009 were also discussed. The TV conference meeting was then held four times with open-ended discussions, before the first Board of Trustees meeting in February 2010.

Theorizing problems of management in international development cooperation projects

The case of E-JUST provides illustrative evidence for this chapter's central premise: namely, that management is a functional necessity of international development cooperation projects.[11] Elaborating this management-in-international-cooperation-projects premise involves movement along two pathways. Along the first pathway, the task is to characterize *international development projects* in a way that allows for a discussion of management-related necessities. Along the second pathway, the task is to identify appropriate lines of theorizing about *management*. As we will see, the two pathways intersect.

What a development cooperation project *is* depends on the style of theorizing. Here the style is purposive and design-oriented. Viewed from stratospheric heights, international development cooperation projects generically consist in a "triad"[12] of mechanisms. One element of the triad is self-evident: the project through which support for a partner organization is delivered. As technical assistance is a major feature of such projects, we call this part of the triad a "technical assistance project." In the E-JUST case, this feature was JICA's technical assistance project to support the establishment of E-JUST. Another element of the triad is almost as self-evident: it's the partner organization, in this case, E-JUST. A third element of the triad is the nexus to which a project's various key stakeholders belong. In indicative terms, the partners belonging to the Japan/Egypt/E-JUST partnership-nexus were JICA's Human Resource Development Department, leaders of the universities most active in the technical assistance project in support of E-JUST's establishment, Egypt's minister of international cooperation and its minister of higher education and scientific research, and Executive Committee for the establishment of E-JUST and its successor, the superstructure within E-JUST's organizational configuration. In sum, an international development cooperation project is a development-project-triad, a unified functioning whole made up of a technical assistance project, a partner organization, and a partnership-nexus.

Having sketched and formalized the idea of development-project-triads, let us now move along the pathway on management, before reaching the junction where the idea of *management* will intersect with the *development-project-triad* idea. Along this second pathway, there are many riches to sample, even within the genre of purposive, design-oriented theorizing. Henri Fayol's way of theorizing what he called "enterprises," in the classic volume, *General and Industrial Management*,[13] belongs to this genre. Fayol's theorizing adopted usual placeholders for the intent of commercial enterprises. Fayol focused on necessities that are inherent in any enterprise and, in that sense, are uniform across all enterprises.

He implicitly likened the idea of an enterprise's necessities to the idea that any type of organism has functions that need to be performed for it to survive and thrive.[14] Accordingly, he phrased the idea of an enterprise's necessities as its functions. We can refer to them as functional necessities. Under this direction of theorizing, an enterprise will fall short of whatever intent on which it fixes in the event that any of its functional necessities is not satisfied. The items on Fayol's original list of functional necessities were technical, commercial, accounting, financial, security, and management.[15]

Fayol held that management is a functional necessity of enterprises. (The less compact version of the idea is that organizations are mechanisms for realization of the intent of enterprises, and management is a functional necessity of organizations.) Fayol's management-function was a gestalt-concept in that the meaning of its elements was tied to the pattern of which they were a part.[16] As a list, the elements of management included planning, directing, coordination, and controlling. The gestalt-like character of the concept is easily seen. If planning does not lead to the making of decisions that direct the organization to be guided by some plans, then the function of management will not have been adequately carried out. If directing is not supported by some systematic use of information and accumulated intelligence, then, again, the performance of the management function will be deficient. If plans do not exist, then there would be no clear basis for performing the controlling function, and it would be much harder to coordinate, as well.

We have come full-circle, back to the premise with which this section began: namely, that management is a functional necessity of international development cooperation projects, when the specific intent includes capacity-building in the partner-organization. But now it should be clearer what the statement means, particularly as the terms "functional necessity" and "intent" had not been discussed beforehand. Further, international development cooperation projects have been described as development-project-triads. The result is that the original premise can be re-stated thus: management is a functional necessity of *development-project-triads*, no less so when the intent includes organization-strengthening. For the sake of complete clarity, the explicit rational argument[17] behind this premise has the form of a syllogism and runs as follows:

> Major premise: Management is a functional necessity for any enterprise.
> Minor premise: Development-project-triads are enterprises.
> Conclusion: Management is a functional necessity of development-project-triads.[18]

Our theorizing journey has not only come full circle, but the ground on which these ideas rest is also more fully apparent. A simple extension of this theorizing is to presume that what is true of the development-project-triad as-a-whole is also true of each of its elements, with the implication being that management is a functional necessity of a triad's technical assistance project, its partner-organization, and its partnership-nexus. Given what management means in this context, this statement leads to the idea that planning, directing, coordinating, and controlling are presumably involved in each element of the whole.

Purposive, design-oriented theorizing about organizations sometimes point to abstract scenarios where something goes wrong with the organization-as-mechanism, so that it falls further short of its intent than would otherwise be the case. Such scenarios are known as "traps." A famous example of a trap in the management is the competency trap.[19] The basic idea of this trap is that there is a robust tendency for organizations and their members to get better and better at tasks that are similar to each other, which will make the organization better than other organizations in relation to doing that spectrum of things. However, it may turn out that being good at that spectrum of things will not translate into business success for "ego," because organizations doing other things ("alters") have out-competed "ego" in the industry context. Traps are pragmatic ideas: they suggest dilemmas that might be a route to insight[20] and ultimately more intelligent decisions and practices.[21]

With that in mind, consider the well-established critique that technical assistance projects, in the interest of their intent being realized, tended to make participants in the recipient country quite dependent on the development agency's dispatched technical experts. Call this the *TA-dependency trap*, with TA plainly being a reference to technical assistance. A question to ponder is whether a scenario similar to the TA-dependency trap is inherent in projects with an organization-strengthening intent. The dynamic might be that the overall development-project-triad is so keen for the partner-organization to be successful that, in the face of deficiencies in the latter, the "mechanism" for performing the partner-organization's management function increasingly lies in other parts of the development-project-triad than the partner-organization. The harmful consequence would presumably be the partner-organization's overreliance on the other partners. In terms of realizing the intent of organization-strengthening, that consequence would be harmful. Call this the *managerial-dependency trap*.

There are hints of the managerial-dependency trap having been at work in the E-JUST case. However, there is also evidence that JICA staff were sensitive to the practical dilemmas posed by this trap. More interestingly, there is clear evidence of measures taken to ease the dilemma and to neutralize the managerial-dependency trap. Neutralizing the trap involved creative ways of performing the management function for the E-JUST project-triad; it eased the dilemma faced by the partners in the project, and, especially, by JICA.

Structuring problems of management in international development cooperation projects

With all this in mind, let us establish a clear link between this chapter's purposive, design-oriented theorizing of management within international development cooperation projects and the fact-pattern in the E-JUST case. The general idea is to outline the practical argumentation (and thus instrumental reasoning) behind the problem-solving effort in a clear and compact form. Some theorists of problem-solving label such outlining as problem-structuring.[22] Accordingly, what follows is an exercise to structure the problem faced by E-JUST's Japanese partners. The exercise involves formalizing the presumptions within a practical argument and then stating practical conclusions that follow from them.[23] To wit:

> Premise 1: The E-JUST project-intent includes (a) creating public value through E-JUST's education, research, and joint work with industry and (b) E-JUST becoming a capable organization.
>
> Premise 2: It is rational for the members of the E-JUST partnership-nexus – including Japanese members acting on behalf of JICA and the Japan Supporting University Consortium (JSUC) – to bear responsibility for this project-intent being realized.
>
> Premise 3: E-JUST's functional necessities – among them, technical and management – need to be satisfied adequately if E-JUST's project-intent is to be realized.
>
>> Premise 3a: E-JUST's technical-functions – education, research, industrial outreach, student recruitment, student administration, facilities procurement, campus development, laboratory supply and maintenance – need to be performed adequately.
>>
>> Premise 3b: E-JUST's human resource management, accounting, finance, and security functions need to be performed adequately.
>>
>> Premise 3c: For E-JUST's technical, human resource, accounting, finance, and security functions to be performed adequately, E-JUST's management-function needs to be performed adequately.
>
> Premise 4: E-JUST's problem-solving activity and decision-making system is the mechanism that performs E-JUST's management function; an aspect of which is the role-structure within E-JUST's organization, especially its superstructure: to be specific, the acting president role and committee system roles.
>
> Conclusion: This line of practical reasoning leads to two practical conclusions:
>
>> Conclusion 1 (general): If Japanese partners have reservations or more serious concerns about whether any of E-JUST's functional necessities are being adequately satisfied, it is rational for them to proceed to deal with the problem-situation they have encountered.
>>
>> Conclusion 2 (specific): If Japanese partners have reservations or serious concerns about E-JUST's management-functions being performed adequately, then it is rational for them to intervene.

The bottom line here is that the Japanese partners in E-JUST considered it rational to intervene with the intent of effectuating the more adequate performance of E-JUST's management-function, specifically within a time-horizon of months, not years. In philosophical terms, the Japanese partners considered they had "conclusive reasons"[24] for acting on their intent. However, there's more to problem-structuring than deciding on an agenda. The implication is that a client or designer should state a *problem-solving challenge* in such a way as to effectuate the design activity on which the creation of truly adequate solutions depends.[25] Accordingly, what follows is an exercise to state the problem-solving challenge as faced by E-JUST's Japanese partners. To wit:

> *Problem-situation*: As of mid-2009, six months into E-JUST's start-up phase, designs and plans for mechanisms to perform E-JUST's technical functions were

not adequately specified and approved, given the time-scale of plans for start-up. E-JUST could not create public value unless and until the situation changed for the better (given Premise 1).

Problem-diagnosis: Specification and approval of technical-function plans and designs, as a general matter, depend on the management-function being performed; insufficient specification and approval of such plans and designs implies deficiencies in the performance of E-JUST's management-function (given Premise 3).

Decision-dilemma: Japanese partners had reason to intervene to correct the deficiency in the management-function's performance (given Premise 2). However, correcting the deficiency could have the unintended consequence[26] of actualizing the managerial-dependency trap, thereby jeopardizing the E-JUST project's organization-strengthening intent. In sum, there was a reason for Japanese partners to intervene (given the situation, diagnosis, and Premise 2) *and* a reason for them not to (given Premise 1b and the theorized managerial-dependency trap). Japanese partners thus faced a decision-dilemma.

Problem-solving challenge: Devise a Japanese partner intervention that corrects E-JUST's management-function deficiency, while keeping the theorized managerial-dependency trap from being actualized to the point of jeopardizing the project's organizational-strengthening intent.

Solving management problems: case analysis preliminaries

Let us now characterize the intervention – the Strategic TV Conference – that came to exist as a response to this problem-solving challenge. The focus here is on the practice itself rather than on the way in which it came onto the scene. In characterizing it, we adopt a well-known conceptual scheme in the program planning and evaluation literature, due to Pawson and Tilley.[27] This scheme exemplifies purposive, design-oriented theorizing and case analysis.

In its most compact form, Pawson and Tilley's generic schema for programs was presented symbolically as: $C + M = O$. In this metaphorical arithmetic expression, the letter O stands for the idea of "program outcome," though the vocabulary of "program intent" would be more apt. On the left-hand side, the letter M stands for the idea of "program mechanism," while the letter C stands for the idea of "program's context."

The schema includes only essential elements. If O were excluded, the schema would represent what a program consists in, but would not indicate what it is for. Second, if M were excluded, the schema would provide no indication of how the program's intent is to be fulfilled. Third, if C were excluded, the schema would overlook the effect of program context on what eventuates from a program mechanism's configuration and operation. In sum, this core and compact idea is that the fulfillment of intent is "effectuated"[28] by M as situated in C. In our view, Pawson and Tilley provided a highly serviceable template for developing a *model of the case* that is consistent with the purposive, design-oriented theorization of management in international development cooperation projects that is part and parcel of this study.

As a preliminary point, let us consider how to refer to M for purposes of this chapter.[29] Two options are self-evident. One is to refer to M as the Strategic TV Conference; the other is to stick with M. Referring to M as the Strategic TV Conference has two merits. First, seeing this word-string presumably makes for a more pleasing reading experience, for this chapter's audience, than seeing the letter M repeatedly; and "pleasing" is a reader-response whose importance in academic writing is hard to overstate.[30] The second reason is authenticity. The participant-members used this term in referring to the empirical phenomenon we are analyzing in this case study, after having called it the "E-J University Strategic Coordination Meeting" for the first three meetings. However, we wish to avoid the qualitative-research-trap of naturalizing the very phenomenon we are trying to understand.[31] Repetition of the word-string for the Strategic TV Conference, in the context of this chapter's purposive and design-oriented style of case analysis, could easily lead this naturalizing trap to take hold. We thus face a decision-dilemma and, hence, a reason to seek a third option.

In acting on this reason, what comes first to mind is to identify various aspects of the feature under analysis and present the whole (arbitrarily truncated) list each time reference is being made to the feature. This option would presumably neutralize the qualitative-research-trap of naturalizing the phenomena being studied, but at a high cost in terms of word count and aesthetics. We thus reformulate the dilemma into a problem-solving challenge, that is, to craft of form of words that not only uses the authentic label, Strategic TV Conference, but also reminds the reader that the object of analysis is an empirical phenomenon that relates to what Pawson and Tilley labeled as M. A form of words that would satisfy both criteria is the "M-like Strategic TV Conference," which we adopt.

A further set of preliminary remarks concerns C in Pawson and Tilley's purposive theorizing scheme. Recall that what effectuates the realization of intent is the *concatenation of context and mechanism*, although Pawson and Tilley rather cheekily portrayed this idea as an additive relation, $C + M$. Given that purposive case analysis pivots around the issue of what gives M leverage over O, it is difficult to say much that is general about context. However, as we seek to understand what effectuates the realization of intent in the present study, a reasonable "placeholder" for C is the development-project triad.

The triad idea points to the partnership-nexus as a context factor, which we will now explore illustratively by focusing on the Japan University Supporting Consortium (JSUC). We take JSUC as a context factor in two senses. First, JSUC was what some sociologists would call a "site for organizing"[32] within Japan's university sector. Enough organizing went on at this site – mainly by high-echelon university officials in concert with JICA's Human Development Department – for JSUC's member-universities to become a collective, constitutive part of E-JUST's development-project-triad. In relational and reciprocal fashion, JSUC's status as a constitutive part of the triad endowed certain individuals representing its member-universities with "actor-hood" in the triad.[33]

That actor-hood status was contextual vis-à-vis the Strategic TV Conference's mechanism in two senses. First, the actor-hood of Professor Hashimoto and Professor Miki did not arise from the Strategic TV Conference and, to that extent, the context was autonomous from the mechanism. Second, realization of the Japanese partners' intent depended on the concatenation of the actor-hood of these individuals (C), on the one hand, with these biological individuals being participant-members of the meeting (M), on the other. Analytically, if JSUC's being part of the triad is viewed in *isolation* from the mechanism features, it is hard to see its significance for the Strategic TV Conference; but if it is viewed in *relation* to the mechanism-features of Professor Hashimoto and Professor Miki's participation, then JSUC's significance is clear and substantial.

In sum, these remarks are preliminary in character, because our immediate intent is to underscore the point that the analysis of the E-JUST case, and specifically the Strategic TV Conference, works in part because of the conceptual constraint of the ideas symbolized as $C + M = O$, when they are properly construed, with the aid of processual sociology's theorizing mindset.[34]

Analysis

Table 7.1 presents an analysis of the Strategic TV Conference case. The three rows present questions that exemplify mechanism-intent thinking about a purposeful phenomenon: what it is for; what it consists in; and how it works. The two columns exemplify mechanism-intent thinking in the professional discipline of engineering. A conceptual design represents a purposeful phenomenon's character, intent, and constitutive functions; to the extent that a conceptual design represents mechanisms, few specifics are mentioned. By contrast, an embodiment design identifies process design features or other conditions that shape a mechanism's context-activity-outcome profile. Thus, the conceptual design column furnishes a high-level, generic representation, while the embodiment design column furnishes a detailed, specific one. The two columns together give a professional practitioner flexibility when using the Strategic TV Conference as a design-precedent for another organization-strengthening international cooperation project. At an early stage, the high-level representation, drawn from the conceptual design column, will be more relevant than a detailed one; and vice versa for a later stage.

We will now run through the rows. The Strategic TV Conference involved two linked-enterprises: (a) the international cooperation project involving Japan and Egypt, and (b) the public organization, E-JUST. The Strategic TV Conference was for effectuating enterprise-intent in two respects: (a) to effectuate E-JUST's "start-up transition"[35] and (b) to strengthen E-JUST as an organization. The other entries in this row reflect mechanism-intent thinking about public management: the idea is that enterprises will struggle to effectuate their intent, insofar as their enterprise-functions are deficiently performed. As analyzed here, the Strategic TV Conference's conceptual design was to perform the management function of (a) the Japan–Egypt international cooperation project and (b) E-JUST, in certain respects. Specifically, the conceptual design of the Strategic TV Conference was to perform "coordination," a constitutive function of management, for both the international cooperation project and for E-JUST. It was not designed to perform E-JUST's directing function. Rather, the conceptual design was to enable

Table 7.1 Mechanism-intent analysis of the Japan–E-JUST Strategic TV Conference

	What was the Strategic TV Conference's conceptual design?	What was the Strategic TV Conference's embodiment design?
What was the Strategic TV Conference for?	*Enterprises:* (a) the Japan–Egypt international development cooperation project (b) the public organization, E-JUST. *Intent:* (a) effectuate E-JUST's successful start-up transition; (b) strengthen E-JUST as an organization. *Functions:* (a) Management, specifically, coordination.	*Scenario-process mechanism:* (a) *Preparation* included: (i) interaction between JICA E-JUST Office and members of E-JUST committees, (ii) interaction between JICA HQ, JICA E-JUST Office, and SWG. (b) *Video tele-conference sessions,* chaired by Provost of Waseda University, with opposite number being Acting E-JUST President, with JICA staff in attendance, on a monthly basis, lasting one hour. (c) *Follow-up* included drafting meeting minutes, jointly between JICA E-JUST Office staff and E-JUST faculty.
What did the Strategic TV Conference consist in?	*Scenario-process mechanism:* Flow within and between meeting cycles (composed of preparation, tele-conference sessions, and follow-up steps).	*Organization-design mechanism:* (a) *Japan side:* (i) Strategic Working Group (SWG) of university consortium, (ii) JICA HQ and JICA E-JUST Office. (b) *Egypt side:* (i) E-JUST "University Council," headed by Acting President; (ii) E-JUST faculty, beyond University Council.
	Organization-design mechanism: Liaison device, between Japan universities, JICA, and E-JUST. *Labeling mechanism:* Coordination meeting (initially), Strategic TV Conference (later).	
How did the Strategic TV Conference work?	*Activated the social mechanisms of* (a) frame alignment, (b) homo- and hetero-phily in networks (c) performance feedback (arising from successive iterations of the scenario-process).	(Detailed analysis of the scenario-process mechanism's context-activity-outcome dynamics, discussed in relation to the conceptual design.)

the performance of the management function within E-JUST, in its totality, so as to effectuate E-JUST's start-up transition.

Let's turn now to the middle-row, concerned with the mechanism aspect of the Strategic TV Conference. The theoretical approach here is to view a mechanism primarily as being constituted by its scenario-process (with its context-activity-outcome dynamics). The scenario-process' high-level structure was that of a meeting cycle, with each cycle consisting in steps for preparation, the video tele-conference session, and follow-up. The cycles were connected, as the video tele-conference session inputs resulted from performing tasks that had been commissioned during a previous such session. The standard monthly periodicity of the video tele-conference sessions, as well as their standard one-hour duration, were marked process design features. The profile of pre-meeting activity included agenda-formulation, involving intensive communication between some E-JUST personnel and the JICA E-JUST Office; between the JICA E-JUST Office head (Dr. Tsunoda) and the JICA HQ official with lead responsibility for E-JUST (Mr. Ueda); and between JICA and members of the universities' Strategic Working Group. The profile of the conference sessions included chairing by Professor Shuji Hashimoto, the Provost of Waseda University, in his capacity as chair of the universities' Strategic Working Group, as well as active participation by Professor Chitoshi Miki, of Tokyo Tech. The Strategic Working Group members addressed the Acting E-JUST President, Professor Khairy, as their direct counterpart. Reports were received from other members of E-JUST's University Council and their associates, drawn from the small initial faculty. The profile of the follow-up activities included formulating minutes of the video tele-conference meetings, with initial drafting being conducted by JICA E-JUST Office staff and their counterparts within E-JUST (specifically, Dr. Etawil, a faculty member).

The Strategic TV Conference's organization-design mechanism was a liaison device. Within Mintzberg's theory of organizational design,[36] liaison devices are formalized venues for regular interaction among representatives of different institutional hierarchies. In this case, the venue established regular interaction between E-JUST, the universities' Strategic Working Group, and JICA. It also created an additional, effectively external, role to be played by E-JUST's *internal* liaison device, its University Council, as that grouping formed part of the Strategic TV Conference.

The labeling mechanism initially involved the verbal sign of a "coordination meeting," but the term Strategic TV Conference took hold after a few iterations of the scenario-process. The original label highlighted the mechanism's function, while the replacement label highlighted a distinctive mechanism-feature (the video teleconference).

Finally, let's turn to the bottom-row, concerned with how the Strategic TV Conference worked. Saying how this phenomenon worked requires causal insight, which, in turn, requires explanatory argumentation.[37] The approach to explanation taken here is mechanism-based,[38] with explanatory mechanisms essentially being causal (and descriptive) idealizations that form part of a discipline or substantive field of knowledge.[39] The concepts used here to formulate mechanism-based explanations fall within the category of social mechanisms: they are frame-alignment, homo- and hetero-phily in networks, and performance feedback. The general argument is that the Strategic TV Conference would have failed to perform the management/coordination function for the Japan–Egypt international cooperation project and for E-JUST as an enterprise, if these social mechanisms had not been causal influences within the Strategic TV Conference's scenario-process.

The idea of frame-alignment – originating in the Chicago School of Sociology – concerns how a situation is "defined" by the people who experience it.[40] A situation's definition is influenced by the way it is framed, with a frame essentially being a stereotype. A frame channels how participants in a situation act toward anything in the situation, including other participants; the experience of those actions then validate, or challenge, the definition of the situation. When the definition of a situation for some participants clashes with that of other participants, then the interaction will tend to involve rivalrous claims-making about what the situation is. When participants come to define the situation in similar ways, there's a tendency for a pattern of activity and interaction to take hold, as participants' actions conform to the situational definition. Frame-alignment is a trajectory toward a pattern of interaction with consistent, frame-based, situational definitions.

The idea of homo- and hetero-phily in networks concerns relations among participants in a social situation. Homo-phily involves recognition of social similarity between two individuals, relative to their context. An example of similarity concerns occupational role and status. A typical effect of homo-phily is the strengthening of ties between the individuals who recognize themselves as being socially similar. Two actors may give close attention to each other because they play similar roles in the same network and/or they play similar roles in different networks.[41] By contrast, hetero-phily involves recognition of social difference between two individuals, relative to their context. An example of dissimilarity is not having worked in the same country over the course of a career. A typical effect of hetero-phily is to be interested in the perspective of individuals who are different in such respects, as it might be instructive.

The idea of performance feedback concerns scenario-processes and, especially, how upstream and downstream ones are connected.[42] Performance feedback involves assessment of scenario-outcomes. A favorable assessment of a given iteration tends to enhance commitment to the scenario-process, which tends to be reflected in patterns of interaction in subsequent iterations. The mechanism operates in part through the validation of scenario-participants, which enhances the emotional energy they experience when involved in iterations of the scenario-process.[43]

These social mechanisms are sources of causal insight into how the Strategic TV Conference worked. In broad terms, frame-alignment had the effect of creating a common definition of the Strategic TV Conference and participation in it. The definition involved the need for more coordination (and direction) inside E-JUST, in order to effectuate the soft-opening. It also involved a sense of the appropriateness of regular support from the Japanese side, especially in respect to methods of coordination and the involvement of top officials of prestigious Japanese universities. As to how frames came to be aligned, we can point to the presentation of the Strategic TV Conference's specified process design features, as well as to the strength of the pre-existing frame that E-JUST was a Japan–Egypt collaboration – a frame rooted in the experience of several years of planning and approval work.

The homo-phily mechanism was activated by social similarity between Professors Hashimoto, Miki, and Khairy. As Professor Hashimoto agreed to chair the TV conference sessions, Professor Khairy was more inclined to participate routinely. During the sessions, Hashimoto, Miki, and Khairy were the highest status individuals present. Homo-phily had the effect of making Professors Hashimoto and Miki a center of attention for Professor Khairy, which, in turn, contributed to the attention accorded to what remarks and advice they stated. The hetero-phily mechanism was activated by social dissimilarity, owing to Professor Hashimoto and Miki's career experience in Japan, while the University Council members' experience included Egypt and, to a lesser extent, the U.K. and U.S. The effect was to increase interest in what the Japanese professors had to say during the sessions.

Finally, the performance feedback mechanism was activated by moving through iterations of the Strategic TV Conference. Commitment to the Strategic TV Conference strengthened as participants on the Egyptian side made effective use of the sessions to put information and issues before Professor Khairy, while his responses were under the guise of Professors Hashimoto and Miki. Commitments also strengthened as participants from JICA, including its E-JUST Office, were able to put issues before Professor Khairy, as Professors Hashimoto and Miki participated. Finally, joint commitment to this scenario-process strengthened as each installment of official minutes of the Strategic TV Conference came to be viewed as expanding the "Common Understanding" between the Japan and Egypt sides (and within E-JUST).

Discussion and conclusion

As can be seen, this discussion doesn't provide a complete explanation of how the Strategic TV Conference worked, but it's not meant to. For one reason, that's not what explanations ever do. The point is that they provide "causal insight." I would suggest that the three mechanisms discussed above are bases for independent (though compatible) lines of theorizing the Strategic TV Conference. The result is a loosely-organized theory of this purposeful phenomenon.

It's important to emphasize what such analysis is meant to be used for. The fundamental idea is to use it – within the professional practice of public management – as a design-precedent for enterprises falling under the description of international cooperation projects, where intent includes both enabling public value creation by partner organizations *and* strengthening them. A reason why design-precedents are useful in respect to organization-strengthening international cooperation projects is that there's only so much that can be said, by way of purposive theorizing, about how to balance the demands of helping a partner organization succeed, against the prospect that doing so will cancel out the effects of actions intended to strengthen them as organizations.

With this consideration in mind, the Strategic TV Conference's overall profile is that it helped E-JUST accomplish its soft-opening, while helping to strengthen (rather than weaken) E-JUST as an organization. The analysis shows that these twin-virtues are due to the judiciousness of the Strategic TV Conference's conceptual design – with its clarity of focus on performing the management/coordination function – and to the way in which the Strategic TV Conference worked. The way it worked, in turn, was due to process design features within the Strategic TV Conference's scenario-process and to the related activation of the social mechanisms of frame alignment, homo- and hetero-phily, and performance feedback; with the specific argument not needing to be repeated here.

If there is a lesson from this case analysis, it is that it's possible to help a partner organization effectuate its intent, while strengthening it as an organization. Beyond that, there's no real lesson, unless one feels compelled to present the study in these terms. If that's true, one lesson is to embody a conceptual design for performing the management/coordination function, along the lines of a "coordination meeting," with a suitably configured scenario-process, complemented by an appropriately designed liaison device and an appropriate labeling. Another lesson can be patterned on Bardach's[44] principle of replicating smart practices in "target sites" based on analysis of "source sites": replicate mechanisms, while adapting features. Such a lesson would be that, in configuring the scenario-process of a "coordination meeting," replicate the mechanisms of frame-alignment, homo- and hetero-phily, and performance feedback, while adapting the features as presented in this case analysis.

NOTES

1 This chapter is drawn from Working Paper 172 of the Japan International Cooperation Agency Research Institute (JICA-RI), whose permission to reproduce it is gratefully acknowledged. The Working Paper was published in March 2018. The final analytical section of the paper was introduced subsequently. As mentioned in the acknowledgments, funding for this work was provided by JICA-RI and by Higher Education Innovation Funding through the London School of Economics.

2 UNDP (2002), Mabuchi and Tsunoda (2006), Miyoshi and Nagayo (2006), JICA Research Institute (2006, 2008), UNDP (2009), Hosono et al. (2011), Sato (2013).

3 See, https://www.jica.go.jp/english/news/focus_on/education/index.html (Accessed: January 3, 2018).

4 Simon (1996), van Aken (2004).

5 Van Aken and Berends (2018).

6 Bardach (1994, 2004).

7 Barzelay (2007).

8 Lawson (2004).

9 http://open_jicareport.jica.go.jp/pdf/12037545_03.pdf, p. 120 (Accessed: April 9, 2019).

10 Mintzberg (1983).

11 The premise may apply with equal force to international development cooperation projects where the intent does not specifically include organizational capacity-building; however, that is not an issue with which this chapter is concerned.

12 Choi and Wu (2009).

13 Fayol (1919/1984).

14 Ariew and Perlman (2002).

15 Fayol's purposive, design-oriented theorizing about enterprises has largely been forgotten, but much of it remains in conscious awareness in the management field thanks to the impact of Michael Porter's

theorizing about enterprises in *Competitive Strategy* (Porter 1985). A feature of Porter's theorizing was an enterprise's value chain. It is roughly the same idea as Fayol's, even though Porter didn't cite Fayol. What Fayol called "functions" within an enterprise, Porter called "value-activities" within firm's "value-chain." Fayol's technical function is similar to six value-chain activities in Porter's scheme: inbound logistics, production, outbound logistics, after-sales service, research and development, and procurement. Fayol's commercial function is similar to Porter's sales value-activity. Looked at the other way around, Porter's corporate infrastructure value-activity is similar to four of Fayol's functions: accounting, finance, security, and management.

16 Lakoff (1987), Morgan (1986).
17 Baggini and Fosl (2010).
18 Note, that these statements would mean the same if the term "organization" were put in place of "enterprise," as, in this context, organizations are the mechanisms of interest within enterprises and management is a functional necessity of organizations.
19 Levitt and March (1988), Levinthal and March (1993).
20 Klein (2013).
21 March (2010). A literature has also developed around a trap that Diane Vaughan theorized through her research into the disastrous Challenger launch decision (Vaughan 2005). The term associated with the trap is the normalization of deviance.
22 Van Aken and Berends (2018).
23 Walton (1992).
24 Raz (1999).
25 Khurana and Rosenthal (1997), Rantanen and Domb (2002), van der Voort et al. (2011), Klein (2013).
26 Merton (1936).
27 Pawson and Tilley (1997).
28 Sarasvathy (2008).
29 Self-conscious exercises in labeling are not uncommon in academic work, not least in philosophy. For an example that inspired this paragraph, see Rescher (1996), where the issue was how to label the very topic of his book.
30 Booth et al. (2003), Becker (1997).
31 Van Maanen (2011), Stake (2010).
32 Fligstein and McAdam (2012).
33 Latour (2005), McAdam, Tarrow, and Tilly (2001).
34 McAdam, Tarrow, and Tilly (2001), Barzelay and Gallego (2006), Abbott (2016).
35 Watkins (2009).
36 Mintzberg (1983).
37 Pawson and Tilley (1997), Bardach (2004), Barzelay (2007).
38 Elster (1989), Craver and Darden (2013), McAdam, Tarrow, and Tilly (2011).
39 Morgan and Morrison (1999).
40 McAdam, Tarrow and Tilly (2001).
41 Kilduff and Tsai (2003: 58).
42 Greve (2003).
43 Collins (2004).
44 Bardach (2004).

8

Designed, not copied: the making of public management as a design-oriented professional discipline

This book, as you know, is about public management. What's public management for? It's for creating public value. What does effectuating public value creation involve? Two lines of theorizing are both pertinent: (a) performing a public organization's enterprise functions, including program-delivery and management, and (b) problem-solving in organizations. The latter is about doing the former better than would otherwise be the case.

What does public management consist in? Two layers of mechanisms,[1] in particular: design-projects and professional activities, both of which are important to problem-solving and performing a public organization's enterprise functions. Design-projects combine designing new enterprise mechanisms, such as systems and plans, with making organizational decisions. Professional activities are a family of mechanisms of professional practice, in relation to which individual professional practitioners are agents, and they include sense-making, designing, argumentation, and dramatization. How well problem-solving is accomplished and how well enterprise functions are performed affect what public management is for: creating public value.[2] Thus, public management is a professional practice, for effectuating the intent of public organizations, consisting in design-projects, as well as a family of professional activities.

What's this book *for*? Broadly, it's to improve public management as a professional practice. What is involved in improving professional practice? It's about fostering a virtuous circle between "doing" and "learning."[3] What does this book *consist in*? It consists in two layers of argumentative discussion. One is about a distinctive system of ideas – labeled as design-oriented public management – that is offered as professional knowledge appropriate for the professional practice of public management. Another is a distinctive view – labeled as a design-oriented professional discipline – about how public management should be thought of as an enterprise for improving professional practice.

These two layers of argumentative discussion fit together, to make a consistent whole, in two respects. First, the very idea of public management as a professional practice, with a distinct design-oriented profile, will *not* become part of the professional life of multiple thousands of individuals working in public organizations, *unless* public management acquires properties of being a professional discipline, patterned on Herbert Simon's vaunted concept of a science of the artificial, but adapted properly to management.[4] Second, without such a professional discipline, professional practitioners won't benefit from the opportunity to examine and use "professional knowledge" as they engage in the doing and learning functions of their professional practice, whether that knowledge about public management consists in purposive theorizing, or in design-precedents.[5] Thus, this book is an argument about the enterprise of public management as a design-oriented professional discipline, one that becomes an institution supporting problem-solving and performing a public organization's enterprise functions, irrespective of place and time.

While there are precedents for what has just been said about public management and professional practice, the overall line taken here hasn't been put forward before. In the light of that statement, I'll offer a few remarks about the novelty and positioning of this book.

Let's take the idea that public organizations effectuate public value creation, most directly by delivering public programs (except in cases when public organizations are in a leadership and/or service role within government). This statement derives from Mark Moore's widely cited 1995 book on public management, in particular the intricately formulated and brilliantly argued Chapter 2 of that volume. In this respect, what's novel about the present book is little more than the labeling of such a discussion as a purposive theory of public organizations and the incorporation of the term "effectuation"[6] as a verbal marker of purposive theorizing, as a distinctive form of argumentative discussion.

Let's turn to the idea that a public organization's intent is effectuated by a multitude of mechanisms, any one of which can be theorized, or represented for practical purposes, as a scenario-process. Although this vocabulary is not universal, the idea is so commonplace that it practically operates as a presupposition within the field of program planning/evaluation as well as within the field of management and organizations – if not in public management. Reference to some classics makes the point.

A classic in program planning/evaluation is Pawson and Tilley's *Realistic Evaluation*.[7] One of its premises – and take-aways – is that any program can be represented, for either design or evaluation purposes, by the formula, $C + M = O$. Pawson and Tilley's formula appears to symbolize the virtues of understanding how a program works to effectuate program intent by observing and analyzing how a combination of program context and program activity eventuates in program outcomes. (You'll have to overlook their troublesome use of the term "mechanism" to avoid stumbling as you read the previous statement.)

A classic about organizations is Mintzberg's *Designing Effective Organizations: Structures in Fives*.[8] Mintzberg posits that no organization can be effective if it is deficient in coordinating its working parts and the tasks they carry out. Among other things, Mintzberg identified distinct forms of scenario-processes that are *for* performing an organization's coordination function, labeling them "coordination mechanisms." These different forms of coordination-performing mechanisms were, characteristically, five-fold: direct supervision, standardization by procedure, standardization by output, standardization by skill, and mutual adjustment. He also discussed how an organization's use of such mechanisms tends to form patterns, shaping and reinforcing power balances within bureaucracies, private or public. Mintzberg's book on organization design clearly illustrates mechanism-intent theorizing about organizations.

Another classic is Michael Porter's *Competitive Advantage*.[9] Among other things, Porter identified the configuration of an enterprise's value chain as a mechanism to create value for the purchaser/users of a business' products and services, while neutralizing the ill-effects of competition on a company's profits. Here, a business' value chain configuration is a multitude of mechanisms, which perform each and all of its functions (which Porter termed a business' value activities), so as to effectuate company intent, revolving around profitability. A value-chain's multitude of mechanisms, in turn, consists in scenario-processes (as in research and development) and conversion-processes (as in production).

In mentioning these classics, my well sign-posted point is to suggest that this book's style of theorizing public organizations is deeply rooted in precedent. The connection to precedent is, however, not that easy to see, because those who engage in mechanism-intent, purposive theorizing in management tend to be coy about presenting the ideas that "stand above" the ideas that they offer up. This book's novelty lies in part in its retrieval and use of forms of theorizing that have long been prevalent, even if they are not altogether fashionable.

That said, this book goes further than its precedents in theorizing scenario-processes along lines known within sociology as "processual sociology."[10] Seeing organizations as consisting in scenario-processes is hardly original: within organization studies, there's more than one intellectual tradition for doing so – for example, one focusing on decision-making in organizations, as well as ones that take cues from structuration theory[11] or actor-network theory.[12] However, in my view, works about management that engage fully with purposive theorizing – like the two classics just discussed – tend not to engage fully with processual sociology. Conversely, works that engage fully with processual sociology don't tend to engage fully with purposive theorizing about management. There are plenty of exceptions to this broad pattern; two were presented in Chapter 4, Bryson's[13] book on strategic planning and my book with Campbell on strategic planning in the U.S. Air Force.[14] But the pattern is broadly evident. The reasons lie in path-dependencies in the management field and in the complex relation between management and social science, reasons that are not "lost to history."[15] In any case, I seek to position this book by claiming that it engages equally with purposive theorizing of public organizations and with processual sociology, unlike a very large fraction of literature on management or public management.

In dealing with the general issue of this book's novelty and positioning, the idea of design science requires some depth of discussion, as Herbert Simon's

Sciences of the Artificial has served as both a precedent and a contrast, and as some academics along the years have proposed that public management be cast as a design science. Some context needs to be provided in advance of this discussion, as suggested in Chapter 2, in particular.

As a matter of historical fact, Simon didn't say that management should be cast as a design science; he listed management – almost in passing – as a science of the artificial, alongside the exemplary cases of engineering and architecture. As widely known, Simon did put forward the term "design science." However, he coined this term to refer to research work that ought to be done to generate fundamental knowledge about problem-solving, and specifically about the creation of artificial systems through designing and organizational decision-making. In calling for a science of design, Simon was trying to neutralize stiff opposition to teaching design in some engineering programs and to teaching problem-solving in some management programs (including those at his own university). The basis of opposition was attributed to the accepted doctrine that proper professional practice derives from a practitioner's skillful application of knowledge that derives ultimately from scientific investigation.[16] Thus, a science of design was envisioned as a means to generate the fundamental knowledge on which teachers of engineering and management could draw, in both fashioning – and legitimating – courses on design in engineering schools and problem-solving in the modern management school.

Perhaps the most common meaning of a design science in management is that theory based on cumulative inquiry about human behavior in organizations should be applied directly by professional practitioners when they deliberate over choices between alternative mechanisms for coordinating and motivating human activity in organizations.[17] However, this idea is far from Simon's idea of a design science; and it is not wholly in tune with his idea that problem-solving is the essence of the professional practice of management. For Simon, problem-solving wasn't about using theory for applied purposes, or about solving problems on the basis of theory – not that Simon would have scorned any of those ideas. Problem-solving was about participating in scenario-processes, whose initial conditions include individual insights, but collective ignorance, about an enterprise's problems and solutions. The scenario-process he had in mind was a design-project, constituted by the activities of designing and decision-making. Thus, disambiguation is needed when the term design science is invoked in the field of management.

Let me say how I position this book relative to Simon's ideas as put forward in *Sciences of the Artificial*. I'll start with two points of agreement. First, management ought to be a professional discipline that teaches designing enterprises, and problem-solving more generally, to professional practitioners. More stridently, the professional discipline of management should be engaged with preparing professional practitioners for problem-solving for enterprises, not just with decision-making for one or another functional domain, like finance, marketing, or production. Second, it should develop professional practitioners' competences for problem-solving, as well as their professional knowledge about the enterprises that they will be involved in creating, through design-projects, or otherwise. These two points of agreement head toward an implication: academic institutions in the field of management should encourage faculty to develop a design-oriented professional discipline, concerned with creating professional knowledge about management, problem-solving, and the relation between the two, as well as with developing professional practitioners' competence in problem-solving for enterprises.

This implication is stretched here to apply to *public* management, as follows: academic institutions should encourage faculty to develop a design-oriented professional discipline, concerned with creating professional knowledge about management, problem-solving, and the relation between the two, as well as with developing professional practitioners' competence in problem-solving for public organizations within governmental and societal institutions. A similar statement can be made for government-based schools of public administration.

By way of positioning, I would now like to note some contrasts between this book's idea of a design-oriented professional discipline of public management and Simon's views about management as a professional discipline, as far as these views are evident. They are to do with purposive theorizing, learning from experience, and competences of professional practitioners. I'll take them up, in turn.

This book makes a big deal of purposive theorizing. However, there's no mention of this term in *Sciences of the Artificial*, and there's no other term in that volume that has the same significance. I believe that purposive theorizing is important to the professional practice of management, and to the professional discipline of public management. In public management, purposive theorizing concerns the purposeful phenomena of public organizations, design-projects, and professional activities – taken individually and together. For professional practice, such purposive theorizing has specific practical implications for professional activities. For example, purposive theories of public organizations have practical implications for what observations and assessments to make as a professional practitioner engages in sense-making. For example, the idea that a public organization depends on support from its authorizing environment implies that sense-making should eventuate in observations about the interests and power of a public organization's multitude of stakeholders. Similarly, the idea that a public organization's functions include program delivery and management implies that sense-making should eventuate in observations about its value-chain configuration. Similar kinds of points can be made about the other professional activities: for example, designing should eventuate in an adequate value chain configuration – and its corresponding scenario- or conversion-processes – for whatever functions fall within the scope of the design-project at issue. As another example: dramatization should eventuate in a "routine" that projects ideas about design-oriented problem-solving, the mechanism of design-projects, and the professional activity of designing.

At the risk of digression, I don't see high-level statements about administrative philosophies[18] like cameralism, progressive public administration, the post-bureaucratic paradigm, new public management, public value governance, network governance, and the like as particularly good examples of purposive theorizing about public organizations. But I do think that serious critical examinations of administrative philosophies, including these, using a range of standard principles and methods of analyzing practical argumentation, can eventuate in contributions to what I call purposive theorizing of public management: see, for example, my *New Public Management*,[19] chapters 4 and 5, and, with caveats, my *Breaking Through Bureaucracy*,[20] chapters 2, 7, and 8.

By comparison, Simon's stereotypical writings about management-related topics were downbeat on purposive theorizing. Take, for example, Simon's famous article, "The proverbs of administration,"[21] which took aim at classical administrative theorizing about organizational design. To say this critique of principles of administration was downbeat on purposive theorizing is nothing short of an understatement. Indeed, in that reputation-establishing piece, Simon didn't even bother to use standard principles of critical assessment of practical argumentation, such as being charitable toward an opponent's presentation of an argument, as you are interpreting and representing it, in order to avoid committing the strawman fallacy. When it came to setting out the idea of "administrative analysis," in the same piece, Simon didn't point out that he was using some established purposive theories, like aspects of scientific management, to warrant some of his own position. It shouldn't be overlooked that Simon wrote this article before the renaissance of philosophical work on practical argumentation, the beginning of which is often credited to Stephen Toulmin's *Uses of Argument*,[22] which eventually made huge inroads into discussions of public policy analysis and public administration. And even Simon's own late-career work – *Reason in Human Affairs*[23] – reflected the argumentative turn. Still, the stereotype of Simon, within public administration, is that of being scornful of purposive theorizing, at least when he wasn't discussing decision-making.

Simon's attitude toward purposive theorizing in *Sciences of the Artificial* isn't easy to discern. Consider his adopted idea that designing is constituted by analysis and synthesis –two interlocking scenario-processes with contrasting context-action-outcome profiles, in the language of this book. Analysis was presented as being channeled by knowledge of some range of domains that came to be identified as relevant to the design-project at issue. The term "domain knowledge" later came into use as a handy reference to this idea. In the context of *Sciences of the Artificial*, which was heavily concerned with engineering design, domain knowledge connoted technical knowledge and expertise. From that volume, it's not really clear what Simon thought would be "domain knowledge" for management, apart from his own theorizing about organizational design and decision-making (which, in any event, he appeared to assign to the category of design knowledge). What is clear is the following: purposive theorizing of enterprises was not Simon's cup of tea, while *Sciences of the Artificial* was not centrally concerned with the professional discipline or practice of management.

Bottom line: When I say that purposive theorizing about enterprises, including public organizations, counts as professional (or domain) knowledge for management, or public management, I am presenting a view that diverges from stereotypes of Simon's idea of sciences of the artificial, that is, his term for design-oriented professional disciplines. It is also out-of-tune with respect to the tenor of much of his writing about management. However, I don't think there is a fundamental clash – or incompatibility – in perspective. My view is there is much to be gained from energetically updating Simon's theorizing about professional disciplines, including management, so that it makes sense, and can thrive, after the argumentative turn in social science, philosophy, and beyond.

Learning from experience is a second point of dissonance or departure. This point was discussed at some length in Chapter 6. Suffice it to say here that Simon's theorization of designing as a professional activity, and of the analysis aspect of design-projects, was essentially silent on this topic. In this respect, his theorization of designing was thin, to put the point gingerly. There are reasons of intellectual history that explain this deficit; some of which have to do with the setting within which Simon did his earlier work and some have to do with his focus on decision-making as a theoretical frame about management. Be that as it may, the position taken in this book is that design-precedents count as professional (or domain) knowledge, as does purposive theorizing. That position points toward a wide-open challenge of studying past manifestations of purposeful phenomena, within a professional discipline, with a view to creating design-precedents.

I don't see any clash between this position and Simon's, even though the creation and use of design-precedents isn't stereotypical of the ideas in *Sciences of the Artificial*. (I'm ignoring here a few salient passages in the first chapter, which suggest that the study of artificial phenomena should include methods for analyzing past artifacts, so that, as the saying goes, humankind is not damned to reinventing the wheel, repeatedly.) That said, it seems to me that what's truly missing from Simon's account of design-oriented professional disciplines is how to investigate past manifestations of purposeful phenomena, so that the material I call a design-precedent is meaningful, in the course of design-projects, when it is being used in *combination with* purposive theories.

Bottom line: in my view, the understandable silence on purposive theorizing, *combined with* strange silence on design-precedents, makes Simon's *Sciences of the Artificial*, altogether, a weak precedent for a design-oriented professional discipline of management or public management. We need such a discipline: Simon, however, doesn't provide the blueprint, after all. If it's going to happen, we need to develop it ourselves. That's a big ask: about which, more later.

A third contrast with Simon concerns professional competences. The contrast is not altogether stark – certainly less so than the contrast between *Sciences of the Artificial* and this book's position on purposive theorizing and design-precedents. Here's the common ground. First, Simon theorized professional competences by putting the emphasis on how thinking and communicating played roles in the emergent processes (to effectuate problem-solving) that eventuate in scenario outcomes; in this respect, his general approach to theorizing professional competences was quite in line with processual sociology – unsurprisingly, as they stemmed from a common source, not least the philosophical pragmatism of John Dewey. (The commonplace idea that competences consist in knowledge, skills, and attitudes is cut from different philosophical cloth.) Second, Simon put great store in *designing* as being a professional competence. Its attributes include the ability to make good choices about how to "search" for knowledge and information, as well as to judge its relevance and implications for problem-solving, during further stages of a design-project. Third, Simon considered creativity to be a kind of professional competence, though one that is a bit hard to teach. Fourth, Simon saw being able to participate in design-projects *within organizations* as a competence: hence, he emphasized that engineers had to learn about how decision-making in organizations works. Finally, Simon implicitly put a high value on the competence of framing, formulating, and expressing a practical argument; though he didn't use the words, it's clear that his purposive theory of decision-making in organizations was in line with this view.

This book's purposive theorizing about public management takes all of this on board. The resulting form was evident in Chapter 4 – specifically, the audio guide presentation of the mezzanine and lower floors of the Public Management Gallery. The gallery layout made a distinction between design-projects (presented on the mezzanine floor) and professional activities (presented on the lower floor). In this theorization, designing is a professional activity, while a design-project is its context. Put the other way around, designing as a professional activity is a constitutive mechanism of a design-project. Both design-projects and designing have their complementary roles in this line of purposive theorizing about public management.

Disentangling design-projects from designing allows us to see that Simon's theorization of professional-competences-for-problem-solving was too narrow. The natural remedy is to expand the theoretical scheme, with the result being a construct consisting in the professional activities of sense-making, designing, argumentation, and dramatization. As mentioned, this idea was introduced toward the end of Chapter 4; it is developed slightly further and presented in tabular form, in Table 8.1.

The contrast between this table and Simon's idea of the competences of a professional practitioner are muted, insofar as one's attention is limited to sense-making, designing, and argumentation. However, the contrast becomes striking as soon as one gazes at the column titled "dramatization." The view taken here is that problem-solving isn't effectuated by (a) creating representations of object-designs, plus (b) formulating practical arguments, unless (c) the participating professional practitioners dramatize agendas, context, actors, action, conceptual and embodiment designs, choice alternatives, authoritative actions, and more. That's a quite conventional view, with plenty of theoretical and empirical precedents in processual sociology (where one might pigeonhole Goffman), and elsewhere. But it's not stereotypical of Simon's idea of design-oriented professional practice; because his processualism was more philosophical (along the lines of Dewey) than sociological (along the lines of the Chicago School of Sociology), as much lamented by his 1950s collaborator, James G. March. With a nod in the latter direction, there's no reason to be constrained by such path-dependencies in the field of management. Hence, this book's idea of professional practice includes the professional activity of dramatization, seen in mechanism-intent terms, as a constitutive mechanism of design-projects and, more inclusively, of public organizations.

Bottom-line: Simon's *Sciences of the Artificial* is a huge precedent for this book;

Table 8.1 Mechanism-intent analysis of professional activities in public management

Professional activity	Sense-making	Designing	Argumentation	Dramatization
What's it for?	Effectuating design-projects; Problem-solving; Performing functions; Creating public value	Effectuating design-projects; Problem-solving; Performing functions; Creating public value	Effectuating design-projects; Problem-solving; Performing functions; Creating public value	Effectuating design-projects; Problem-solving; Performing functions; Creating public value
What's the outcome?	Observations about a public organization; Ideas for problem-solving;	Coherent conceptual and embodiment designs for a public organization; Alternatives for decision-making	Arguments about problems, solutions, and decisions concerning a public organization	Collective representations of agendas, context, actors, action, conceptual and embodiment designs, choice alternatives, and authoritative actions
What conditions channel it?	Events leading to the present; Professional knowledge	Outcomes of sense-making; Professional knowledge (including design precedents); Initiated design-projects	Outcomes of sense-making and designing; Professional knowledge	Outcomes of sense-making, designing, and argumentation; events leading to the present

but it is an insufficient – and in some ways, weak – basis for theorizing public management as a design-oriented professional discipline. Apart from the fact that figuring this out took me a decade of my professional life, that's fine. That's no burden for you. You now have something better to work with than I had when I started down this path.

The final step in positioning this book has to do with the idea that public management is a professional discipline. To be clear, I am not presenting public management as a profession, with manifest jurisdictional claims over membership, knowledge, and practice. Indeed, I haven't even discussed the relationship between public management, public administration, public policy, and management. I am hoping to draw people to the idea, irrespective of whether they happen to be placed institutionally within public administration, management, or public policy – or for that matter, outside academia. That raises a question about how to position this book's argumentation, in relation to the idea of a professional discipline.

As you can tell by now, the main precedent I have in mind is Simon's idea of a science of the artificial, which is a very high-level idea about a professional discipline. Not only is it high-level, Simon's idea is essentially presented in mechanism-intent terms, rather than in institutional ones. That is equally true of the way I presented public management as a professional discipline in this book, all the way back to Chapter 1. There, I presented it, first, in terms of a program results chain, and then as two mutually enabling "enterprises," one for discipline-development and the other for teaching and learning. This abstract representation should be meaningful to anyone who aligns with the idea of public management being a design-oriented professional discipline.

You would rightly ask whether anyone has previously called for public management to be a design-oriented professional discipline, in as many words. To my knowledge, the answer is no. You can confirm this with a Google search, with the search-string of "public management design oriented professional discipline."

There was once a call for *public administration* to be a *design science*, in a piece by Shangraw, Crow, and Overman, in *Public Administration Review*.[24] They stated:

> As a design science, public administration can be separated from the behavioral sciences such as political science, psychology, or economics. In those fields of inquiry, the goal is to understand and predict particular types of human behavior in individual and social settings. . . .. Public administration, alternatively, draws knowledge from these fields and others, for the purpose of designing, constructing, and evaluating institutions and mechanisms for the public good. . . .. Defining public administration as a design science means that the role of the field is to design and evaluate institutions, mechanisms, and processes that convert collective will and public resources into social profit. (p. 156)

To me, the authors here are using the term "design science" merely to establish similarity between public administration and Simon's idea of a professional discipline concerned with purposeful phenomena. They display some mechanism-intent theorizing of public administration. Public administration is *for* creating "social profit." Public administration *consists in* institutions and mechanisms, as well as their design and evaluation. However, there's little more to the similarity with Simon's idea of a science of the artificial than that. In fact, there's a bit less: the way they write about "the field" undercuts the distinction between a professional discipline – involving research and education – and actual practice. Indeed, the implication seems to be that the *practice* of public administration is a design-science, which has nothing to do with Simon's idea of a science of the artificial: as noted above, a design science is not a property of problem-solving; it's a basis for formulating and legitimating a course that teaches designing in engineering and problem-solving in management. All in all, the historical piece by Shangraw, Crow, and Overman is a *negative precedent* as far as this book is concerned. (Beware of "design science" as a label for public management as a professional discipline.)

While no one has previously called for public management to be a design-oriented professional discipline, there are precedents for (a) the idea that designing is a distinctive professional activity within the professional practice of public management, and for (b) the idea that public management is a professional discipline. I consider these works as design-precedents for this book – and to this extent, they are relevant for positioning.

To my mind, the precedent for the idea that designing is a distinctive professional activity within the professional practice of public management is a pair of writings by Eugene Bardach, now professor emeritus of public policy at University of California, Berkeley. The writings are *Getting Agencies to Work Together: The Practice and Theory of Managerial Craftsmanship*,[25] and "Presidential Address: The extrapolation problem – how can we learn from the experience of others?"[26] As suggested by its title, the book presents the idea of designing as a professional activity using the terminology of managerial craftsmanship. The presidential address, discussed at some length in Chapter 6, illustrates the idea of mechanism-intent thinking when the purposeful phenomena are programs and when the mechanisms for performing a program's functions are analyzed as scenario-processes, with context-activity-outcome dynamics. The argument is that professional practitioners should engage in such thinking when they practice public management – specifically, when they (a) observe, analyze, and assess a program's source site, (b) extrapolate the results of this learning scenario to the challenge and situation in a program's target site, and (c) when they actually engage in specifying a program design there. Bardach's presidential address was also a precedent for my earlier article on case study research,[27] which developed into the idea of design-focused case studies and design-precedents in this book, as presented in Chapter 6.

The precedent for the idea that public management is a professional discipline is Lawrence Lynn's *Public Management as Art, Science, and Profession.*[28] Indeed, Lynn's book is a precedent in two senses. First, it was a book about a *discipline* that he calls public management: he argues that it is profession-like, however much of the research supporting it is scientific. Second, Lynn's book took a clear line about the doing of public management: namely that it's a professional practice, however much it might be instructive to probe an analogy between practicing public management and practicing an art. These similarities between Lynn's book and the present one are huge. I don't know of any other work that argues these two positions together, though there are some older works in public administration – not too well known – that can be cited as strong precedents.[29]

While Lynn's book was an abiding precedent for this one, it's really different in substance. First, its scope of discussion is vastly wider, as evident from how Lynn defined public management, that is, as performing the executive function in government. The phrasing as well as Lynn's commentary on the definition made clear that his book was concerned broadly with public administration. To that extent, Lynn was using the label "public management" to refer to what a decade or two earlier would have been labeled as "public administration." That's not to say that Lynn's book didn't deal with matters that figure centrally in public management: indeed, it includes a chapter that beautifully illustrates mechanism-intent thinking about change in a public organization – and that could be seen as an essay on the difference between drawing lessons from a case and formulating a design-precedent. However, when Lynn presented his broad pronouncements about public management being a professional discipline, these features of the book's discussion were essentially invisible. Bottom-line: the present book is exclusively about public management, while Lynn's was about public administration and public management, in varying proportions.

Second, Lynn's idea of a professional discipline was cut from different cloth than the idea that is presented here, under the label of a design-oriented professional discipline – particularly as he presented his thinking in the final, most programmatic chapter. Among the lines he took is that professional education in public management should consist in learning about a range of theories within a variety of disciplines, as well as in educational activities whose function is to make a practitioner more skillful at public management. To illustrate, some of the theories would be from institutional and organizational economics, while some others would be from political and legal theory. Skills would be built up from application exercises. So, you might ask: from what cloth was Lynn's position cut?

A step in answering this question is to be clear what fabric Lynn steered away from. The first is obvious: along the course of the book, Lynn made his disdain for Harvard case- and problem-based teaching painfully clear. There's also no evidence that Lynn had any interest in the intellectual tradition that formed the precedents for the content of such teaching, including the sort of mechanism-intent thinking that was ushered into the field of administration by Henri Fayol. The second is less obvious: Herbert Simon's idea of sciences of the artificial, as it applies to management. Simon's idea of management as a professional discipline included teaching problem-solving. That's just not there.

Lynn's idea of a professional discipline seems to have come from elsewhere: a different sort of step is required to pinpoint it. That step is to look at the history of management in business schools in the U.S. – and specifically the immensely revealing volume by Mie Augier and James G. March.[30]

Augier and March lay out the rivalry between the "modern management school," embodied during the 1950s in the Graduate School of Industrial Administration at Carnegie Institute of Technology, and Harvard Business School's longer-standing approach. They also point out that the modern management school included a dominant and a heterodox position. The dominant position was modeled on the modern medical school, focused on developing a range of functional disciplines of management (e.g., finance and marketing) through theory development and empirical research aligned closely with economics and/or psychology. The heterodox position was that of Herbert Simon and his close collaborators (like March), focused as it was on problem-solving *about* enterprises – and *within* organizations. The line taken by "the modern medical school" wing was that becoming a professional practitioner requires the study of relevant scientific disciplines, followed by applications to gain skill in applying that knowledge in the making of business decisions.

The inference I draw is that Lynn's idea of public management as a professional discipline was cut from the cloth of the modern medical school. By contrast, the present book's idea of a design-oriented professional discipline was cut from the *two rival traditions* of the modern medical school, as it took form in the field of management: namely, the Harvard and Simon ones. Thus, Lynn's book is a precedent for the present book by virtue of its form (i.e., a full-length discussion of public management as a professional discipline), but not in its content.

I haven't sought to position this book in relation to recent publications in the business management field. One of the reasons is that I don't know of any book that actually works out a coherent position on business management as a design-oriented professional discipline. There are widely recognized works on design thinking, as an approach to product and service design: that relates to the professional activity of designing and, to a limited extent, to design-projects. But that's all. The volume that has the most topical similarity to the present book is an edited book by Richard Boland and Fred Collopy,[31] entitled *Managing as Designing*. This book claims to develop the idea of bringing a design attitude to management, one that contrasts with "the more traditionally accepted and practiced decision attitude." It's clear that this book builds on Simon's idea of a design-project, which trades on the design/decision distinction. It's also majestic in style. But I wouldn't say that it works out the idea of a design-oriented professional discipline of business management in the way that the present volume does for public management. I've spotted some other successor works, but my assessment is similar.

The bottom line is that, while you could have surmised from this book's title what it is *for*, you couldn't have guessed what it *consists in*. The underlying reasons are, as follows. First, you can't find a precedent in the public management literature that is a full-dress discussion of public management as a design-oriented professional discipline. Second, this book's approach to public management is not closely aligned with any stereotypical reference point – not in business management, not with evidence-based policy or management, not with New Public Management, not with traditional public administration, and not even entirely with *Sciences of the Artificial*.

The point lingering in the shadows is this: public management should not be seen as a discipline whose future has been foretold by the other disciplines with which it is institutionally and historically aligned. Public management need not be a follower of developments in other fields: as a discipline, we can lead the way to learning how to embody the idea of a design-oriented professional discipline, involving management and public administration, in universities and government-based schools of public administration.

This book has extensive implications for the discipline-development and teaching-and-learning enterprises of the design-oriented professional discipline of public management. Indeed, I've "laid it out there" throughout this book, especially in the dialogues centered around Marshall, the barely fictionalized professor of public management, who you first met in Chapter 1. As you can tell by those dialogues, as well as every chapter of this book, I'm asking a lot of many hundreds of real-world Marshalls, Noras, Oliviers, and Petras. My hope is that what today looks like a Big Ask will seem – in retrospect – a rather modest one. That's an appropriate test of progress for the design-oriented professional discipline of public management.

NOTES

1 Craver and Darden (2013).
2 Moore (1995).
3 Schön (1983).
4 Simon (1996).
5 Lawson (2004).
6 Sarasvathy (2008).
7 Pawson and Tilley (1997).
8 Mintzberg (1983).
9 Porter (1985).
10 Abbott (2016).
11 Giddens (1984).
12 Latour (2005).
13 Bryson (2018).
14 Barzelay and Campbell (2003).
15 Augier and March (2011).
16 Simon (1996), Schön (1983).
17 Rousseau (2006).
18 Hood (1991), Hood and Jackson (1991).
19 Barzelay (2001).
20 Barzelay (1992).
21 Simon (1946).
22 Toulmin (1958).
23 Simon (1990).
24 Shangraw, Crow, and Overman (1989).
25 Bardach (1998).
26 Bardach (2004).
27 Barzelay (2007).
28 Lynn (1996).
29 Jun (2006).
30 Augier and March (2011).
31 Boland and Collopy (2004).

References

Abbott, Andrew (1992). From causes to events: notes on narrative positivism. *Sociological Methods and Research*, 20(4), 428-455.

Abbott, Andrew (2001). *Time Matters*. Chicago, IL: University of Chicago Press.

Abbott, Andrew (2005). The idea of outcome in U.S. sociology. In Adams, J., Keane, W., and Dutton, M. (Eds), *The Politics of Method in the Human Sciences: Positivism and its Epistemological Others*. Raleigh, NC: Duke University Press, 393-426.

Abbott, Andrew (2016). *Processual Sociology*. Chicago, IL: University of Chicago Press.

Alexander, Jeffrey, Ishikawa, Sara, and Silverstein, Murray (1977). *A Pattern Language: Towns, Buildings, Construction*. New York: Oxford University Press.

Allison, Graham T. (1971). *Essence of Decision*. Boston, MA: Little, Brown.

Ariew, André and Perlman, Mark (2002). Introduction. In Ariew, A., Cummins, R., and Perlman, M. (Eds), *Functions: New Essays in the Philosophy of Psychology and Biology*. Oxford: Oxford University Press, 1-25.

Augier, Mie and March, James G. (2011). *The Roots, Rituals, and Rhetorics of Change: North American Business Schools After the Second World War*. Stanford, CA: Stanford Business Books.

Baggini, Julian and Fosl, Peter S. (2003). *The Philosopher's Toolkit: A Compendium of Philosophical Concepts and Methods*. Malden, MA: Blackwell.

Baggini, Julian and Fosl, Peter S. (2010). *The Philosopher's Toolkit: A Compendium of Philosophical Concepts and Methods*, 2nd edn. Chichester: Wiley Blackwell.

Bardach, Eugene (1994). Comment: The problem of 'best practice' research. *Journal of Policy Analysis and Management*, 13(2), 260-268.

Bardach, Eugene (1998). *Getting Agencies to Work Together: The Practice and Theory of Managerial Craftsmanship*. Washington, DC: Brookings Institution.

Bardach, Eugene (2004). Presidential address: The extrapolation problem – how can we learn from the experience of others. *Journal of Policy Analysis and Management*, 23(2), 205-220.

Barnard, Chester I. (1938/1968). *The Functions of the Executive*. Cambridge, MA: Harvard University Press.

Barzelay, Michael (1992). *Breaking Through Bureaucracy: A New Vision for Managing in Government*. Berkeley, CA: University of California Press.

Barzelay, Michael (2001). *The New Public Management: Improving Research and Policy Dialogue*. Berkeley, CA: University of California Press.

Barzelay, M. (2007). Learning from second-hand experience: methodology for extrapolation-oriented case research. *Governance*, 20(3), 521-543.

Barzelay, Michael (2012). The study of public management: reference points for a design science approach. In Tria, G. and Valotti, G. (Eds), *Reforming the Public Sector: How to Achieve Better Transparency, Service, and Leadership*. Washington, DC: Brookings Institution Press, 219-339.

Barzelay, Michael and Campbell, Colin (2003). *Preparing for the Future: Strategic Planning in the U.S. Air Force*. Washington, DC: Brookings Institution Press.

Barzelay, Michael and Gallego, Raquel (2010). The comparative historical analysis of public management policy cycles in France, Italy, and Spain: Symposium introduction. *Governance*, 23(2), 209-223.

Becker, Howard S. (1997). *Tricks of the Trade: How to Think About Your Research While You're Doing It*. Chicago, IL: University of Chicago Press.

Boland, Richard J. and Collopy, Fred (Eds) (2004). *Managing as Designing.* Stanford, CA: Stanford University Press.

Booth, Wayne C., Colomb, Gregory G., and Williams, Joseph M. (2008). *The Craft of Research,* 3rd edn. Chicago, IL: University of Chicago Press.

Brown, Tim (2009). *Change by Design: How Design Thinking Transforms Organizations and Inspires Innovation.* New York: Harper Collins.

Bryson, John M. (2018). *Strategic Planning for Public and Non-Profit Organizations: A Guide to Strengthening and Sustaining Organizational Achievement,* 5th edn. Hoboken, NJ: Wiley.

Choi, Thomas Y. and Wu, Zhaohui (2009). Triads in supply networks: theorizing buyer–supplier–supplier relationships. *Journal of Supply Chain Management,* 45(1), 8-25.

Cialdini, Robert B. (2016). *Pre-suasion: A Revolutionary Way to Influence and Persuade.* New York: Simon & Schuster.

Colebatch, H.K. (2002). *Policy: Concepts in the Social Sciences,* 2nd edn. Maidenhead: Open University Press.

Collins, Randall (2004). *Interaction Ritual Chains.* Princeton, NJ: Princeton University Press.

Craver, Carl F. and Darden, Lindley (2013). *In Search of Mechanisms: Discoveries Across the Life Sciences.* Chicago, IL: University of Chicago Press.

Cross, Nigel (2008). *Engineering Design Methods: Strategies for Product Design,* 4th edn. Chichester: Wiley.

Droste, Magdelena (2011). *Bauhaus, 1919-1933.* Cologne: Taschen.

Dunn, William N. (2015). *Public Policy Analysis,* 3rd edn. London: Routledge.

Dym, Clive L. (1994). *Engineering Design: A Synthesis of Views.* Cambridge: Cambridge University Press.

Elster, Jon (1989). *Nuts and Bolts for the Social Sciences.* Cambridge: Cambridge University Press.

Fauconnier, Giles and Turner, Marc (2002). *The Way We Think: Conceptual Blending and the Mind's Hidden Complexities.* New York: Basic Books.

Fayol, Henri (1919/1984). *General and Industrial Management,* revised by Irwin Gray. New York: The Institute of Electrical and Electronics Engineers.

Fligstein, Neil and McAdam, Doug (2012). *A Theory of Fields.* Oxford: Oxford University Press.

Funnell, Sue C. and Rogers, Patricia J. (2011). *Purposeful Program Theory: Effective Use of Theories of Change and Logic Models.* New York: John Wiley & Sons.

Giddens, Anthony (1984). *The Constitution of Society: Outline of Structuration Theory.* Cambridge: Polity Press.

Goel, Vinod (1995). *Sketches of Thought.* Cambridge, MA: MIT Press.

Goffman, Erving (1959). *The Presentation of Self in Everyday Life.* New York: Anchor Books.

González Asis, Maria and Woolcock, Michael (2015). *Operationalizing the Science of Delivery Agenda to Enhance Development Results.* Washington, DC: World Bank (available at goo.gl/ffMjPb).

Goodman, Paul S. (2000). *Missing Organizational Linkages: Tools for Cross-Level Research.* Thousand Oaks, CA: Sage.

Greve, Henrich R. (2003). *Organizational Learning from Performance Feedback: A Behavioral Perspective on Innovation and Change.* Cambridge: Cambridge University Press.

Guillén, Mauro F. (1994). *Models of Management: Work, Authority, and Organization in Comparative Perspective.* Chicago, IL: University of Chicago Press.

Hamel, Gary and Prahalad, C.K. (1995). *Competing for the Future.* Boston, MA: Harvard Business School Press.

Heath, Chip and Heath, Dan (2008). *Made to Stick: Why Some Ideas Take Hold and Others Come Unstuck.* London: Random House/Arrow Books.

Hedström, Peter (2005). *Dissecting the Social: On the Principles of Analytical Sociology.* Cambridge: Cambridge University Press.

Hedström, Peter and Swedberg, Richard (Eds) (1998). *Social Mechanisms: An Analytical Approach to Social Theory.* Cambridge: Cambridge University Press.

Hilgartner, Stephen (2000). *Science on Stage: Expert Advice as Public Drama*. Stanford, CA: Stanford University Press.

Hirschman, Albert O. (1973). *Journeys Toward Progress: Studies of Economic Policy-making in Latin America*. New York: W.W. Norton.

Hirschman, Albert O. (1991). *The Rhetorics of Reaction: Perversity, Futility, Jeopardy*. Cambridge, MA: Belknap Press of Harvard University Press.

Hood, Christopher (1991). A public management for all seasons? *Public Administration*, 69(1), 3-19.

Hood, Christopher and Jackson, Michael (1991). *Administrative Argument*. Aldershot: Dartmouth.

Hopp, Wallace J. and Spearman, Mark L. (1996). *Factory Physics: Foundations of Manufacturing Management*. Boston, MA: Irwin McGraw-Hill.

Hosono, A., Honda, S., Sato, M., and Ono, M. (2011). Inside the black box of capacity development. In Kharas, H., Makino, K., and Jung, W. (Eds), *Catalyzing Development: A New Vision for Aid*. Washington, DC: Brookings Institution Press, 179-201.

JICA Research Institute (2006). *Joint Study on Effective Technical Cooperation for Capacity Development: Synthesis Report*. https://www.jica.go.jp/cdstudy/about/output/pdf/SynthesisReport_04.pdf (Accessed April 26, 2019).

JICA Research Institute (2008). *Capacity Assessment Handbook: Project Management for Realizing Capacity Development*. Tokyo: JICA-RI. http://jica-ri.jica.go.jp/IFIC_and_JBICI-Studies/english/publications/reports/study/capacity/200809/index.html (Accessed August 12, 2016).

Jonsen, Albert R. and Toulmin, Stephen (1988). *The Abuse of Casuistry: A History of Moral Reasoning*. Berkeley, CA: University of California Press.

Jun, Jong S. (2006). *The Social Construction of Public Administration: Interpretive and Critical Perspectives*. Albany, NY: SUNY Press.

Kaufer, David S. and Butler, Brian S. (1996). *Rhetoric and the Arts of Design*. Mahwah, NJ: Erlbaum.

Khurana, A. and Rosenthal, S.R. (1997). Integrating the fuzzy front end of new product development. *IEEE Engineering Management Review*, 25(4), 35-49.

Kilduff, Martin and Tsai, Wenpin (2003). *Social Networks and Organizations*. London: Sage.

Klein, Gary (2013). *Seeing What Others Don't*. London: Hodder & Stoughton.

Konnikova, Maria (2013). *Mastermind: How to Think Like Sherlock Holmes*. New York: Viking.

Lahlou, Saadi (2017). *Installation Theory: The Societal Construction and Regulation of Behaviour*. Cambridge: Cambridge University Press.

Lakoff, George (1987). *Women, Fire and Dangerous Things: What Categories Reveal about the Mind*. Chicago, IL: University of Chicago Press.

Lakoff, George and Johnson, Mark L. (1980). *Metaphors We Live By*. Chicago, IL: University of Chicago Press.

Lakoff, George and Johnson, Mark L. (1999). *Philosophy in the Flesh: The Embodied Mind and its Challenge to Western Thought*. New York: Basic Books.

Lasswell, Harold E. (1971). *A Preview of Policy Science*. Chicago, IL: Elsevier.

Latour, Bruno (2005). *Reassembling the Social: An Introduction to Actor-Network Theory*. Oxford: Oxford University Press.

Lawson, Bryan (2004). *What Designers Know*. Oxford: Architectural Press.

Leroi, Armand M. (2014). *The Lagoon: How Aristotle Invented Science*. New York: Viking.

Levinthal, Danial A. and March, James G. (1993). The myopia of learning. *Strategic Management Journal*, 14(S2), 95-112.

Levitt, Barbara and March, James G. (1988). Organizational learning. *Annual Review of Sociology*, 14(1), 319-338.

Lindblom, Charles E. (1959). The science of muddling through. *Public Administration Review*, 19(2), 79-88.

Lindblom, Charles E. (1990). *Inquiry and Change: The Troubled Attempt to Understand and Shape Society*. New Haven, CT: Yale University Press.

Lynn, Laurence E., Jr. (1996). *Public Management as Art, Science, and Profession*. Chatham, NJ: Chatham House.

Mabuchi, Shunsuke and Tsunoda, Manabu (2006). Capacity development in regional development – Sokoine University of Agriculture, Centre for Sustainable Rural Development Project. *Technology and Development*, 19, 25-35. http://jica-ri.jica.go.jp/IFIC_and_JBICI-Studies/english/publications/reports/study/technology/pdf/19.pdf (Accessed August 3, 2016).

Majone, Giandomenico (1989). *Evidence, Argument, and Persuasion in the Policy Process*. New Haven, CT: Yale University Press.

March, James G. (2010). *The Ambiguities of Experience*. Ithaca, NY: Cornell University Press.

March, James G. and Simon, Herbert, A. (1958). *Organizations*. Oxford: Wiley.

March, James G., Sproull, Lee S., and Tamuz, Michal (1991). Learning from samples of one or fewer. *Organization Science*, 2(1), 1-13.

Marshall, Sandra P. (1995). *Schemas in Problem Solving*. Cambridge: Cambridge University Press.

Mashaw, Jerry L. (1981). *Bureaucratic Justice: Managing Social Security Disability Claims*. New Haven, CT: Yale University Press.

McAdam, Doug, Tarrow, Sidney, and Tilly, Charles (2001). *Dynamics of Contention*. Cambridge: Cambridge University Press.

Merton, Robert K. (1936). The unanticipated consequences of purposive social action. *American Sociological Review*, 1(6), 894-904.

Mintzberg, Henry (1983). *Designing Effective Organizations: Structures in Fives*. Englewood Cliffs, NJ: Prentice Hall.

Miyoshi, Takahiro and Nagayo, Narihide (2006). A Study of the Effectiveness and Problems of JICA's Technical Cooperation from a Capacity Development Perspective: Case Study of Support for Ghana's Irrigated Agriculture. Tokyo: Institute for International Cooperation, JICA. http://jica-ri.jica.go.jp/IFIC_and_JBICI-Studies/english/publications/reports/study/capacity/200609/index.html (Accessed August 12, 2016).

Moore, Mark H. (1995). *Creating Public Value: Strategic Management in Government*. Cambridge, MA: Harvard University Press.

Morgan, Gareth (1986). *Images of Organization*. Beverly Hills, CA: Sage.

Morgan, Mary S. and Morrison, Margaret (Eds) (1999). *Models as Mediators: Perspectives on Natural and Social Science*. Cambridge: Cambridge University Press.

Murphy, Gregory L. (2002). *The Big Book of Concepts*. Cambridge, MA: MIT Press.

Pahl, Gerhard and Beitz, Wolfgang (1999). *Engineering Design: A Systematic Approach*. London: Springer Verlag.

Patton, Michael Quinn (2011). *Developmental Evaluation: Applying Complexity Concepts to Enhance Innovation and Use*. New York: Guilford Press.

Pawson, Ray and Tilley, Nick (1997). *Realistic Evaluation*. Los Angeles, CA: Sage.

Perrow, Charles (1986). *Complex Organizations: A Critical Perspective*, 2nd edn. New York: McGraw Hill.

Porter, Michael E. (1985). *Competitive Advantage*. New York: Free Press.

Ragin, Charles C. (1987). *The Comparative Method: Moving Beyond Qualitative and Quantitative Strategies*. Berkeley, CA: University of California Press.

Ragin, Charles C. and Becker, Howard S. (Eds) (1992). *What is a Case? Exploring the Foundations of Social Inquiry*. Cambridge: Cambridge University Press.

Rantanen, Kalevi and Domb, Ellen (2002). *Simplified TRIZ: New Problem-Solving Applications for Engineers and Manufacturing Professionals*. Boca Raton, FL: CRC Press.

Ravetz, Jerome R. (1971). *Scientific Knowledge and its Social Problems*. New York: Oxford University Press.

Raz, Joseph (1999). *Practical Reason and Norms*. Oxford: Oxford University Press.

Rehg, W. (2009). Cogency in motion: critical contextualism and relevance. *Argumentation*, 23, 39-59.

Rescher, Nicholas (1996). *Process Metaphysics: An Introduction to Process Philosophy*. Albany, NY: SUNY University Press.

Rousseau, D.M. (2006). Is there such a thing as 'evidence-based management'? *Academy of Management Review*, 31(2), 256-269.

Rumelt, Richard P., Schendel, Dan E., and Teece, David J. (1994). *Fundamental Issues in Strategy: A Research Agenda*. Boston, MA: Harvard Business School Press.

Sarasvathy, Saras D. (2008). *Effectuation: Elements of Entrepreneurial Expertise*. Cheltenham, UK and Northampton, MA, USA: Edward Elgar Publishing.

Sato, Mine (2013). A fresh look at capacity development from insiders' perspectives: a case study of an urban redevelopment project in Medellín, Colombia. JICA Research Institute Working Paper, Number 60 https://jicari.repo.nii.ac.jp/?action=pages_view_main&active_action= repository_view_main_item_detail&item_id=669&item_no=1&page_id=13&block_id=21 (Accessed July 9, 2019).

Schelling, Thomas C. (1978). *Micromotives and Macrobehavior*. New York: Norton.

Schön, Donald A. (1983). *The Reflective Practitioner: How Professionals Think in Action*. New York: Basic Books.

Shangraw, R.F. Jr., Crow, M.M., and Overman, E.S. (1989). Public administration as a design science. *Public Administration Review*, 49(2), 153-160.

Simon, Herbert A. (1946). The proverbs of administration. *Public Administration Review*, 6, 53-67.

Simon, Herbert A. (1947/1968). *Administrative Behavior*. New York: Free Press.

Simon, Herbert A. (1990). *Reason in Human Affairs*. Stanford, CA: Stanford University Press.

Simon, Herbert A. (1996). *The Sciences of the Artificial*, 3rd edn. Cambridge, MA: MIT Press.

Simons, Herbert W. (2001). *Persuasion in Society*. Thousand Oaks, CA: Sage.

Skocpol, Theda (1979). *States and Social Revolutions: A Comparative Analysis of France, Russia and China*. Cambridge: Cambridge University Press.

Stake, Robert E. (1995). *The Art of Case Study Research*. Thousand Oaks, CA: Sage.

Stake, Robert E. (2010). *Qualitative Research: Studying How Things Work*. New York: Guilford Press.

Tendler, Judith (1997). *Good Government in the Tropics*. Baltimore, MD: Johns Hopkins University Press.

Tendler, Judith and Freedheim, Sara (1994). Trust in a rent-seeking world: health and government transformed in Northeast Brazil. *World Development*, 22(12), 1771-1791.

Tilly, Charles (2006). *Why? What Happens When People Give Reasons, and Why*. Princeton, NJ: Princeton University Press.

Toulmin, Stephen (1958). *The Uses of Argument*. Cambridge: Cambridge University Press.

United Nations Development Programme (2002). Capacity for development: new solutions to old problems http://www.undp.org/content/dam/aplaws/publication/en/publications/ capacity-development/capacity-for-development-new-solutions-to-old-problems-full-text/ Capacity-Dev-NewSolutions-OldProbs-FULL.pdf (Accessed April 26, 2019).

United Nations Development Programme (2009). Supporting capacity development: the UNDP approach http://www.undp.org/content/dam/aplaws/publication/en/publications/capacity-development/support-capacity-development-the-undp-approach/CDG_Brochure_2009.pdf# search='undp+capacity+development' (Accessed April 26, 2019).

van Aken, Joan E. (2004). Management research based on the paradigm of the design sciences: the quest for field-tested and grounded technological rules. *Journal of Management Studies*, 41(2), 219-246.

van Aken, Joan E. and Berends, Hans (2018). *Problem-Solving in Organizations: A Methodological Handbook for Business Students*. Cambridge: Cambridge University Press.

van der Voort, Haiko, Koppenjan, Joop F.M., ten Heuvelhof, Ernst, Leijten, Martijn, and Veeneman, Wijnand. (2011). Competing values in the management of innovative projects: the case of the RandstadRail Project. In Bekkers, V., Edelenbos, J., and Steijn, B. (Eds), *Innovation in the Public Sector: Linking Capacity and Leadership*. Basingstoke: Palgrave Macmillan, 134-154.

van Maanen, John (2011). *Tales of the Field: On Writing Ethnography*. Chicago, IL: University of Chicago Press.

Vaughan, D. (2005). Organizational rituals of risk and error. In Power, M. and Hutter, B.N. (Eds), *Organizational Encounters with Risk*. Oxford: Oxford University Press, 33-66.

Vickers, Geoffrey (1965/1983). *The Art of Judgment: A Study of Policy Making*. London: Harper & Row.

Walton, Douglas N. (1992). *Plausible Argument in Everyday Conversation*. Albany, NY: SUNY Press.

Watkins, Michael D. (2009). Picking the right transition strategy. *Harvard Business Review* 87(1), 46-53.

Weick, Karl E. (1979). *The Social Psychology of Organizing*. Reading, MA: Addison-Wesley.

Williamson, Oliver E. (Ed.) (1995). *Organization Theory: From Chester Barnard to the Present and Beyond*. New York: Oxford University Press.

Wilson, James Q. (1989). *Bureaucracy: What Government Agencies Do, and Why They Do It*. New York: Basic Books.

Wimsatt, W. (1997). Functional organization, functional analogy, and functional inference. *Evolution and Cognition*, 3(2), 102-132.

Yin, Robert K. (2014). *Case Study Research: Design and Methods*, 4th edn. Los Angeles, CA: Sage.

Glossary of terms and names

Abbott, Andrew. A leading professor of sociology, long based at the University of Chicago, who has theorized sociology in a distinctive way that he calls processual sociology (Abbott 2001, 2016).

Argumentation. This is one of four professional activities within a purposive theory of public management, along with sense-making, designing, and dramatization. Argumentation has long been theorized within philosophy, which brings out the character of practical (as opposed to scientific) argumentation. Going back to Aristotle, practical argumentation has been understood to move forward through inexact reasoning on the basis of presumptions that are more like opinions than facts or laws. Such ideas about practical argumentation have been formalized over the last few generations, starting with Toulmin (1958). Argumentation theorists, such as Douglas Walton, have emphasized that practical reasoning is a social phenomenon in being goal-oriented and cooperative. Ideas about argumentation have been combined with ideas about social relations and studied more empirically by sociologists. Chapter 4 identifies argumentation with a sociological theorist, Charles Tilly.

Bardach, Eugene. A major figure in the fields of public policy and public management, now an emeritus professor at the Graduate School of Public Policy of the University of California, Berkeley, where he was based for his entire academic career. Bardach's writings about public management, and especially about research, represent the starting point for developing this book's ideas about public management as a design-oriented professional discipline. These writings, especially, Bardach (1994) and Bardach (2004), are discussed at some length in this book, especially in Chapter 6.

Bryson, John. A leading figure in the professional discipline of public management, and McKnight Presidential Professor of Planning and Public Affairs at the University of Minnesota's Hubert H. Humphrey School of Public Affairs. He is best known by practitioners for his multi-edition book on strategic planning in public and non-profit organizations, which exemplifies mechanism-intent thinking about public organizations and professional practice. This book is featured in the Public Management Gallery Tour, presented in Chapter 4, in the section on purposive theories of public organizations.

C + *M* = *O*. A symbolic representation drawn from Pawson and Tilley's (1997) book, *Realistic Evaluation*. C stands for context, M for mechanism, and O for outcome. The arithmetic symbols indicate that outcomes are due to both context and mechanisms. In terms of the present book, C + M = O is a way to represent public programs as purposeful phenomena, focusing on their embodiment designs, with the expression being about the totality of scenario-processes in which a program consists. These ideas are discussed in Chapters 7 and 8.

Conceptual designs. This term is drawn from purposive theorizing about engineering design (Cross 2008). Dating back to late nineteenth-century Germany, this purposive theory holds that designing consists in a sequential stage process. As theorized, the outcome of any given stage within a design process is a "design," that is, a *representation* of the machine or, more broadly, the purposeful phenomenon, with which the design process is concerned. The sequential stage process theory of engineering design holds that the first stage should eventuate in a conceptual design. A proper conceptual design is meant to be clear about some, but not all, aspects of the purposeful phenomenon with which it is concerned. In simple terms, a proper conceptual design is clear about what the purposeful phenomenon is for, while not resolving the issue of what the purposeful phenomenon should consist in. The essential reason for this view is that it's best for the designer and the client to be in agreement on what a purposeful phenomenon is for, before they move toward settling on the specifics of a technical system, thereby implementing the conceptual design so as to effectuate the phenomenon's purpose. Accordingly, a proper conceptual design – insofar as it represents a purposeful phenomenon's technical system – does so in a high-level way, with emphasis placed on what functionality is needed for the purpose to be effectuated; accordingly, a technical system's outcome pattern, as it operates, would be relevant to a proper conceptual design, whereas a technical system's physical features and its spatial organization would be out-of-place. This idea is pertinent to a design-oriented professional discipline of public management, because it takes public organizations to be purposeful phenomena, to which this discipline is tied. The conceptual bridge from engineering design to public management consists in two steps. The first is the idea that enterprises are purposeful phenomena, which Fayol (1919/1984) developed. The second is that public organizations are enterprises, which Moore (1995) developed. A proper conceptual design of an enterprise (and thus of a public organization) is clear about enterprise-intent. A proper conceptual design of an enterprise is also clear about the totality of enterprise-functions that need to be performed to effectuate enterprise-intent. Further, an enterprise's conceptual design – following Fayol, and illustrated by Porter (1985) and Bryson (2018) – presents a functional breakdown, along with statements about how the performance of one function depends on the performance of one or more other functions. On the other hand, a proper conceptual design of an enterprise is not definitive about the mechanisms for effectuating enterprise intent. Nevertheless, a proper conceptual design of an enterprise can contemplate its enterprise-mechanisms, by presenting them in a "high-level" way. For example, a conceptual design may outline the scenario-processes in which enterprise-mechanisms consist, pointing to what social mechanisms (as theorized in processual sociology) would be helpful to activate, or pointing to a scenario-process' desired outcome pattern.

Context. This term is part of the idea of a scenario-process. A scenario-process is a way of representing the embodiment design of purposeful phenomena in public organizations. A scenario process plays the role of mechanism in relation to fulfilling a public organization's intent. The context-activity relation is understood through modeling, drawing on theoretical ideas from processual sociology. The term "context" in this discussion is specifically a reference to dynamically stable properties of scenario-processes. Their causal role is to channel the activity within a scenario-process, which, in turn, is viewed as the direct source of scenario-process outcomes.

Coordination. An idea in Henri Fayol's purposive theory of enterprises. In this theory, performing the management function of an enterprise is necessary in effectuating the intent of an enterprise. Coordination is a constitutive function of management, as is planning, directing, and controlling. Coordination is also an idea in Henry Mintzberg's (1983) theory of organization design. That theory is unlike Fayol's in that it is about organizations, as contrasted with enterprises. The idea that coordination is a necessary function in organizations lies at the heart of Mintzberg's purposive theory of organizations. Coordination is discussed specifically in Chapter 7.

Creating public value. An idea in Mark Moore's (1995) purposive theory of government, public programs, organizational strategy, and executive leadership at the apex of public organizations. In this theory, creating public value is what public programs properly do; it is their proper function; it is what they effectuate. This idea is meant to be just as true of public programs that deliver obligations to the entire citizenry as it is to public programs that provide services to populations of individuals. From that idea, Moore's theorizing moves in two directions. One was to be more specific about what is the proper function of programs generically; another was to be more specific about the costs of programs generically. In his theory, the proper function of public programs is to fulfill a citizenry's collective political aspirations about conditions prevailing in the society; it is decidedly not to satisfy individual wants and needs. When collective political aspirations are realized, public value has thereby been created. It follows that the intent of any specific public program is properly to realize such political aspirations. Turning to the other direction of theorizing, a program's adequacy as an effectuator of intent depends on the costs generated by its functioning. In Moore's theory, the idea of cost includes such effects as a reduction of individual consumption due to the need for the government to fund a program; reduction of individual liberty, arising specifically when the program delivers obligations to the citizenry; and a residual category of costs that are borne by citizens in co-producing public services or complying with obligations. In straightforward economizing terms, the higher the cost, the less public value is created, all things considered. This purposive theory provides a very general framework for idea-tion and deliberation about the intent of any specific public program, as well as a general guide for specifying a program's system-designs and plans. The idea of public value creation has gradually become widely referred to in the field of public administration, though this specific theorization of it has not always been preserved. These matters are discussed primarily in Chapter 2.

Design-focused case studies. Case studies conducted within a professional discipline, tied to a kind of purposeful phenomenon. In public management, design-focused case studies are about public organizations, design-projects, and/or the professional activities of sense-making, designing, argumentation, and designing. Design-focused case studies are unlike stereotypical case stud-ies in being about kinds of purposeful as distinct from empirical phenomena. Design-focused case studies answer questions such as what was a purposeful phenomenon for; what did it consist in; and how did it work. Answers to such questions reflect mechanism-intent style purposive theorizing about the kind of purposeful phenomenon of which the case is a token. A design-focused case study's "take-aways" are not lessons but are rather design-precedents (Lawson 2004) within a professional discipline. Drawing analogies between historically-existing purposeful phenomena – that is, design precedents – and purposeful phenomena-in-the-making is a significant part of the professional activity of designing. These ideas are discussed in Chapters 6 and 7.

Design-precedent. An idea in the purposive theory of public management. Design-precedents are used in channeling the professional activity of designing. The use involves generative, critical thinking, typically involving exploration of close and distant analogies between a given historical purposeful phenomenon and another that is still being formulated (or designed). In a professional disci-pline, design-precedents result from design-focused case studies. (See the entry on that term, above.) This idea is discussed primarily in Chapter 6.

Design-projects. This term refers to ideas discussed by Herbert Simon (1996) in Chapter 5 of *Sciences of the Artificial*. Simon discussed how designs for artificial systems are created within organizations, to the point that decisions are made to construct, fabricate, or otherwise realize them. From the standpoint of this book, Simon presented a purposive theory of "design-projects" within enterprises. This terminology is used even though Simon did not phrase his discussion in terms of projects – and even though design-projects include decision-making in organiza-tions. While the present book borrows the idea of design-projects from Simon, it develops this idea in concert with other aspects of its purposive theorizing of enterprises, generally, and of public organizations, more specifically. For instance, in Chapter 4 and 5, design-projects are presented as mechanisms *for* performing the enterprise-functions that effectuate enterprise-intent; further, design-projects are presented as *consisting in* designing and decision-making scenario-processes; and, beyond that, design-projects are presented as being *constituted by* the profes-sional activities of sense-making, designing, argumentation, and dramatization.

The idea of design-projects is also used to formulate a neo-Simonean/post-Moore synthesis of purposive theorizing about public management, discussed in Chapters 2 and 3. Design-projects are discussed at length in Chapter 4, where the literature featured consists in Simon (1996), van Aken and Berends (2018), and Barzelay and Campbell (2003).

Designing. This is one of four professional activities within a purposive theory of public management, along with sense-making, argumentation, and dramatization. Designing plays an important role within design-projects. Designing – considered as a professional activity – involves generative, critical thinking about professional knowledge within a professional discipline, whether such knowledge takes the form of purposive theories or design-precedents. The literature on designing provides many lines of purposive theorizing of designing; lively debates about creating purposeful phenomena, and artificial systems specifically, can be found there. Chapter 4 calls attention to a purposive theory of designing as formulated by Nigel Cross (2008), while emphasizing his ideas about problem- and solution-structuring, presented in Chapter 1 of his book.

Dramatization. This is one of four professional activities within a purposive theory of public management, along with sense-making, designing, and argumentation. Dramatization creates social realities through the stage-managed projection of verbal and non-verbal signs, some of which represent relationships among actors in scenes. This professional activity has, in effect, been theorized by Erving Goffman (1959), and it has been discussed in the literature on rhetoric (e.g., Simons 2001, Kaufer and Butler 1996). This theorization has not generally entered into mechanism-intent style purposive theorizing of public organizations and professional practice, though there are definitely traces of this in literature that furnish design-precedents about public organizations (e.g., Mashaw 1981, Hilgartner 2000). A brief discussion of dramatization is placed toward the end of Chapter 4.

Embodiment designs. This term, like conceptual designs (see above), is drawn from purposive theorizing about engineering design (Cross 2008). Dating back to late nineteenth-century Germany, this purposive theory theorizes designing as a sequential stage process. This theory holds that the second stage should eventuate in a purposeful phenomenon's embodiment design. A proper embodiment design *fits with* a conceptual design, with the relation being that a purposeful phenomenon's embodiment design's role is *to implement* a settled conceptual design. The two representations are meant to be complementary, in being continuous in substance but different in degree of specificity. A proper embodiment design is specific in ways that a proper conceptual design is not. A proper embodiment design is more specific than a proper conceptual design about what a given purposive phenomenon consists in and how it works. In the design-oriented professional discipline of public management, mechanisms are theorized as scenario-processes with context-activity-outcome dynamics. A proper embodiment design is reasonably specific, but not totally definitive, about such scenario-processes and their interconnections in place and time.

Enterprise-Functions. An idea in Henri Fayol's purposive theory of enterprises. Fayol's enterprise-functions were management, technical, commercial, security, accounting, and finance. This purposive theory is based on an analogy between enterprises and organisms as they have been theorized in biology since the work of Aristotle (see Ariew and Perlman 2002). For a given organism, it is necessary that its functions (e.g., respiration) be performed adequately if it is to survive and thrive; uncorrected deficiencies can be disabling or fatal. Also in biology, functional necessities are uniform within a species. In biology, the mechanisms for performing an organism's respective functions are uniform within the species. In Fayol's purposive theory, enterprises are uniform in their functional necessities, but not uniform in the mechanisms for performing them. (There is no one best way.) This has the implication that the enterprise-functions in Fayol's theory are not as clearly differentiated compared with the differentiation of organism-functions in biological research; as such Fayol's enterprise-functions and management-functions are more like lists than a system analysis. But they are useful as a loose taxonomic framework within the sort of purposive theory that Fayol's theory is meant to be. These matters are discussed primarily in Chapters 2, 3, and 5.

Enterprises. The overarching idea in Henri Fayol's theory of enterprises. In this purposive theory, all enterprises have functional necessities, among which one is management. By this argument, an enterprise will have lower prospects of fulfilling its purposes if the performance of its necessary functions is deficient. Enterprises consist in intent-effectuating mechanisms, some of which are artificial systems, with predictable input-activity-output profiles, some of which are scenario-like purposeful phenomena, with patterns of context-activity-outcome dynamics. Enterprises are sites for professional practice. An elaborate mechanism-intent, purposive theory of business enterprises is Porter (1985). A thematically focused mechanism-intent, purposive theory of public organizations is Bryson (2018). A different style of purposive theorizing of public organizations, with casuistical overtones, is Moore (1995). These matters are discussed primarily in Chapters 2, 3, and 5.

Fayol, Henri. Best known as a late nineteenth-century theorist of enterprises. See, *enterprises.*

Goffman, Erving. A leading North American sociology professor until his untimely death in 1983, associated with the so-called Chicago School of Sociology. Author of *The Presentation of Self in Everyday Life* (1959). Goffmann originated a current of micro-sociological theorizing and case study research, with which the term "dramaturgical" is associated. This line of theorizing concentrates on how social realities, as experienced by individuals, result from how and what people, to an extent deliberately, present to others as "true" about social entities and processes. It also concentrates on how social realities, so constructed, affect the course of social life, by virtue of the meaning individuals attribute to scenes and social relations. In the present book, Goffman's dramaturgical theory is the basis for purposive theorizing about the professional activity of dramatization. These matters are briefly discussed at the end of Chapter 4.

Intent. An idea that plays a significant role in such representations of a purposeful phenomenon. The role points to a state of affairs, or continuing process, whose effectuation is sought through a purposeful phenomenon's mechanisms. In the design-oriented professional discipline of public management, the intent of public organizations, generically, is to create public value.

Lynn, Laurence E., Jr. An American professor of public policy, who holds emeritus appointments at Texas A & M University and the University of Chicago. Lynn entered the field of public policy through economics: he obtained his PhD in Economics at Yale University, and he then worked in the U.S. Federal government in positions for program planning and evaluation from the late 1960s through the late 1970s. During the late 1970s through the start of the 1980s, Lynn was a professor of public policy at Harvard's Kennedy School of Government. He subsequently moved to the University of Chicago, holding appointments in two professional schools: public policy and social administration. Lynn served as Dean for the latter. During the 1990s, Lynn became an outspoken critic of certain approaches to both teaching and researching on public management, which were somewhat prevalent within public policy schools – most prominently so at the Kennedy School. Lynn's first book-length statement of his views on this matter appeared in *Public Management as Art, Science, and Profession* (1996). That book is a reference point for the present one, *Public Management as Design-Oriented Professional Discipline*. Lynn's book was similar to the present book in identifying public management as a professional discipline; however, these books' substantive views about public management, as a professional discipline, are sharply divergent, as discussed in Chapter 8.

Management-function. An idea in Henri Fayol's purposive theory of enterprises. In this theory, an enterprise's six functions include the management-function, as well as technical, commercial, finance, accounting, and security functions. The management-function is enabling of the performance of these other functions. The constitutive functions of management are planning, directing, coordinating, and controlling. Any of these functions is performed by mechanisms, which can be theorized as interlocking scenario processes within organizations. Planning is distinctive in that it eventuates in standards and plans, as well as other representations of intent and mechanisms to effectuate them. The term is not currently fashionable: designing is more fashionable. Directing is also not currently fashionable; leadership is more so. Controlling is distinctive in comparison with coordination in that it is based on standards, which can come from plans or other sources. Controlling is not currently fashionable; monitoring is more so. These matters are discussed generally in Chapters 2 and 3, and they are illustrated concretely in Chapter 7.

Mechanism-intent thinking. A style of theorizing purposeful phenomena, whether types or particulars. Standard questions discussed in such theorizing concern what a purposeful phenomenon is for; what it consists in; and how it works. The answers reflect lineages and precedents within a professional discipline. Not all purposive theorizing and analysis of purposeful phenomena is guided by these ideas of mechanism-intent theorizing. The mechanism-intent style of purposive theorizing and case analysis is characteristic of a design-oriented professional discipline. The idea is introduced implicitly in Chapter 1 and explicitly in Chapter 3.

Mechanisms. An idea that plays a key role in mechanism-intent thinking about purposeful phenomena. A purposeful phenomenon's mechanisms effectuate its intent. In some purposive theories of enterprises, mechanisms effectuate intent by performing one or more of its constitutive functions. Mechanisms consist in processes, some of which are theorized as scenario-processes. Scenario-processes begin with their initial conditions and terminate in their outcomes. Scenario-context channels scenario-activity, involving interactions among flows of activity, usually on a range of social scales. Scenario-activity eventuates in scenario-outcomes. These matters are primarily discussed in Chapters 4, 5 and 6.

Modern management school. The purposeful phenomenon to which this term referred first came to exist in North American universities during the late 1940s (Augier and March 2011). A token of this type was the Graduate School of Industrial Administration (GSIA) at Carnegie Institute of Technology, in Pittsburgh, Pennsylvania. As presented by its proponents, the modern management school would do for the field of management (in North America) what the modern medical school had done for the field of medicine, in the half-century since its inception at Johns Hopkins University. The modern management school was pre-dated by the Wharton School at the University of Pennsylvania and the Graduate School of Business Administration at Harvard (HBS). GSIA and HBS became, in effect, rivals. GSIA recruited heavily from the Cowles Commission for Research in Economics at the University of Chicago. Nobel prize-winning work on modern finance theory was undertaken at GSIA. A field of marketing was developed along lines reflecting disciplinary research in economics and psychology. GSIA's initial faculty included Herbert Simon, who had connections to the Cowles Commission, but who had done his doctoral work in political science and had worked to develop, in effect, a professional discipline of public administration. Simon became an internal critic of the modern management school; he was not enamored with the idea that the modern medical school provided a suitable template for a professional discipline within the field of management (Augier and March 2011). He set off to develop fundamental knowledge about decision-making in organizations, and he parlayed this work into an approach to management as problem-solving, especially involving the creation of novelty. The present book steers wide of the modern management school notion of management as a professional discipline, while incorporating Simon's ideas, which were consonant with neither the modern medical school nor with the HBS approach. These matters are discussed in Chapters 2 and 8.

Moore, Mark. Author of *Creating Public Value: Strategic Management in Government* (Moore 1995). During his entire academic career, Moore was based at Harvard University, primarily at the Kennedy School of Government, but he was also associated with the Graduate School of Education and Harvard Business School. He has had major involvements with public management teaching outside the U.S., especially with the Australia–New Zealand School of Government. *Creating Public Value* exemplifies a Harvard-style approach to theorizing enterprises and the professional practice of management, and it constitutes a Harvard-style approach to theorizing public organizations and the action profile of individuals in a role theorized as that of a public manager. This book is featured in the Public Management Gallery Tour, presented in Chapter 4, in the section on purposive theories of public organizations.

Pattern language. This term refers to a body of conventions for representing mechanism-intent thinking about enterprise-like purposeful phenomena, including public organizations. These conventions can be placed in two groups, by drawing on the distinction, notable in the professional discipline of engineering, between a machine-like system's conceptual design and its embodiment design. Reflecting Fayol, the conceptual design of enterprises involves the identification of enterprise-intent, on the one hand, and enterprise-functions, on the other. Within the pattern language, performing an enterprise's functions effectuates an enterprise's intent. In such thinking, the performance of a given function is dependent on the performance of one or more other functions (as is true of organisms, as well). Under the conventions of pattern language, this relation of inter-functional dependency is expressed in terms of functions enabling other functions. Thus, overall pattern language of an enterprise's conceptual design goes along the lines of: *functions effectuate intent*, while *functions enable functions*. Turning to the second group of conventions, the embodiment designs of enterprises are constituted by mechanisms and their inter-relations. A given mechanism, viewed in isolation from other mechanisms, is a scenario-process with a distinct context-activities-outcome profile. When detail is added to the characterization of a scenario-process, clarity about how *contexts channel activities* and how *activities eventuate in outcomes* is achieved – making the causal properties of scenario-processes more explicit. An embodiment design is constituted by relations among the totality of its scenario-processes. The pattern language express this idea in terms of one scenario-process *structuring* another. The pattern language also expresses the relation between an enterprise's embodiment and conceptual designs: the former *implements* the latter, in service of effectuating enterprise-intent, as presented in its conceptual design. These matters are discussed in Chapter 3 and the ideas are illustrated concretely in Chapter 7.

Process context factors. Within purposive theorizing of enterprises, these are aspects of mechanisms – specifically, of scenario-processes. (The term comes from Barzelay 2007.) In relation to scenario-process activity, process context factors are dynamically stable conditions – specifically those whose presence in the scenario is due to scenario-processes that are cast as being contextual in relation to those on which attention is focused, for analytical or problem-solving purposes. This idea is discussed in Chapters 6 and 7.

Process design features. Within purposive theorizing of enterprises, these are aspects of mechanisms – specifically, of scenario-processes. (The term comes from Barzelay 2007.) In relation to scenario-process activity, process design features are dynamically stable conditions – specifically those whose presence in a scenario-process is central to the line of purposive theorizing that is being examined. This idea is discussed in Chapters 6 and 7.

Processual sociology. A school of thought in sociology with deep roots in the Chicago School of Sociology. Major intellectual statements of this school of thought include Abbott (2001) and Abbott (2016). While this school of thought does not lay out purposive, design-oriented theorizing or case analysis, it has much to offer in analyzing and designing scenario-processes, because its theoretical ideas can be used to make explicit how scenario-context channels scenario-activities and how scenario-activities eventuate in scenario-outcomes. Processual sociology provides a tradition and precedents for theorizing such process dynamics. Part of processual sociology revolves around the idea that causation in social processes can be theorized in terms of social mechanisms, with examples of such mechanisms being frame alignment (McAdam, Tarrow, and Tilly 2001), actor certification (McAdam, Tarrow and Tilly 2001), opportunity attribution (McAdam, Tarrow, and Tilly 2001), homophily and heterophily in networks (Kilduff and Tsai 2003), and performance feedback (Greve 2003). The relevance of these ideas to design-focused case studies was presented in Barzelay (2007) and, in the present volume, is discussed in Chapter 6 and demonstrated in Chapter 7.

Professional discipline of public management. This book furthers the idea that public management is (or, can be) a professional discipline (Lynn 1996). Any professional discipline is essentially constituted by two linked enterprises: discipline-development and teaching-and-learning for would-be and actual professional practitioners. As represented here, the teaching-and-learning enterprise effectuates better professional practice, encompassing professional activities, design-projects, and performing the management function within public organizations. It also effectuates an expanding community of professional practitioners who tackle opportunities and challenges through design-focused public management practice. The teaching-and-learning enterprise's constitutive functions are acquiring professional knowledge, improving professional abilities, and strengthening professional competence. As for the discipline-development enterprise, it has a role in enabling the teaching-and-learning enterprise, while its constitutive functions are strengthening disciplinary identity, expanding professional knowledge, and faculty development.

Professional disciplines. A professional discipline is a domain within networks of institutions of higher education and research. Unlike scientific disciplines, which are generally focused on kinds of *empirical* phenomena, professional disciplines are generally focused on kinds of *purposeful* phenomena, as well as on teaching and learning about professional practice concerned with them. A professional discipline can be classified as a science of the artificial (Simon 1996) when its kinds of purposeful phenomena are artificial systems, like machines and buildings. Professional disciplines that are not sciences of the artificial do not have a standard label. The term "profession" on its own is problematic for many professional disciplines (Abbott 2016 and Schön 1983), including management (Augier and March 2011). Any professional discipline is essentially constituted by two linked enterprises: discipline-development and teaching-and-learning for would-be and actual professional practitioners. As represented here, the constitutive functions of a professional discipline's teaching-and-learning enterprise are acquiring professional knowledge, improving professional abilities, and strengthening professional competence. The discipline-development enterprise enables the teaching-and-learning enterprise. Its constitutive functions are strengthening disciplinary identity, expanding professional knowledge, and faculty development. The term "*design-oriented* professional disciplines" refers to professional disciplines that (a) are tied to kinds of purposeful phenomena and (b) are concerned with the creation of novelty, to the point that their teaching-and-learning and discipline-development enterprises are strongly concerned with design-projects and the professional activity of designing. The category, design-oriented professional disciplines – a term in this book – includes the category, sciences of the artificial (Simon 1996), but it is wider: it includes professional disciplines whose kinds of purposeful phenomena are enterprises, an example of which is public organizations.

Professional knowledge. The state of debate within a professional discipline about the purposeful phenomena to which they are tied, as well as about professional practice as it relates to that discipline. Forms of professional knowledge within a professional discipline include purposive theorizing and design-precedents. This idea is discussed throughout the book, but comes into particular focus in Chapters 1 and 8.

Public organizations. A term borrowed from Moore (1995). In that book, public organizations are purposeful phenomena, as is appropriate to a study within the professional discipline of public management, rather than empirical phenomena, as would be appropriate to a study within social science disciplines. In theorizing public organizations as purposeful phenomena, Moore borrows ideas that have been used to theorize enterprises generally. In doing so, he theorizes that public organizations are *for* creating public value. Aligned with this way of theorizing public organizations, public programs are presented as one of their most significant aspects. In his theory, public organizations create public value by combining operational capacity with support from their authorizing environment. Whether the term "public organizations" is the best label for this purposeful phenomenon, as theorized, is a debatable point; but Moore's book establishes a convention for using this label for the enterprise-like purposeful phenomenon being theorized. These matters are discussed in Chapters 2, 3, and 4.

Purposeful phenomena. A term that widens Herbert Simon's (1996) idea of artificial phenomena. As presented in *Sciences of the Artificial*, artificial phenomena include artificial systems and the design-projects that create them. Purposeful phenomena are tied to professional disciplines. Public management's purposeful phenomena include public organizations, design-projects, and the professional activities of sense-making, designing, argumentation, and dramatization.

Purposive theory. Theories of purposeful phenomena are formulated (and critically examined) within professional disciplines, for use in professional practice. In public management, purposive theorizing concerned public organizations, design-projects, and such professional activities as sense-making, designing, argumentation, and dramatization. Purposive theories constitute professional knowledge and, as such, are appropriate items of critical discussion in the teaching and learning enterprise of the public management discipline. This idea is examined in some depth in Chapters 2-5.

Scenario-processes. See *mechanisms*.

Sciences of the artificial. A collection of professional disciplines concerned with professional practice in creating types of artificial systems, whether physical or digital. The term is also the title of a book by Herbert A. Simon (1996). In the present book, Simon's idea of a science of the artificial is a precedent for the idea of public management as a design-oriented professional discipline; see, especially, Chapter 8.

Sense-making. This is one of four professional activities within a purposive theory of public management, along with designing, argumentation, and dramatization. The outcome of sense-making activities include observations about specific situations and directions for problem-solving. In public management, the substance of such observations and problem-solving ideas reflects purposive theories of public organizations and of design projects, as they are used in professional practice. Sense-making is discussed briefly in Chapter 4.

Simon, Herbert A. A leading twentieth-century academic in social science. Studied for a PhD in Political Science from the University of Chicago in the 1930s and 1940s, with a focus on public administration. During the 1940s and 1950s, Simon was a professor at the Graduate School of Industrial Administration of Carnegie Institute of Technology. During the 1960s to his death in 1991, Simon was professor of computer science and psychology at Carnegie-Mellon University. He is most known in the social sciences for developing positive theories of human decision-making in which rationality is procedural and concerned with incomplete information, ignorance, and limits to the calculative capacities of the human mind. The single-word term that became the standard way to refer to this theory is satisficing. Simon was awarded the Nobel Prize in Economics in 1978 for this work. What is relevant for the present book is Simon's *Sciences of the Artificial*, the final edition of which came out in 1996. Simon argued that fields of research and education that are tied to professional practice, as in engineering, architecture, and management, ought to be concerned with designing. In Chapter 5, Simon outlined (what we call here) a purposive theory of designing that, in being abstract and generic, was meant to apply uniformly to any field of professional practice. What Simon wrote proved influential as the interdisciplinary field of design studies developed; and this field, in turn, has come to influence the field of management, though only to a degree. These considerations are discussed here in Chapters 2, 3, and 8.

Social mechanisms. Within sociology, a social mechanism is a robust, but not law-like empirical phenomenon. Social mechanisms can be discovered through theorization and empirical study. Once they have been identified, they can be used to gain causal insight into kinds of social entities and processes, by way of explanatory argumentation of particular entities and episodes. Many mechanisms in sociology provide causal and descriptive idealizations of scenario-processes, whose outcomes eventuate from combinations of time-specific factors, some of which are contextual in being dynamically stable properties of situations, while others are constitutive of activities. Examples of such mechanisms are frame alignment, homo- and hetero-phily in networks, and performance feedback (see Chapter 7).

Index